BuzzFeed

UNSOLVED

S U P E R N A T U R A L

101 True Tales of Hauntings, Demons, and the Paranormal

Ryan Bergara

Shane Madej

and Anna Katz

RUNNING PRESS
PHILADELPHIA

Running Press
Hachette Book Group
1290 Avenue of the Americas, New York, NY 10104
www.runningpress.com
@Running_Press

Printed in Canada

First Edition: September 2022

Published by Running Press, an imprint of Perseus Books, LLC, a subsidiary of Hachette Book Group, Inc. The Running Press name and logo are trademarks of the Hachette Book Group.

The Hachette Speakers Bureau provides a wide range of authors for speaking events. To find out more, go to www.hachettespeakersbureau.com or call (866) 376-6591.

The publisher is not responsible for websites (or their content) that are not owned by the publisher.

Illustrations shown in black (except pages 118, 174, and 228) by Matthew Hollings

Print book cover and interior design by Rachel Peckman.

Photos provided courtesy of BuzzFeed, Shane, and Ryan: front cover, back cover, pages 4, 26, 34, 73, 77, 91, 152, 162, 200, 204, 207, 209, 214, 216, 225, 229

The following images are copyright © by Getty Images Plus collection.
pages vi-1: cwinegarden; page 17: Pimpay; page 31: Yevhenii Dorofieiev; page 36: ZU_09 (DigitalVisionVectors); pages 38-39: shutter18; page 46: Marina Dekhnik; page 52: BRPH; page 56: Kreatiw; page 58: Lindsay Guido; page 62: gregobagel; page 64: f11photo; page 68: ilbusca; page 70: andipantz; page 74: longboardlola; page 76: Sierra Gaglione; page 80: Tashka; page 82: ottoblotto; page 90: catnap72; page 93: Jupiterimages; page 98: Pimpay; page 100: PhilAugustavo; page 102: Meinzahn; pages 104-105: South_agency; page 114: Olha Saiuk; page 116: ioanmasay and FrankRamspott; page 118: clu (DigitalVisionVectors); page 120: channarongsds; page 121: Hein Nouwens; pages 126-127: laddio1234; page 128: Paulbr; page 130: ChuckSchugPhotography; page 132: Pgiam; page 134: BeachcottagePhotography; page 138: ArtBalitskiy; page 138: Long_Strange_Trip_01; page 140: pastorscott; pages 144-145: spanglish; page 149: FarbaKolerova; page 157: Mafaldita; page 159: Long_Strange_Trip_01; page 163: THEPALMER; page 167: Inna Sinano; pages 168-169: Gill Copeland; page 170: Paul-Briden; page 172: Andrii-Oliinyk; page 174: ilbusca (DigitalVisionVectors); page 178: BleachedPink; page 182: Hein Nouwens; pages 186-197: Mypurgatoryyears; page 188: DenisTangneyJr; page 196-197: powerofforever; page 210: ilbusca; page 215: ilbusca; page 220: Comstock (Stockbyte); page 226: bauhaus1000; page 228: Keith Lance (DigitalVisionVectors); page 230: ilbusca; paper scraps used throughout: Tolga TEZCAN

The following images are copyright © Shutterstock.
page 2: djenkins5; page 5: Maddi Avery; page 24: Orange Grove; page 150: Mr. James Kelley; page 164: Edd Lange; page 199: Natalia BratslavskyInterior

Library of Congress Cataloging-in-Publication Data

Names: Bergara, Ryan, author. | Madej, Shane, author. | Katz, Anna, other.
Title: BuzzFeed unsolved supernatural : 101 true tales of hauntings, demons, and the paranormal / Ryan Bergara, Shane Madej and Anna Katz.
Description: Philadelphia : Running Press, 2022.
Identifiers: LCCN 2022009071 (print) | LCCN 2022009072 (ebook) | ISBN 9780762480203 (paperback) | ISBN 9780762480210 (ebook)
Subjects: LCSH: Ghosts--United States. | Haunted places--United States.
Classification: LCC BF1472.U6 B464 2022 (print) | LCC BF1472.U6 (ebook) | DDC 133.10973--dc23/eng/20220524
LC record available at https://lccn.loc.gov/2022009071
LC ebook record available at https://lccn.loc.gov/2022009072

ISBNs: 978-0-7624-8020-3 (paperback), 978-0-7624-8021-0 (ebook), 978-1-6686-1065-7 (audio)

FRI

10   9   8   7   6   5   4   3   2

For the Boogaras and Shaniacs

Though the following are ghost stories,
some of the details may still be disturbing or
upsetting to readers. Read at your own risk.
That's not to say ghosts aren't real,
because they very much are.

SHANE: NO, THEY'RE NOT.

RYAN: Yes, they are.

SHANE: NO, THEY'RE NOT . . .

RYAN: Just read the book.

CONTENTS

INTRODUCTION

Hey there, demons, it's us! No one really plans on becoming the internet's leading paranormal bad boys, but here we are. What began as a dip of the toe into the world of ghost-hunting inexplicably evolved into a full cannonball, plunging us deep into a proverbial pool of ectoplasm. Make no mistake: It's grueling work and we are heroes for it. With nary a complaint, we have endured nearly six long years of grime and sweat, swatting cobwebs and listening for whispers in the dark as we crawled through some of the world's straight-up freakiest locales. If that all sounds appealing, then bully for you on purchasing this book. Herein you'll find a vast compendium of seriously spooky spots, from harrowing hotels to wicked watering holes and every last nasty ghoul-infested establishment in between. So steel your nerves and thumb on through, and we'll try our best to distract you from the horrifying details and downright depressing history of some of these decrepit destinations with our usual detestable yuck-em-ups.

And also, the fact that this series spawned a book is truly a testament to you guys. Holy moly, thank you. And sorry to inform you that you just made us both "authors." Have fun explaining that one at the pearly gates (if you believe in that sort of thing).

—Ryan *and* SHANE

HAUNTED HOUSES

The Murders That Haunt the
Lizzie Borden House

Fall River, Massachusetts

Lizzie Borden took an ax
And gave her mother forty whacks.
When she saw what she had done,
She gave her father forty-one.

To be accurate, Abby Borden was Lizzie's *step*mother and was given a mere eighteen whacks, while Andrew Borden received only eleven. And the murder weapon was actually a hatchet, not an ax. Also, Lizzie was found not guilty so, per official record, she technically gave zero whacks.

SHANE: THE INACCURACY OF THIS SCHOOLYARD RHYME IS UNNERVING. NEXT YOU'RE GONNA TELL ME THAT WHEN I'M SLIDING INTO FIRST AND I FEEL SOMETHING BURST, IT'S NOT DIARRHEA. (STARTING OFF THIS BOOK STRONG WITH A LITTLE THING WE CALL COMEDY.)

RYAN: Not sure what's stranger—the fact that you referred to that as comedy or the fact that you made a sports reference. Either way, I think once you eclipse more than maybe two whacks, the rest is basically a wash, no?

Still, there's a reason why she attempted a rebrand by calling herself Lizbeth after the trial.

Gotta say, if I'm changing my name to *Poo-pourri* the stench off a double-murder accusation, I'm definitely going more liberal than simply changing from Lizzie to Lizbeth . . . you gotta go with something diametrically opposed, like Shaq.

I THINK YOU'RE THE ONLY OTHER PERSON WHO COULD PULL OFF SHAQ.

Thanks, man.

For the rest of her sixty-six years, infamy would follow her—all the way to her big fancy house on the Hill, a wealthy neighborhood nearby. Those who believe Lizzie was guilty point to money as motive; though she and her family lived on a diet of "warmed-over fish" and mutton, Mr. Borden was a rich man. Perhaps Lizzie had grown tired of her father's famous frugality and so gave him a bunch of whacks while he napped on the sofa in the sitting room.

MY DAD LOVES TINNED SARDINES, BUT I'VE NEVER ONCE KILLED HIM BECAUSE OF IT. JUST MADE ME LOVE SNACKIN' ON THOSE FREAKY LITTLE FISH. (I LIKE THAT YOU CAN FEEL THEIR BONES CRUNCHING UNDER THE WEIGHT OF YOUR TEETH.)

Never had sardines, and tbh, after hearing you describe their bones crunching on my molars, I don't think I ever will.

Perhaps Mrs. Borden then walked in at an inconvenient moment, and so Lizzie was forced to chase her up the stairs and into the guest room to silence her. Mrs. Borden—with whom Lizzie had fallen out five years prior—died on the floor next to the bed, her blood soaking the rug.

RYAN AND I HAVE VISITED THIS LOVELY HOME, AND I REGRET TO INFORM ANY TRUE CRIME SICKOS LOOKING TO GET THEIR PEEPERS ON A VISCERA-STAINED RUG THAT IT LOOKS LIKE THEY CALLED IN STANLEY STEEMER TO SUCK UP ALL THE BLOOD AND BRAINS.

Jesus, man. Also, from a tactical perspective—and I'll preface this with the fact that I've never been chased up the stairs by a hatchet wielding maniac—but if you're getting chased UP stairs, don't you technically have some sort of high-ground advantage after simply turning around? I guess the hatchet negates that? Maybe I've watched that duel on Mustafar from *Revenge of the Sith* too many times. Obi-Wan's (cocky, I might add) high-ground warning still rings in my head to this day.

Mrs. Borden is a central player in another theory featuring Lizzie as killer. According to its proponents, Mrs. Borden discovered Lizzie and the maid, Maggie, doing verboten dirty things to each other and so they killed her. In this version, Mr. Borden is the one who walked in inconveniently and was hence dispatched.

I THINK THIS SERVES AS A FAIR REMINDER FOR ALL PARENTS TO KEEP IN MIND THAT YOUR CHILDREN CAN AND WILL KILL YOU.

I hope you have kids one day.

SWEET OF YOU!

Some blame John V. Morse, the uncle of Lizzie and her sister, Emma. He and Mr. Borden were struggling over a failing shared enterprise. Or maybe it had something to do with Mr. Borden's will. Either way, Mr. Morse's whereabouts are unaccounted for from 9 a.m. to noon on August 4, 1892, the oppressively hot day of the murder.

> Probably at the swimming hole.
>
> EATIN' SOME SLIGHTLY WET SWEET TARTS, GOD WILLIN'.

Then there's the mysterious "Portuguese man" who allegedly stopped by the house to collect wages he was owed. Of course, someone might have noticed a Portuguese man drenched in blood walking down Second Street in broad daylight. To this day, no one knows whodunnit. Lizzie died in 1927 and was buried next to her father, step-mother, and sister, under a gravestone with the name "Lizbeth."

> Tell me this gravestone is not instantly improved by reading "Shaq " instead. I dare you.
>
> RJP SHAQ

Guests can stay in the very same house in which these gruesome murders occurred. Rooms include breakfast "of what the Bordens had that morning" minus the mutton. If you stay in Andrew Borden's room, leave some coins, or at least don't take any—his ghost is known to scratch those who part him from his money.

> PRO TIP TO ALL THE SHANIACS OUT THERE: FREE COINS AT THE BORDEN HOUSE.
>
> I didn't realize we could've had breakfast there.
>
> IT PROBABLY WOULD HAVE BEEN A BETTER OPTION THAN THE OUTBACK STEAKHOUSE WE WENT TO. IN MASSACHUSETTS. A MASSACHUSETTS OUTBACK STEAKHOUSE.
>
> Those Borden bathrooms are now consequently equally haunted.

The Abusive Witch of Bell Witch Farm

Adams, Tennessee

For thirteen years, the Bell family lived comfortably on their new farm along the south bank of the Red River in Robertson County, Tennessee. Then, in 1817, strange animals began to visit the fields, and late at night knocking rattled the walls.

> WHAT BRAND OF STRANGE ARE WE TALKIN' HERE? LIKE A COW WITH SUPER-LONG UDDERS OR SOMETHING EXTRA-FREAKY LIKE AN INSIDE-OUT CHICKEN?
>
> Inside-out chicken is fun, or like a pig with a bacon addiction? Oh shit, do animals who eat their own kind consider themselves cannibals? Like are there Hannibal Lecters in the animal kingdom?

The family awoke to the sounds of choking, stones dropping, chains dragging, dogs fighting, and rats gnawing on the bedpost. But when they lit a candle, the noise ceased.

> PURE NONSENSE SPOUTED BY IMBECILES.
>
> I guess ghosts like it a little more spontaneous. All the ceremony of lighting candles and rose petals and whatnot is a little too try-hard. Noted.

The patriarch, John Bell, was an upstanding citizen and deacon at the Red River Baptist Church

OH, HERE WE GO.

Hahaha.

and did not want word of these disturbances to tarnish his reputation.

Too late.

But eventually, it just got too weird to go it alone, especially as the terrorizing escalated. Labeled the Bell Witch—as in, the Bell's witch—and "Kate," so named after Kate Batts, the eccentric and very much alive wife of a neighbor who claimed that Bell swindled him over the sale of an enslaved girl, the entity targeted John and his youngest daughter, Betsy.

LOVE THAT HE WAS HESITANT TO BRING IT UP TO ANYBODY AND THEN FULLY PIVOTED TO SLAPPIN' HIS NAME ON THAT OL' HAG LIKE A NASCAR SPONSOR.

Love him going two birds one stone here by dunking on his annoying neighbor while naming his demon.

ALSO, IT SHOULD BE STATED: ALL THESE PEOPLE ARE ASSHOLES.

Kinda hope this ghost is actually a demon so it just eats these d-bags. Or possesses them to belly flop onto a pitchfork or something.

By all accounts, Betsy was a babe, and for whatever reason, Kate was adamant that she should not marry a handsome boy by the name of Joshua Gardner.

Don't think I've ever covered a case where a ghost has the hots for someone. Other than the motion picture *Ghost* starring Patrick Swayze, but I only kinda watched that one. Also, I'm pretty sure he was banging his wife's spirit in that one? A little fuzzy on it.

THAT'S AN INSULTINGLY REDUCTIVE DESCRIPTION OF A BEAUTIFUL FILM ABOUT LOVE, LOSS, AND LITTLE SHADOWBABIES FROM HELL.

Just sayin' that paranormal penetration sounds icky.

Kate cussed and threatened and pulled the girl's hair, pinched her and scratched her, slapped her and stuck her with pins and untied her shoes.

WHEN IT COMES TO GHOULS, SLAP ME ALL YOU WANT. SPIT ECTOPLASM IN MY MOUTH FOR ALL I CARE. BUT DON'T UNTIE MY SHOES. CHILDISH BABY SHIT.

Is it 'cause it takes a lot of energy for you to crane all the way down there?

NASTY.

Meanwhile, John experienced bizarre facial tics and felt intermittently that he had "stiffness of the tongue." When eminent community members attempted to intervene, Kate became ruder and ruder, going so far as to call a neighbor Old Sugar Mouth during prayer.

THIS IS RUDE? I FIND IT INCREDIBLY ROMANTIC.

Yeah, strangely, it feels like something you'd call a human songbird. I'd be flattered. But also I keep forgetting these people are dumb as hell.

Eventually, four distinct personalities joined the crew: Blackdog, Mathematics, Crypocryphy, and Jerusalem.

I'M ON A BOWLING TEAM WITH THESE GUYS. HAHAHA, JUST A JOKE. I'M NOT ON A BOWLING TEAM WITH THESE GUYS. NEXT!

On December 20, 1820, John Bell was found dead in his bed, a half-full vial the culprit, as determined by experimenting with the remaining liquid on the cat. Soon thereafter, Betsy broke off her engagement to Joshua. Kate took credit for the family's misfortune yet was apparently unsatisfied—she promised to return to visit John's descendants.

WAIT, IS KATE A SPIRIT ENTITY? NAMED AFTER A WOMAN? OR A CORPOREAL HUMAN LADY? AND IF IT'S THE LATTER, AND SHE'S TAKING CREDIT FOR MURDERING A MAN, SHOULDN'T SHE HAVE BEEN TOSSED DOWN A WELL OR SOMETHING? (TO BE CLEAR: I DO NOT CONDONE TOSSING ANYONE DOWN WELLS. I'M SIMPLY ASSUMING THIS WAS PROTOCOL AT THE TIME.)

Now you can visit the farm, which was placed on the National Historical Registry in 2008. The Bell Witch Cave, a cave carved by the Red River, was part of the family's original acreage, and visitors have reported the sensation of choking or paralysis, the sound of whispers and singing, and the sight of a ghostly figure. Sometimes photos taken in the cave do not develop.

QUICK TIP: NEVER TRUST ANY REPORTS FROM ANYONE WHO GOES OUT OF THEIR WAY TO SPEND TIME AT AN ALLEGEDLY HAUNTED LOCATION. WORD-OF-MOUTH EVIDENCE IS AKIN TO CHEAP SOUVENIRS FROM THE GIFT SHOP. YEAH, I'M BEING STRAIGHT-UP NASTY ABOUT THIS, BUT I'M ONE OF THE GREAT PARANORMAL BAD BOY SKEPTICS OF OUR TIME. SUE ME.

I think experiences can't be discounted. I'm a theme park aficionado, and if I go to Disneyland, I can assure you that all of my trip report is valid.

NO DISNEYLAND SIMPING ALLOWED IN THIS BOOK. THAT'S STRIKE ONE.

The Mystical Villa Montezuma Mansion

San Diego, California

Benjamin Henry Jesse Francis Shepard was born the same year as the Spiritualist Movement, in 1848.

> If I ask you what your name is and you keep talking past, say, three names, we're no longer talking.

While teen sisters Maggie and Kate Fox (aka the "Rochester Rappers") became famous for communicating with the dead via rapping noises in Hydesville, New York, the Shepard family was relocating from Birkenhead, England, to Illinois.

> IS THAT "RAPPING" AS IN "HARK! FROM YONDER WINDOW, A RAPPING!" OR ARE THEY OUT HERE DOING KENDRICK STUFF TO GHOSTS?
>
> Probably the former, but boy do I wish it was the latter. Then again, the "Rochester Rappers" sounds like a mixtape I'd be handed on Hollywood Boulevard, next to a dollar-store *Spider-Man*.

Jesse grew up singing and playing the piano, developing enough confidence in his musical skills to move to Europe at the age of twenty-one to make a name for himself. In Paris, he enjoyed his growing popularity, eventually touring the continent, performing and attracting patrons and staying on lavish estates.

MUST BE NICE!

We're like Jesse in the upside down. Touring run-down homes covered in cobwebs and rat turds in the Bible Belt.

It is believed that Jesse learned how to conduct séances while in St. Petersburg to perform for the czar in 1871. Three years later, he played for Madame Helena Blavatsky, a medium and founder of the Theosophical Society.

WHAT A TIME TO BE ALIVE. "NICE TO MEET YOU. I DID GHOSTS FOR RUSSIA."
"COOL, YEAH, I'M A WELL-RESPECTED PERSON, AND I DO A MADE-UP THING FOR A HORSESHIT SOCIETY."

You're just jealous 'cause it's badass to have "madame" in front of your name. I believe this is used to preface normal folk, but I always have it in my head that it's reserved for fortune tellers or that lady whose head floats around in a crystal ball in the Haunted Mansion at Disneyland.

STRIKE TWO.

He began to claim to channel spirits of the musical greats through his music, a claim supported by his extensive range and extraordinary ability to sing "in two voices."

THERE IS A ZERO PERCENT CHANCE THIS WAS PLEASANT OR ENTERTAINING. PROBABLY SOUNDED LIKE HE WAS BURP-SINGING.

Speak for yourself. I wanna see this dude sing out of his mouth and butthole (assuming that's how he did it). Lol, two mic stands. One tall and one small.

JUST LIKE US!

Very good, very good.

It was through the spiritualism community that he met the High Brothers of San Diego, who funded the construction of a "Palace of the Arts" for him.

I knew twins in college named the High Brothers. But they were from Colorado and High wasn't their last name. They were just the go-to ganj guys on campus.

He and his "companion," Lawrence W. Tonner, moved into Villa Montezuma in 1887.

Of the approximately $19,000 cost of the mansion, $7,000 went into the windows alone. Stained-glass depictions of artists, musicians, saints, and even Jesse himself overlook the rooms' eclectic design.

SAW THESE WINDOWS IN PERSON. I'LL BET THEY LOOK STUNNING WITH DAYLIGHT SUN DAZZLING THROUGH THEM, BUT SOMEONE INSISTS THAT WE GO TO HAUNTED LOCATIONS ONLY AT NIGHT.

Ghosts are like Dracula. Everyone knows that.

Jesse and Lawrence stayed for little more than a year before hitting the road, this time to pursue a new career in writing. Jesse found literary success under the pen name Francis Grierson, though the couple's finances diminished over their forty years together. In 1927, Jesse/Francis died as he lived—upright at the piano after wowing a small crowd of admirers.

ALL I CAN RESPONSIBLY DO IN THIS INSTANCE IS POINT YOU TO THE *UNSOLVED* EPISODE IN WHICH WE HELPLESSLY CRY WITH LAUGHTER AS WE DISRESPECTFULLY MEDITATE UPON THIS MAN PASSING AWAY WHILE PLAYING A FUNNY LITTLE TUNE ON HIS PIANO.

And possibly pooping himself. It sounds juvenile. Mainly 'cause it is. But I do recommend you watch the ep if you haven't.

The villa was sold again and again until, finally, the San Diego History Center purchased it in 1970. This very turnover has been attributed to a curse, perhaps the same one that stunts plants' growth in a particular corner.

WEAK-ASS CURSE. A POX! A POX UPON THIS HOME! MAY THEIR SCHEFFLERAS WITHER EVERMORE!

Today, the Villa Montezuma Museum denies the rumors that the villa is haunted. But others claim to hear piano music from the locked séance room where the original owner contacted spirits, and one little girl told the tour guide that she heard a chorus and organ music in Jesse's bathroom.

HERE'S A NICE MOMENT TO DRAW A LINE IN THE SAND. YOU'RE EITHER ON THE SIDE OF SCIENCE OR SOME STUPID LITTLE GIRL WHO HEARD AN ORGAN IN A BATHROOM. (NO DISRESPECT TO THE STUPID LITTLE GIRL.)

Just occurred to me how weird it is that bathrooms haunted by ghosts never seem to stink. If they're stuck in there eternally, what else could they be doing?

Others reported seeing a sad specter in the cupola and a grief-stricken ghost in the observatory tower. It is said that, in his stained-glass portrait, the beard of Flemish Baroque painter Peter Paul Rubens is slowly turning gray.

IF I HAD A NICKEL FOR EVERY "IT IS SAID THAT..." I COULD BUY SEASON TICKETS TO BLUE MAN GROUP.

Doubt it. BMG season tix have a waiting list.

The Visions of Woodburn Mansion

Dover, Delaware

Built by Charles Hillyard III in 1798, the Woodburn Mansion has changed hands many times, becoming the official residence of the governor in 1965. Its first female governor, Ruth Ann Minner, moved in, in 2001. She was twice widowed at the time, which is presumably why her husbands' portraits aren't included on the "Wall of First Ladies."

I GUESS YOU CAN CHALK BEING TWICE WIDOWED UP TO UNFORTUNATE CIRCUMSTANCES. BUT ONCE YOU HIT THRICE WIDOWED...THAT'S WHEN THE SHANESTER'S GONNA START KEEPING AN EYE ON HIS OATMEAL AROUND YOU.

Yeah, it probably has nothing to do with her, but if I'm Ruth, I'm definitely leaving that little factoid off my dating profile on Hinge.

The seven-bedroom Middle Period Georgian house is just a half mile from the Delaware state capitol. One of its gubernatorial traditions involves the planting of trees by each new occupant and his or her family. It is in one of these trees that a mean ghost lurks.

THIS GENUINELY SOUNDS LIKE A LOVELY TRADITION! I PLANTED A BALD CYPRESS IN MY PARENTS' BACKYARD A DECADE AGO, AND I LOVE TO SEE HOW HUGE THAT LITTLE FUCKER'S GOTTEN. IT SPROUTED KNEES THIS YEAR. CYPRESS KNEES. IT'S A WHOLE THING. WE DON'T NEED TO GET INTO IT. BACK TO THE GHOSTS.

If I were a governor, I'd put "gubernatorial" in front of everything. As much as I could. "It's time for my gubernatorial nap," or "it's time for my gubernatorial snack." It's just too fun to say. Even more fun when you imagine Arnie Schwarzenegger saying it.

IF YOU EVER HELD THE OFFICE, YOU COULD GO BY RYAN BERGUBERNATOR. OR, AHEM, SHAQ BERGUBERNATOR.

Bergubernator is a solid alias. Might have to take that for a test drive off the lot.

George Alfred Townsend's book *The Entailed Hat* was published in 1884, creating a chicken-or-egg debate. In it, a character based on Patty Cannon, illegal slave trader and the "wickedest woman in America," hunted escaped slaves taking refuge in the "Cowgill House"—Woodburn was owned by the Cowgill family at the time. So it is from this book that the legend comes, or maybe the legend inspired the book. Either way, one ghost is reported to be that of a slave raider, who arrived to suss out people sheltered in the cellar of this Underground Railroad safe haven. He hid in a poplar tree to lurk and spy, hoping to catch an enslaved person venturing aboveground. But he slipped and somehow his head got caught in the tree and he died. To this day, his apparition occasionally is seen still hanging from the tree, moaning and flailing about.

THE THOUGHT OF THIS DUMB ASSHOLE SUFFERING FOR ALL OF ETERNITY IS ENOUGH FOR ME TO WISH THAT GHOSTS WERE REAL.

Otherwise, the ghosts tend to be mild mannered. A young girl in a gingham dress and bonnet walks around the reflecting pool, carrying a lit candle.

COOLEST GHOST WE'VE ENCOUNTERED IN THIS BOOK SO FAR. ASPIRATIONAL, TO HAUNT A POOL. I'D PROBABLY DO ALL OF THE ABOVE BUT ALSO BE DOWNING A VIENNA BEEF HOT DOG SLATHERED IN MUSTARD.

If I saw a ghostly little girl face lit by candlelight, I'd have a heart attack.

Another ghost is believed to be that of the original owner. The first sighting was in 1815, when a Methodist preacher named Lorenzo Dow reported that he'd seen an older gentleman in the attire of an earlier era—ruffled shirt, knee britches, powdered wig, the whole nine yards.

Very amusing to have a dude from 1815 talk about a ghost in EVEN OLDER attire.

"HIS SHIRT WAS *MUCH* MORE RUFFLED THAN *MY* RUFFLED SHIRT! GHASTLY!"

Per his description, the lady of the house determined that this was her father, Mr. Charles Hillyard III, who, according to lore, knew it was always five o'clock somewhere. Apparently, if current residents leave a full glass of wine downstairs at night, he'll empty it by morning.

YO, NO. PROVE THIS SHIT. POINT A NANNY CAM AT A BIG GULP FULL OF FRANZIA, GET YOUR ASS TO BED, AND I'LL BE THERE IN THE MORNING TO WATCH THE FOOTAGE OF CASPER GETTING HAMBONED. UNTIL THEN, NOT BUYIN' IT.

Also, if my house were haunted, I'd much rather have that spirit stack chairs or some shit. Drinking all of the Bergooze's booze as I sleep is a one-way ticket to the after afterlife.

The Scratching Demon
of the Sallie House

Atchison, Kansas

Debra and Tony Pickman and their baby moved into the house on 508 North Second Street on December 31, 1992. Built by the Finney family in 1871, the site has three recorded deaths: that of Michael Finney in 1872, William True in 1918, and Agnes True in 1939. But those three deaths don't account for the evil that torments ye who enter there.

HERE WE GO. BASICALLY, A VACATION HOME FOR US AT THIS POINT. WE GOT IN THERE, DID OUR THING, CLEARED IT. GOD-TIER INTERNET CONTENT, SURE, BUT IT WAS JUST ANOTHER HONEST DAY'S WORK FOR THE GHOUL BROTHERS.

This house blows.

For the Pickmans, things were weird from the start: Lights dimmed and went on in the night, pictures on the wall were turned upside down, the dog barked incessantly at the nursery doorway, and a wind-up musical toy spontaneously played. Their newborn woke up every hour (though the Pickmans would not be the first parents to attribute their baby's sleep schedule to demonic forces).

BAD DOG, BAD TOY, BAD BABY. NEXT.

Wonder if the Pickmans ever tried hanging their photos upside down? Work smarter not harder, ya know?

On July 14, 1993, Tony, Debra, and her sister, Karen, discovered all the stuffed animals arranged back-to-back in a circle in the middle of the floor of the nursery.

Holy shit, I don't know how I've missed this in the two times we've covered this but . . . is this proof that *Toy Story* is real?

They tidied up and went downstairs, but when they returned, the light was on, and a stuffed bear was laying on the ground. The next morning, Tony's brother approached the bear with his camera, and as he clicked the shutter, the bear spun around right before their eyes. With that, they packed up and fled. Tony felt a sharp sting on his back while they were leaving and, later, he discovered three long scratches.

NOT SAYING WE SHOULDN'T FEEL SYMPATHY FOR THE SCRATCHED, BUT THEY *ARE* ALL LIARS. YOUR NASTY BOY SHANE HAS SPENT FIVE YEARS DUNKIN' ON THE WORLD'S GNARLIEST GHOULS AND NARY A SCRAPE TO BE SEEN.

I do have to concede that this is true. He's never been scratched. We even offered our belly buttons to Sallie in the last episode, and she did nothing. Despite knowing how weird and uncomfortable it feels to poke it.

IT REMAINS A SHOCK THAT THE BELLY BUTTON SMACKING SCENE GOT CUT FROM THE SERIES FINALE.

Even for us, it was far too much. And that's saying a lot.

Tony continued to get viciously scratched, and in one instance, a scratch manifested on camera. There were spontaneous fires in the nursery. On the morning of October 31, 1993, Tony saw a full apparition in the form of a little girl in early 1900s clothing, a bow in her hair.

Still very funny to me that a demon picked out this appearance for its Sim. Just picturing the demon trying different looks in the mirror: "Bonnet? Hmmm . . . no, not really doing it for me. Oh shit, they have bows? Oh yeah. That's it. I can work with that."

He ran upstairs to sketch the presence a psychic had told them was named Sallie. The torment soon escalated beyond the physical. Tony said, "When I was in the house, I could not think any happy thought. It was just strictly I wanted to hurt her [Debra] . . . I had planned on slitting her throat." The Pickmans moved out twenty-two months after moving in.

LOOK, THE THROAT-SLITTING THING—IT'S A CONCERNING THOUGHT TO HAVE IN THE FIRST PLACE, BUT EVEN MORE ALARMING TO ADMIT ALOUD. SURELY ALL THE BOOGARAS ARE SAYING, "BUT THE GHOSTS MADE HIM THINK THAT!" BUT TO THE SHANIACS, THIS IS JUST A MAN THINKING, "GOSH, I REALLY WANT TO SLIT A THROAT," AND BLAMING IT ON SOMETHING IMAGINARY. REALLY WILD SHIT.

It's crazy. I've thought of slitting your throat for years, and not once have I said it aloud.

YOU USUALLY SAY IT IN YOUR SLEEP ANYTIME WE DO AN OVERNIGHT AT ONE OF THESE PLACES. I HAVE RECORDINGS.

Eleven years later, a former resident said, "The whole time we lived here, my daughter was five at the time, she had an imaginary friend, Sallie. I would scold her for something, and she would come back and tell me, 'I didn't do that, Sallie did it' or 'Sallie told me to do it.'" When shown Tony's drawing, the daughter identified her "imaginary friend" from her childhood.

I HATE TO POINT THIS OUT BUT... CHILDREN ARE NOT VERY SMART.

Well, in this case, it's a person recounting their childhood. Not a story from a child. I still find this pretty creepy. And to echo earlier, it really shows that the demon made the right choices with his Sim. That's some staying power!

So who, exactly, is Sallie? Records show that a Sallie Isabel Hall did indeed live in the house in 1905. Only problem is that she was a thirty-four-year-old Black woman and not a little white girl. The only logical answer is that Sallie is a demon in disguise. It's reported that spirits captured on audio recordings often refer to another more dominant presence that even scared them. Today, the Sallie House continues to be one of the most haunted places in America.

ALL WE CAN SAY WITH CERTAINTY IS THAT THE ENTITY KNOWN AS SALLIE WHO ALLEGEDLY HAUNTS THIS HUMBLE ABODE IS A STRAIGHT-UP ZERO WHO GOT PUBLICLY CLOWNED ON TWO OCCASIONS BY THE GREATEST GHOST HUNTERS WHO EVER LIVED.

Now that we are safely out of the house, never to return again, I concur.

The Betrayal at the Oliver Estate

Middleborough, Massachusetts

> Right off the bat, hell of a title.

It was the eighteenth century in the colonies, and State Supreme Court Chief Justice Peter Oliver was a Tory who took a salary from the crown. He'd also made a bundle from the ironworks on the Nemasket River, and when his son, Peter Jr., married the governor's daughter, Sally Hutchinson, in 1769, he built a glorious Georgian manse for them near his own as a wedding gift.

> This family had two mansions?! Does his ghost hop between the two? I've never heard of a pair of haunted mansions.

The entire family were Loyalists, a political stance that was going out of style. Someone—probably an underpaid or enslaved chambermaid—got their hands on some letters between the Hutchinson and Oliver families and employees of the crown, and an angry mob of Sons of Liberty (or "Sons of Anarchy," depending on who you ask) descended on the house, forcing the Olivers to flee in 1774. Everything inside was confiscated and sold, the proceeds going toward the launch of the Revolutionary War. Legend has it that the shot of "Shot Heard Around the World" fame came from the Oliver Mill.

> I THINK IT'S FUNNY TO MAKE RICH PEOPLE FLEE THEIR HOMES. I'M SURE THEY MOSTLY JUST FLEE TO THEIR OTHER HOMES, BUT IF WE ALL KEEP AT IT, EVENTUALLY THEY GOTTA RUN OUT OF HOMES.

> Well, in this case, per earlier, he has a mansion next door.

Patriots burned Judge Oliver's house to the ground in 1778, but Junior's house survived the war and was eventually converted back into a single-family residence.

> Well, there you go.

The Olivers themselves were long gone, returned to the loving bosom of Mother England. The Weston family owned the home from 1798 to 1893, the entirety of Bethania (Weston) Sproat's life. She and her husband, Earle, lost three of their six children within a few years—two infants and toddler Abigail, who died of complications from third-degree burns. Earle died of tuberculosis; Bethania died of old age.

> Pearly gates were basically saloon doors back then. People coming and going like hockey substitutions.

Today, the Oliver Estate is a museum; its upkeep is funded, in part, by ghost tours. Bethania seems to be the most outgoing ghost of the bunch, which makes sense given all that tragedy and grief she suffered within the house, though her haunting appears to be pleasant.

"SHE'S A BLAST! AND HAS SUFFERED COUNTLESS SHATTERING TRAGEDIES!"

She's probably just happy to have people in the home.

An apparition believed to be the chambermaid who allegedly found those damning letters has been seen in the closet of her mistress.

Btw, love a chambermaid dunking on her lord. I don't blame her for taking an ethereal victory lap.

There's also a lot of paranormal energy and shadowy figures moving around, plus the mysterious relocation of objects and the sound of disembodied voices. Others claim to have seen little baby ghost Abby cruising around.

NAH. NO BABY GHOSTS. VETOING BABY GHOSTS. NEXT!

But wait, what do you mean cruising around? Like on Heelys?

SEEMS LIKE ANYBODY CAN CLAIM ANYTHING ABOUT THESE PLACES, SO I'LL JUST CLOSE BY STATING THAT, SURE, THE OLIVER ESTATE IS DEFINITELY HAUNTED BY A TINY LITTLE BABY GHOST ON AN ITTY-BITTY SEGWAY.

Sure, I'll cosign that.

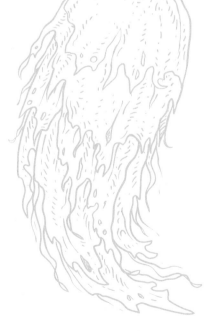

The Spirits of the Whaley House

San Diego, California

Only after he retired did the police officer reveal what he'd seen. A concerned citizen had called 911 to report a woman crying outside the Whaley House Museum in Old Town San Diego, and when the officer arrived, he had found her sobbing inconsolably. She was in period clothing. When he asked if she was alright, she turned around and smiled, then vanished into the night.

SOUNDS LIKE THIS LITTLE PIGGY'S BEEN HITTIN' THE SAUCE. HEHEHE, JAH FEEL, RYAN?

Jah don't feel. Sounds like he saw a fuggin' ghost.

It has been theorized that this was the apparition of Violet Whaley, the second-to-youngest offspring of Thomas and Anna Whaley. In 1885, after a short marriage and divorce, Violet shot herself in the heart and, with her father by her side, died in the parlor. Hers was not the first death at the family's home on 2476 San Diego Avenue.

GOD, THESE STORIES ARE ALL THE SAME. "THIS PERSON HAD PARENTS, BUT THEY ALSO HAD COUSINS AND EVEN A SIBLING OR TWO. THERE WAS A MARRIAGE SOMEHOW, BUT TO WHOM? YOU GUESSED IT! ANOTHER PERSON! WHO WAS THEN KILLED! BUT SOMETIMES PEOPLE HEAR A MEOWING AND SEE THE SHADOW OF A CLOWN!"

Shooting yourself in the heart is very Shakespearean. But also, divorce is tough . . . Wait a second, I just reread the last paragraph. She survived long enough for her father to come to her side??? Her heart ate a bullet. How is that possible?

That occurred in 1852, before the first brick had even been laid, with the hanging of an inveterate thief by the name of Yankee Jim on a gallows on the back of a wagon.

Can you blame the guy for wanting to steal a boat? I bet San Diego was as dusty and hot as every western I've seen. He just wanted to cruise on nature's highway. Is that so bad?

Thomas Whaley was allegedly in attendance yet decided to purchase the property a few years later. As soon as the two-story house he'd designed was built and the family had moved in, they heard the sound of heavy footsteps, which they agreed were made by the ghostly feet of Yankee Jim.

WEIRD TO RETURN TO THE SITE OF A THIEF'S EXECUTION AND DECIDE YOU'D LIKE TO SETTLE DOWN THERE. ALSO BIG UPS TO YANKEE JIM. WE'VE LONG BEEN HUGE FANS.

Anna Whaley believed the property was cursed.

WHY? WERE HER ALOE PLANTS NOT THRIVING, HAHA!

Woof.

Thomas Jr., her second child, died of scarlet fever at eighteen months, the same year that an arsonist burned down Thomas Sr.'s general store.

OH.

Do you not remember anything from our adventures??

The family soon moved to San Francisco, but misfortune tailed them, and after the 6.8 magnitude Hayward earthquake in 1868, they were forced to return to San Diego Avenue.

If I moved to SF to start over and was immediately greeted by a 6.8 earth shaker, I'd think I was cursed, too.

Seventeen years later, Violet took her own life. Anna died at home in 1913, followed by Thomas's brother, Francis, in 1914. By the time the youngest daughter, Corinne Lillian, died in 1953, the house had fallen into disrepair.

I GUESS THE TELLING OF ANY FAMILY HISTORY COULD EASILY BE DISTILLED INTO "THEY ALL DIED." WE CAN PROBABLY TAKE SOME SOLACE IN TRUSTING THAT THEIR LIVES WEREN'T NONSTOP MISERY. MAYBE THEY HEARD A FUNNY JOKE AT THE SODA SHOP ONCE OR SOMETHING.

Yeah, I like that.

Along with the sound of Yankee Jim's footsteps, an infant's cries are often heard, as well as the sounds of vaudeville music and laughter from the front upstairs bedroom once rented by the Tanner Troupe Theater and a gavel striking in what was once a makeshift courtroom. Visitors claim to have seen the ghost of Thomas, in a frock coat and pantaloons, on the upper landing and the ghost of Anna, in a green gingham dress, sipping tea in the parlor.

Btw, for the record, I did have to Google "pantaloons" and can confirm they are as fun to look at as they are to say.

KEEP IT IN YOUR PANTS, SHAQ.

A ghost dog chases a ghost cat in the garden.

Glad to see this chase continue in the afterlife.

On the second floor, the feeling of "profound sorrow" resides—this is where Violet spent much of her unhappy time before her early death.

BEEN TO THAT SECOND FLOOR. DIDN'T CLOCK ANY PROFOUND SORROW. ONLY FELT LOVE AND RESPECT FOR MY MAN YANKEE JIM.

"Profound sorrow" is also how I'd describe Shane and myself when we returned to the Whaley House in 2018, expecting them to welcome us back with open arms, only for them to point us in the direction of the ticket booth if we wanted to come in.

WE EXPECTED A HERO'S WELCOME AND INSTEAD WERE DIRECTED TO GET IN LINE WITH COMMON SCUM.

The Eternal Betrothed of the
Daniel Benton Homestead

Tolland, Connecticut

Daniel Benton's dad gave him the lovely gift of forty acres for homesteading in 1719. Daniel added a bunch more land a couple of years later, making him a highly eligible bachelor and catching the fancy of one Mary Skinner, with whom he had a couple of kids.

> SEEMS NICE TO OWN LAND. THE DREAM. WAKING UP AND LOOKING OUT TO SEE BLADES OF SUNSHINE CUTTING THROUGH THE LEAVES OF YOUR OWN TREES, KISSING DROPS OF MORNING DEW ON ACRES UPON ACRES OF SOFT GRASS. A BIG-ASS VOLCANO BAY-CALIBER LAZY RIVER CARVED DIRECTLY THROUGH THE PROPERTY WITH A SWIM-UP MARGARITA BAR. ONE DAY.

> I honestly have nothing to improve upon for this beautiful picture you've painted. Maybe swapping the swim-up margarita bar for a swim-up tiki bar, but we can workshop offline.

Daniel Jr. grew up and had seven kids of his own and acquired more land, with close to four hundred acres in total.

> This dude tryna build Disney World?

Elisha was the eldest and the favorite. He grew up to be a landowning eligible bachelor himself, which made his romantic feelings toward Jemima Barrows, the daughter of a landless furniture maker, less than ideal. His folks nixed the match.

> THAT'S A PERFECT MATCH! LAND NEEDS FURNITURE! LAWN CHAIRS! CHAISE LOUNGES! FUTONS!

> Rocking chairs! Patio tables! This might be a stretch (I'm not familiar with her craftsmanship capabilities), but a fuggin' gazebo?! That's technically furniture, right? Regardless, agreed, big guy! This feels symbiotic af to me!

> WOULD LOOOOOOOVE A GAZEBO!

Then the Revolutionary War broke out, and Elisha and four of his brothers enlisted. He and brother Azariah were captured at the Battle of Long Island and held aboard a British prison ship in Long Island Sound. These prison ships were aggressively gross in part because that's war and in part as a recruitment strategy—they'd be starved to the brink of death, then offered food in exchange for allegiance to the crown.

> NO DISRESPECT TO OUR FRIENDS ACROSS THE POND, BUT IF I WERE STARVING ON A PRISON SHIP AND OFFERED BRITISH CUISINE, I MIGHT JUST TAKE MY CHANCES INVESTIGATING THE NUTRITIONAL VALUE OF THE SCUM UNDER MY TOENAILS.

Disease ran rampant, and during their four-month imprisonment, the young men contracted smallpox, a nasty disease that was eradicated by a global immunization campaign in 1980. Azariah died on December 29, 1776, at the age of twenty-two. Elisha was traded for a British POW and sent home, bringing the highly contagious infection with him. The Bentons built a wall within the house to quarantine him; his beloved Jemima Barrows heard news of his return and hastened to the Benton homestead, sneaking into Elisha's stopgap sickroom so that, by the time she was discovered, she was already contaminated and she'd just have to ride out the quarantine with him.

I'LL BET THEY RODE IT OUT ALRIGHT! LMAO.

Hope that wall they built was soundproof!

Elisha died less than three weeks after his release from captivity and was buried next to the carriage road that ran along the property. As feared, Jemima sickened and died five weeks later, alone and in mourning.

OH. WELL, NICE THAT THEY ENDED UP TOGETHER. WHO KNOWS? MAYBE THEIR FINAL WEEKS WERE ONES OF UNRESTRAINED ANIMALISTIC ECSTASY. I'D LIKE TO THINK SO.

Well, following our last aside, this is quite brutal news. But as my colleague theorized, I, too, hope that they went out in a blaze of passionate glory.

The two weren't actually married, and it was considered indecent for them to be buried next to each other, so the family buried Jemima on the other side of the road, about forty feet from her star-crossed lover. A plaque commemorating her reads, "His betrothed, who herself died vainly attempting to nurse him back to health."

WHAT! THAT'S THE RUDEST SHIT EVER PUT TO A PLAQUE! GET A LOAD OF THIS ASSHOLE TRYING TO HELP ANOTHER HUMAN!

RIP to Jemima, a real one.

Today, a "dead" feeling pervades the bedroom, and one tour guide reported her watch suddenly stopping while inside. A ghost in a white wedding dress walks through the house, crying for her lost love.

SOUNDS COOL. SOMEBODY SHOULD GET THAT ON CAMERA. NEXT!

I hope these two are doing whatever they want in the afterlife.

The Cold Case of the Nell Cropsey House

Elizabeth City, North Carolina

Beautiful Ella Maud "Nell" Cropsey and James Wilcox, the county sheriff's son, had been dating for going on three years, and he had yet to put a ring on it. She was cute and knew it, and so she finally decided to seek out other suitors. Jim was not stoked, and after a bad fight in early November 1901, the couple broke up.

> Ya snooze ya lose, Jim!

But he was back at the sixty-five-acre plantation known as Seven Pines a couple weeks later, hat in hand. Nell's cousin, Carrie; her older sister, Ollie; and Ollie's beau, Roy Crawford, were there, but Roy bailed and the gals headed up to bed around 11 p.m. when Jim asked to speak to Nell alone on the porch.

> Always so awkward when people exit a room so two people can sort out their shit.

An hour later, the family was awakened by a ruckus of barking and a neighbor shouting that someone was trying to steal the pigs.

THAT'S HOW WE WAKE UP EVERY MORNING IN MY HOMETOWN OF SCHAUMBURG, ILLINOIS.

Explains a lot.

Nell's papa, William, grabbed his rifle and raced outside. Satisfied that everything was in order after searching the premises, William returned to the house, where he did another check. Nell's room was empty.

The town joined in the search, but to no avail. William even hired a team of bloodhounds, who got no farther than the porch, where Jim claimed to have left the young lady the night before, sobbing but safe.

MAYBE THE BLOODHOUNDS WERE JUST A LITTLE *TRUE CRIMED* OUT, Y'KNOW?

Nah, bloodhounds will do anything for a buck . . . or should I say a BONE! Hahaha . . . But no, bloodhounds actually love money.

He also suggested that Nell died by suicide—a hypothesis that everyone who knew her quickly dismissed. Five weeks later, a fisherman spotted her body floating face-down in the Pasquotank River, near the shore adjacent to her family's home. She had a gash on the side of her head and no water in her lungs; the coroner ruled it murder.

Not looking good for Jimbo, here.

I'D LIKE TO DIE FLOATING ONE WAY OR ANOTHER. MAYBE HAVE MY FUNERAL IN A WAVE POOL, MY LIFELESS LIMBS TOPPLING IN THE TIDE. GET CREATIVE.

Jim went to trial twice and was found guilty both times, while Elizabeth City citizens clamored for his hanging. He proclaimed his innocence over the next fourteen years, until he was pardoned by Governor Thomas Walter Bickett himself in 1918. Apparently, the sheriff's son had a private conference with newspaper editor W. O. Saunders, but whatever new information he revealed never saw the light of day. He shot himself in the head, and the editor died in a car accident soon after their meeting.

YOU'VE GOT TO LOVE STORIES. LOVE TO HEAR ABOUT THINGS THAT HAVE HAPPENED. THINGS LIKE THIS.

If Beyoncé's "Single Ladies" had been contemporary for this time, you have to wonder if any of this would have happened.

Today, a shadowy figure believed to be Nell wanders along the riverbank where she was found. She has been spotted in an upstairs window of Seven Pines, where the lights go on and off, doors and windows bang shut at random, and a cold draft announces an ethereal presence.

SOMEONE SHOULD ASK HER WHAT HAPPENED.

And that's why, when it comes to ghoul hunting, you're the best of the best, Madej.

The Mystery of the Winchester House

San Jose, California

Sarah Lockwood Pardee and William Wirt Winchester wed in 1862. The well-educated, upper-middle-class twenty-two-year-old woman was decidedly marrying up, at least in monetary terms. Over the next decades, the Winchester rifle sold in the millions and became the favorite of famous gunslingers like Annie Oakley, Buffalo Bill, and POTUS Theodore Roosevelt. Upon his death in 1881, William left his wife $20 million and 50 percent of the Winchester Repeating Arms Company, making Sarah one of the richest women in the world. Her income was roughly $1,000 to $1,500 per day—the equivalent of approximately $29,000 today—and about one-thousand times the average daily income of the hoi polloi.

> WITH THAT KINDA MONEY, YOU COULD HIRE THE BLUE MAN GROUP FOR A FULL-TIME
> IN-HOUSE RESIDENCY. THEIR DRUMMING COULD POTENTIALLY DROWN OUT THE
> HAMMERING A BIT, TOO. TWO BIRDS, ONE STONE.
>
> Lmfao. That's the dream right there. God, do I love to watch those blue
> dudes drum.

As the legend goes, after Sarah Winchester's husband died, she hired renowned psychic Adam Coons to help her contact her late husband and her daughter lost in infancy. Instead, the psychic told her that she was cursed by the multitudes killed by Winchester rifles, and that she must buy a house and remodel it in perpetuity—if the hammers ever cease, she would die.

MEAN-ASS PRANK TO PULL ON AN OLD LADY.

This psychic's family must own a contracting business.

But obscene wealth is not necessarily a balm for grief, nor can it reverse a curse. Sarah moved from the East Coast to California and, over the next forty years, occupied herself spending all that money on converting an eight-room, two-story farmhouse set on 161 acres of orchard into a ginormous, labyrinthine manse. She hired contractors to hammer around the clock, paying them three times the going rate.

THIS HONESTLY SOUNDS LIKE A PLOY ARRANGED BY THE LOCAL TRADESFOLK AND SARAH'S PSYCHIC TO REDISTRIBUTE HER FAT STACK OF MURDERPENNIES.

Or she just really believed in feng shui.

Every night at 2 a.m., Sarah allegedly held a séance in a special room to which only she had the key in order to receive messages about what to build the following day.

Having been in Zoom calls with more than ten people, I can confirm that a nightly séance with thousands would drive anyone insane. No wonder she built stairs that led straight into the ceiling.

Eventually, the house expanded to seven stories and twenty-four thousand square feet, with ten thousand windows, forty-seven fireplaces, and 161 rooms.

WOULD LOVE TO SET A ROOMBA LOOSE IN THAT PLACE AND JUST FIND ITS RUSTED CORPSE FIFTEEN YEARS LATER IN DINING ROOM #37.

Oh, you may have stumbled onto something there. Maybe that's why she continually built rooms; she hated cleaning. Don't need to clean a room if you just build a new one.

GALAXY BRAIN SHIT.

But that's not what made this house famous—it's the many nonsensical features, like a dead-end staircase, a door that opens to a two-story drop, doors that lead to walls, chimneys shy of the ceiling, and smaller rooms inside larger rooms. Sarah had a thing for thirteen: thirteen bedrooms, thirteen bathrooms, rooms with thirteen windows, windows with thirteen panes, stairs with thirteen steps.

I KNOW SHE WAS "GRIEVING," BUT IT FEELS LIKE A BIT OF A MISSED OPPORTUNITY THAT SHE DIDN'T HAVE MORE FUN WITH HER GRIEF HOUSE. SURE, THERE'S A DOOR OR TWO THAT GO NOWHERE, BUT WHY NOT A BATHROOM WITH A RAINFALL SHOWER THAT SPOUTS PEPSI OR A KITCHEN WHERE THE FLOOR IS A TRAMPOLINE, MAYBE? GOOD LUCK WITH YOUR OMELETS IN THERE! NOT MARRIED TO ANY OF THESE IDEAS, BY THE WAY.

I like where your head's at. How about a fridge that leads into an igloo? Or a fireman pole that drops to hell?

OR A BATHTUB YOU CAN SLEEP IN, YEAH.

That just sounds like a looong night after a college party.

Apparently, Sarah wandered the halls and slept in different rooms until her peaceful death in 1922. Whether this was to evade vengeful ghosts or simply because she had the time, space, and a desire for solitude is up for debate. Today, the friendly ghost of caretaker Clyde pushes a wheelbarrow near the coal chute in the basement. An apparition of a small elderly woman sits at the table in the empty kitchen that sometimes smells like simmering chicken soup. Sounds of whispers, footsteps, and even organ music have been heard in the house that guns built.

I'LL TAKE THIS OPPORTUNITY TO GENUINELY ENCOURAGE READERS TO VISIT THE WINCHESTER HOUSE. GHOSTS ASIDE, IT'S BEAUTIFUL AND WEIRD. AND THERE'S ROCK CANDY IN THE GIFT SHOP. TELL THEM THE BOYS SENT YOU, AND BASK IN A BLANK STARE.

Agreed, this place truly does rule. Also, definitely haunted.

The Gruesome Murders of the Villisca House

Villisca, Iowa

BOY, did I hate this place.

On June 10, 1912, the morning after the Children's Day service at the local Presbyterian church, Mary Peckham noticed that the nearby Moore home seemed strangely quiet. Usually the family of six—Sarah and Josiah and their kids, Herman, Katherine, Boyd, and Paul—would be out bright and early. The elderly neighbor called Joe's brother, who arrived to discover a gruesome scene.

Spoiler alert, this gets much worse.

Later it would be determined that, at around midnight, someone had taken Joe's ax from the yard, entered the house, and bludgeoned each family member plus Lena and Ina Stillinger, two girls who were sleeping over that night.

THAT IS *NOT* WHAT CHILDREN'S DAY IS ABOUT.

The killer then left the ax leaning against the wall next to a four-pound slab of bacon, covered the mirrors and glass in the entryway with clothing taken from the family's dressers, and left a plate of uneaten food and a basin of bloody water on the kitchen table.

~JUST MIDWEST THINGS~

The crime was never solved despite an abundance of suspects. Was it State Senator Frank Jones, who sought revenge after Joe Moore left his employ to open his own implement company? Was it William Mansfield, hired as hitman by State Senator Jones? What about Reverend Lyn George Jacklin Kelly, who told police that God told him to "suffer the children to come unto me" but then later recanted his confession?

Lol, WUT? Reverends get less reverent with every tale I hear about them.

Or transient Andy Sawyer, bloodstained Joe Ricks, prisoner George Meyers? Then there's Reverend J.J. Burris, who received the deathbed confession of the killer . . . too bad he couldn't remember the man's name.

> In a list of ax murder suspects, I'd say the one covered in blood is the most suspicious.
>
> **HUGE RED FLAG.**

Of the bunch, Henry Lee Moore—no relation to the victims—seemed the most promising. He was convicted of the ax murder of his mother and grandmother months after the Villisca killings,

> In a list of ax-murder suspects, I'd say the one with a history of ax murdering is the most suspicious.
>
> **A SIMILARLY LARGE RED FLAG. MAYBE A DIFFERENT SHAPE BUT RED AS HELL, AND IT'S A FLAG, BABY.**

and he just so happened to have been working on the railroad during a two-year slew of more than two dozen similar murders across the Midwest.

> **OKAY, SO IT SOUNDS LIKE IOWA WAS PRIMARILY INHABITED BY WOULD-BE MURDERERS. I WOULD ADD "AT THAT POINT IN TIME," BUT HAVING DRIVEN THROUGH IOWA NUMEROUS TIMES IN MY LIFE, I'M NOT SURE MUCH HAS CHANGED.**
>
> Don't bring your Illinois-Iowa turf war bs into our book.
>
> **THEY THINK THEY'RE SO FANCY WITH THEIR FRENCH-ASS STATE FLAG.**

Over the decades, the house changed hands until Martha and Darwin Linn purchased and set about restoring it in 1994. Now you can visit the cemetery where the Moore family and the Stillinger sisters are laid to rest, or stop by the house and even spend the night. Visitors report that doors open and close on their own, lamps spontaneously fall, ladders move, flashlights turn on and off. Many claim to have experienced the sensation of being watched. Some have heard the laughter of children.

> What kind of psychos would visit this place?!

The Specter Residents
of the Riddle House

West Palm Beach, Florida

On the concrete arch above the West Palm Beach Woodlawn Cemetery, an inscription reads: "That which is so universal as death must be a blessing."

Would have gone with "dilly dilly" myself.

SHOCKER THAT BIG CEMETERY™ IS PUSHING A "HEY, PRETTY COOL TO BE DEAD, HUH?" AGENDA.

Through that entryway, in what used to be pineapple fields, rest a number of notable bodies,

Tough break for those fields.

SHOULDA JUST KEPT BOTH OPERATIONS RUNNING! YOU CAN WEEP OVER THE GRAVE OF A LOST LOVED ONE WHILE TAKING BIG-ASS JUICY BITES OF THOSE TROPICAL DRIBBLERS. THEY COULD SELL BIBS AT THE GATE. IS THIS A GREAT IDEA???

It's a great idea.

including that of Postmistress Lena M.T. Clarke, who stole $32,000 from a registered mail sack and then shot her married lover and coworker through the heart;

Did she know that sack had 32K in it?? Or did she just unknowingly grab a sack to open it up and be like, "HOLY SHIT!"

IT'S KIND OF A GAMBLE TO STEAL A SACK NOT KNOWING WHAT'S IN IT. I GUESS IT DEPENDS WHERE YOU STEAL IT FROM, THOUGH. STEAL A SACK FROM GRANDMA'S SHED? A LOW-RISK OPERATION, BUT THAT THING'S PROBABLY FULL OF POSSUM BONES. STEAL A SACK FROM A BANK? HUGE RISK, AND THERE'S STILL A CHANCE YOU'LL END UP WITH A BAG FULL OF THOSE PENS WITH CHAINS ON THEM. KNOW WHAT SACK YOU'RE AFTER, IS MY POINT.

You've always had stellar sack awareness. If you ever passed (tragically), the first thing I'd say at the funeral is, "You know one thing about Shane? That dude knew a lot about sacks."

School Superintendent Guy Metcalf, who was accused of misappropriating $333.49 of school funds and, rather than face the music, shot himself; Judge Curtis Chillingworth and his wife, Marjorie, who were kidnapped and forced into the sea by thugs hired by a competing judge; and, in a mass grave, white victims of the 1928 hurricane. Black victims are buried three miles away.

Yeesh, racism even postmortem. But from the sound of it, I wouldn't want to be buried with this bunch anyway. Well, mainly the mail thief and the sleazeball school superintendent.

One year after industrialist and real estate developer Henry Flagler created the Wood-lawn Cemetery, in 1904, he commissioned the construction of a two-story Victorian house across the street, at 327 Acacia Street. Its proximity allowed overseers to keep an eye out for graverobbers and other miscreants. It also served as a funeral parlor, where bodies were prepared for interment.

Slap that selling point on Zillow.

I'VE ALWAYS WANTED TO BE A CEMETERY MISCREANT. I'M NOT SURE WHAT THAT ENTAILS, THOUGH. SMOKING FUNNY CIGARETTES AMONG THE HEADSTONES? SMOOCHING IN THE MAUSOLEUM?

This something you just thought up on your own?

With all that neighboring death and corporal transit, it's no surprise that the house is haunted. One ghost goes by the name of Buck. Cemetery employee and known lush, Buck regularly patronized the local tavern and, on occasion, turned belligerent. One evening, a bar brawl proved fatal; he continues to wander the grounds.

Buck is a name that predestines you for alcoholism.

Eventually, Karl Riddle and family took up residence, when he became West Palm Beach's first city manager, county surveyor, and superintendent of public works in the 1920s. Legend has it that Riddle hired a local handyman named Joseph, who then decided to use his employer's attic to escape personal troubles by hanging himself. The family tired of the increasing paranormal incidents, like the sound of rattling chains and murmuring voices, and soon moved on.

As one of the world's preeminent ghost hunters, I can tell you that any haunting described by the sound of "rattling chains" is an immediate red flag. This isn't A Christmas Carol.

OH, THAT'S RICH. EVERY OTHER LOCATION WE'VE GONE TO HAS PEOPLE TELLING US SCROOGE-ASS STORIES ABOUT DICKENSIAN MOPPETS AND SHROUDED OLD WOMEN.

I assure you that all hunt details have been thoroughly and exhaustively fact-checked.

Followed by a number of commercial occupants and a stint as a Palm Beach Atlantic College girls' dormitory, the former funeral parlor was abandoned and fell into disrepair. Rather than demo it, the city donated the building to Karl's cousin John, who moved it to "living history park" Yesteryear Village at the Palm Beach County Fairgrounds in 1995.

HAVING HUNG OUT IN SOME FEMALE FRIENDS' DORM ROOMS DURING COLLEGE, I CAN SEE WHY THE BUILDING FELL INTO DISREPAIR.

Look, I'd never buy a haunted house. But if folks just outright give it to me? I think I'd give it a couple months living there before I cut bait. I just want a house.

The Riddle House's ghosts went with it. During construction after the move, ghosts stole carpenters' tools from the attic and threw them outside, broke windows, and attacked people.

> Not a surprise. If I woke up in my bed and looked out my window to discover my house was mobile on the 405 freeway, I'd be pissed, too.

> THE GHOSTS ARE GOING ALONG FOR THE MOVE NOW? THEY'RE MAKING A QUICK STOP AT 7-ELEVEN FOR GATORADE AND A BAG OF COMBOS AND HOPPING IN THE TRUCK WITH THE "WIDE LOAD" SIGN ON IT?

> I mean, jokes aside, it makes sense.

All this hubbub attracted paranormal investigators' attention, and some have even made contact with the man who hanged himself. Others experience a strange heat near a west window, have seen orbs, or have felt fingers brushing through their hair.

> ZERO RIDDLES TO BE FOUND IN THIS ONE. I CONTINUE TO BE DISAPPOINTED BY THIS WRETCHED BOOK.

> Still plenty of book left.

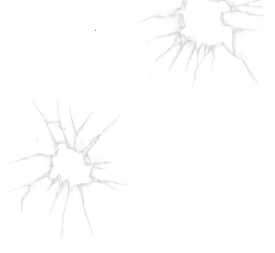

The Demonic Bellaire House

Bellaire, Ohio

Kristen Lee can't sell this 2,280-square-foot, five-bedroom house even if she wanted to—she does and she tried. In fact, the City of Bellaire passed on her asking price of $1.

> Again. Ship that baby to Los Angeles. I'll gladly take it off your hands.
>
> THAT SQUARE FOOTAGE HAS GOT ME HOWLIN' LIKE A CARTOON WOLF.

In 2005, Lee purchased the home on 1699 Belmont Street for $46,000 in a foreclosure sale for what she thought was a killer deal. It wasn't until Lee and her family moved in that she realized there was a reason for the low price.

> She didn't know she was agreeing to live in Ohio?! Jk jk, it's a lovely state and the birthplace of Steven Lim.
>
> A PERFECTLY ACCEPTABLE STATE WHERE I'M SURE ROUGHLY HALF THE PEOPLE ARE NORMAL AND ONLY A FEW ARE SERIAL KILLERS.
>
> Yeah, like I said, Steven Lim.
>
> NASTY. I LOVE IT.

None of the neighbors had seen fit to mention that they'd noticed people wandering inside and peeking out the window, though the house had sat abandoned for years. They also hadn't mentioned nearby ley lines, trails of supernatural energy that crisscross the earth and which Lee credits for the abundance of paranormal activity at this "portal to hell."

> Worth mentioning that Shane and I visited this joint a while back. Happy to discover that they deliver pizza to the portal to hell. Also happy that I don't ever have to go back. Good pizza, though.
>
> WHILE WE'RE ON THE SUBJECT, BIG SHOUT-OUT TO KRISTEN LEE FOR BEING ONE OF THE FEW HAUNTED HOSTS TO HAVE A FRIDGE STOCKED WITH SOME CHILLY BOYS. IT'S A RARE PLEASURE TO CAP OFF A GHOUL HUNT BY CRACKING OPEN A COUPLE WOBBLY POPS, AND I'M GRATEFUL SHE AFFORDED US THAT OPPORTUNITY. (PLEASE DRINK RESPONSIBLY, ESPECIALLY WHILE GHOST HUNTING.)

Lee suspects that there is a mine below the house, which is possible given that Bellaire was a booming coal mining town in the 1800s.

> Shane has long maintained that if ghosts are real, they'd be in a mine. So . . .

THAT'S MOSTLY INFORMED BY MY TIME PLAYING MINECRAFT. SURE, ABOVE GROUND YOU MIGHT RUN INTO A SPIDER OR A CREEPER IF YOU'RE OUT AFTER SUNDOWN, BUT ONCE YOU GET REDSTONE FEVER AND START DIGGING DEEP VEINS INTO THE EARTH, YOU'RE ENTERING A WORLD OF TERROR. SKELETONS LOOSING ARROWS AT YOU, THOSE CREEPY SILVERFISH POPPING OUT OF STONE BLOCKS, ENDERMEN PLOINKING INTO EXISTENCE LEFT AND RIGHT. HORRIFYING. WHAT I'M SAYING IS, WE NEED TO BE LESS DEPENDENT ON FOSSIL FUELS.

That was a wild ride.

That's why Jacob Heatherington wound up there in 1832. An Englishman by birth, he joined the family trade in 1821, when he was just seven years old. The family immigrated to Pennsylvania in 1830 and then on to Ohio, where he and his family of "four sturdy boys" rented a coal bank from steamboat man and coal magnate Captain John Fink.

I, too, am a "steamboat man." I've never captained one, but boy do I love to watch those puppies chug along.

RYAN AND I ARE WRITING THIS BOOK WITH THE PRIMARY INTENTION OF MAKING ENOUGH MONEY TO PURCHASE OUR OWN HAUNTED STEAMBOAT AND CRUISE IT UP AND DOWN THE MISSISSIPPI IN OUR TWILIGHT YEARS. TICKETS WILL BE OUTRAGEOUSLY EXPENSIVE, BUT WE OFFER A BUFFET AND A PUPPET SHOW. (ALSO WE WILL DIE ON THE STEAMBOAT.)

Free popcorn in the captain's quarters, too. +1 to the pseudo Viking/Mark Twain funeral.

Heatherington married Fink's cousin Eliza soon thereafter. She, selfishly, was busy birthing and raising ten children, and so poor Jacob was on his own. That is, until he fell in love with a mule, whom he eponymously named Jack and credited with his burgeoning success. Lee believes that Heatherington owned 1699 Belmont Street, which is possible, since he owned thirty homes in the area.

A mule? Like a drug mule? Or a "hey that kinda looks like a donkey" mule?

A MULE IS ACTUALLY THE SPAWN OF A DONKEY AND A HORSE! MY OL' PAL BOON HOGGANBECK TAUGHT ME THAT.

Oh, I know that, but it still looks like a donkey to me. Put it this way, you'd never mistake it for a horse.

Third-born child, Alex, took over the family business, and his daughter, Lyde, took over from him. Lee believes that Lyde died of a heart attack in front of the dining room's fireplace and, unhinged by grief, her younger brother, Edwin, hired mediums to try to contact her. In doing so, he may have opened some portals best left closed.

ANYTIME PEOPLE AT THESE PLACES TALK ABOUT PORTALS BEING OPENED, I IMAGINE OUR GUY DR. STEPHEN STRANGE DOING HIS FANCY LITTLE TIKTOK HAND DANCES TO OPEN UP THEM SHINY, SHINY HOLES.

If only it was Black Panther who came through said hole. Unfortunately, it's usually a demon named Steve or Sallie.

Since her arrival, Lee was awakened by a man who disappeared into thin air. She experienced paralysis in her bedroom, the same room in which an unseen force threw her dog against a wall. There have been physical assaults—one tour guide was tugged so violently that he almost fell out of a second-story window.

> This demon obviously knows his cinema. I won't lie, I did chuckle when the priest in *The Exorcist* got ragdolled out the window. Spoiler alert, I suppose. It's been out for a while, and odds are, if you're reading this book, you've already seen it.
>
> WE'RE NOT HERE TO TALK ABOUT MOVIES.

Footsteps and voices can be heard in the attic, and the room turns so cold that some visitors can see their breath. Some paranormal investigators have made contact with a demon in the shape of a little girl called Emily Davis.

> Very much in the ballpark of Steve or Sallie. In terms of my fear rankings, based solely on name alone, I'd go Sallie, Emily, and then Steve.

It is because of her presence that Lee has put multiple locks on the door to the attic stairwell.

> I ASSUME IT'S BEEN OMITTED FROM THE DETAILS HERE BECAUSE IT'S ONE OF THE MOST HAIR-RAISING AND SHOCKING MOMENTS EVER CAUGHT ON CAMERA, BUT THIS IS ALSO HOME TO APPLE TATER AND SPAGHETTI, TWO OF THE MOST SINISTER SPECTRAL ENTITIES THE GHOUL BOYS HAVE EVER TANGOED WITH.

> I can't wait for the oral history of just that monumental moment alone.

The Family Suicides of Lemp Mansion

St. Louis, Missouri

The Lemps' sojourn in America started off well. John Adam Lemp was a grocery store owner before founding Lemp Brewery, which was so successful that his son, William J., was able to purchase a sprawling 9,000-square-foot mansion in 1876. He converted several rooms into offices for the business.

> I'M PRETTY JEALOUS OF ANYBODY WHO LIVES IN ST. LOUIS BECAUSE THEY'VE GOT A MCDONALD'S BOAT DOCKED ON THE MISSISSIPPI. YOU READ THAT RIGHT. IT'S A BOAT THAT'S ALSO A MCDONALD'S. NEXT BEST THING TO A FLYING TACO BELL.

> Oh man, those tasty-ass french fries while floating on the river. That's livin'.

Everything was peachy until William J. found Frederick, his twenty-eight-year-old son, dead inside the mansion in 1901. The official cause of death was not made public. Three years later, William J. did not leave a note before picking up a Smith & Wesson .38 revolver and shooting himself in the head.

> HOLD ON. I'VE JUST READ THAT THE FLOATING MCDONALD'S WAS DECOMMISSIONED IN 2000. THIS SIMPLY CANNOT BE TRUE.

> Bummer on the floating arches. Anyways, this story is already very sad.

William Jr., aka Billy, took over the business and the mansion with his wife, Lillian, who apparently only wore lavender and was therefore called the Lavender Lady.

> They didn't spend a lot of time chewing on that one, huh? Also, if your obsession with a certain thing spawns a nickname, it might be time for some moderation. I'd be pretty alarmed if people started calling me Root Beer Float Man.

Billy desired a more colorful lifestyle, and rumor has it that he and a servant produced an illegitimate child, whom he locked in the attic for the ten years of the boy's life. He and Lillian divorced in 1908.

> SURELY IT MUST HAVE BEEN ONE OF THE MOST PROFITABLE MCDONALD'S IN THE NATION IF NOT THE WORLD. YOU COULD SIMULTANEOUSLY HOUSE A BIG MAC AND FEAST YOUR PEEPERS ON THE BIG MUDDY. DID THAT VILE HARLEQUIN RONALD NOT SEE THE APPEAL OF THIS? DID HE DRAW HIS INFAMOUS REVOLVER AND SHOOT HOLES IN THE FLOOR, LEAVING THE EMPLOYEES TO SCRAMBLE FOR THE LIFEBOATS?

> Here I was thinking that only the fictional Dursleys would lock a child in a room.

In 1919, Prohibition greatly diminished the brewing empire, and Billy was forced to close the beer plant and sell off the company for a pittance. One year later, his sister, Elsa, shot herself in the head after a divorce and reconciliation with her husband and a bad bout of insomnia. Two years after that, Billy followed. The mansion got a brief respite from tragedy until 1949, when another brother, the reclusive Charles, shot himself. He is the only one who left a note: "In case I am found dead, blame it on no one but me."

CAN ANY READERS IN ST. LOUIS CONFIRM THAT THE RIVERBOAT MCDONALD'S HAS BEEN SCUTTLED? JUST SAY "YES" OR "NO" ALOUD TO THE BOOK YOU'RE HOLDING, AND WE'LL GET THE MESSAGE. THAT IS SECRETLY HOW BOOKS WORK. ONLY AUTHORS KNOW THIS.

With the Lemp family in disarray and the business gone, the mansion was auctioned off. Its stint as a boardinghouse was short-lived, however, because ghosts—or ghost stories—tended to run off boarders.

Not gonna lie—if it's raining, I'm staying in the haunted house. And mind you, this is coming from me.

Today, guests can enjoy a Lemp Mansion burger or the Chicken Lillian in the downstairs restaurant, then stay in rooms named in honor of the deceased. Many have seen the ghosts of Charles Lemp, the Lavender Lady, a young child, and a servant looking for her son throughout the manse, and some have reported awakening in the dead of night to the sound of a gunshot.

I'VE BEEN A LITTLE DISTRACTED, BUT, SURE, THIS PLACE SOUNDS SCARY. A LOT OF PEOPLE GOT SHOT OR SOMETHING. LET'S CHECK OUT SOME HOTELS!

Yeah, this sounds like an awful, awful place.

HELLISH HOTELS

The Swindled Spirits
of 1886 Crescent Hotel & Spa

Eureka Springs, Arkansas

By the time the "finest hotel west of the Mississippi" (according to the hotel website) welcomed its first guests in May of 1886, there had already been one fatality.

> Interesting alternative to a ribbon-cutting ceremony.

Many more deaths would follow that of an Irish stonemason named Michael, who fell onto a beam in what would become Room 218.

> I ALWAYS FORGET WHERE ARKANSAS IS ON THE MAP. JUST LOOKED IT UP, THOUGH. IT'S OVER THERE.

> In terms of residual hauntings, hearing this death on repeat sounds less than ideal. Like a sack of potatoes falling into a pile of twigs.

For many decades after the hotel's completion, wealthy clientele came to take in the healing waters of Eureka Springs—which purportedly cured everything from hay fever to hysteria to hair loss—and to enjoy the billiard rooms, tennis courts, gardens, and other high-end amenities. Daughters of the southern elite arrived for study in the slow winter months, during which the hotel became an institution of higher education.

> GOD, IT'S SO EASY TO TRICK RICH PEOPLE INTO SPENDING MONEY ON HORSESHIT. THEY WERE GOOPIN' HARD BEFORE GOOP EVER GOOPED.

> I don't care about the "healing" properties. I only know that hot tubs are good for my soul. I'm assuming this is a hot spring, which is essentially like God's hot tub. I gotta dip my bones in one at some point.

> I VISITED ONE IN ANZA-BORREGO. THE SPRING WAS FUNNELED INTO A POOL HOUSED IN A BUILDING THAT HAD ALL THE CHARM OF A JIFFY LUBE. I DON'T RECOMMEND THAT ONE.

> Bad story but ultimately helpful!

Hard times hit with the Great Depression, and Norman Baker, an inventor, former vaudevillian, and infamous charlatan, purchased the hotel in 1937.

> Those are three pretty great things to be known for. Hats off, Norm.

> ALWAYS RISKY TO HATS-OFF ANY PERSON DISCUSSED IN THESE STORIES.

For two years, he operated the Cancer Curing Hospital, offering his very special cures for very special fees. Some were injected with Formula 5—a mixture of alcohol, glycerol, carbolic acid, ground watermelon seed, corn silk, and clover—then went home and died.

> Ah, the ol' "doing my own research" approach.

Others stayed to meet their maker, and so Baker built a morgue in the basement to accommodate them. Baker got busted for mail fraud in 1939, but not before swindling the desperately ill out of hundreds of thousands of dollars.

> Well, hats going back on, Norm.

> SEE.

Today, the Crescent Hotel & Spa is known both for its luxury accommodations and for being one of the most haunted places in the Ozarks.

> A MOIST PART OF AMERICA, THE OZARKS. THESE GHOSTS MUST BE UTTERLY SOPPING.

> Love a wet wraith.

A ghost in a nurse's white uniform wheels a gurney along the third floor late at night when, in the hospital's time, the deceased would be relocated to the morgue's cooler. A cancer patient named Theodora looks for her key to Room 419. Stonemason Michael flickers lights, screams, and reaches out of the mirror in Room 218.

> LAYING IT ON A BIT THICK, MICHAEL.

> Yeah, the other folks definitely understood subtlety. Though, scaring people in the bathroom mirror, making them choke on a mouthful of toothpaste is objectively VERY funny.

A Victorian wedding party dances in the Crystal Dining Room, where one gentleman in nineteenth-century attire awaits the return of a beautiful woman. The screams of a death can be heard at 10:30 p.m. Ghostly butlers carry trays. A little boy apparition might just hold your hand.

> THIS PLACE SOUNDS OFF THE FUCKIN' CHAIN. IS THIS LIKE THE STUDIO 54 OF THE GHOST REALM?

> I'll have to look into vacancies when I die.

Along with the occasional haunting, guests can see a strange collection of jars unearthed in 2019 by a landscaper. These jars hold a clear liquid and tissue and are believed to have been used by Baker as proof of his cure.

> PISS. GOTTA BE.

> My thoughts exactly. That's straight up pee pee, my dude.

The Historic Hauntings
of the Magnolia Hotel

Seguin, Texas

The two-room cabin that would become the Magnolia Hotel was constructed during a time of great upheaval and violence in what is now Seguin, Texas. The Mexican government was fighting Anglo-American settlers who were fighting Tejanos who were fighting Comanches and Apaches, and round and round it went. Like most of the United States' lifespan, it was a hot mess.

Not to be all Jeff Daniels in *Newsroom*, but we do suck.

OG Texas Ranger James Campbell built the cabin in 1839, but soon after completion, he was killed by Comanche Indians outside of San Antonio. According to the hotel website, he was stabbed twenty-seven times and scalped before being left for dead. Some say fellow Texas Rangers buried him near where he fell, while others claim he was buried near his beloved cabin.

NOT AN IDEAL WAY TO GO, BUT PRETTY MUCH ANY PERSON OF MEANS BORN BEFORE THE 1850s DESERVED A GRUESOME DEATH IN ONE WAY OR ANOTHER, SO HELL YEAH.

Scalping is up there with penile injury for me in terms of things I don't even like hearing about. It's very visceral. I can't help but picture it happening to me. I don't want my hair turned into a hat. Unpleasant.

From there, the cabin became the town's stagecoach station and hotel, and, over the years, it continued to be the site of much turmoil. In 1848, slave laborers dug out a raid shelter in the basement, in which women and children hid during conflict between Comanches and white settlers, and for a while it was used as a jail, with a hanging tree conveniently located across the street. The Civil War brought Union soldiers, who used it as a base; even President Ulysses S. Grant stopped by.

I always wonder if ghosts recognize other famous ghosts. Like if I died and saw Jimmy Stewart, I'd definitely be flabberghosted.

LOVE THAT.

Other notable guests include Wilhelm Faust, who stayed in an upstairs room on the night he rode to nearby New Braunfels and accidentally ax-murdered a twelve-year-old girl while trying to on-purpose ax-murder his wife. During the trial in 1875, he admitted to committing several more murders.

I AM NOT A LAWYER, BUT I THINK IF YOU ACCIDENTALLY AX-MURDER SOMEONE WHILE ATTEMPTING TO INTENTIONALLY AX-MURDER SOMEONE ELSE, WE SHOULD JUST LUMP THAT IN AS A FULL-ON MURDER.

Thanks for clarifying that you're not a lawyer. Also, sustained.

The 1880s was a good decade for the hotel, which was transformed into a grand establishment for a little while, but soon it fell into disrepair yet again. After many more iterations, the building was left vacant, open to vandalism and people looking for a secluded place to do drugs.

THEY'RE HARD TO FIND!!!

I won't lie—if I didn't know a place was haunted and I was high as balls, I wouldn't assume a ghost was in fact a ghost. I'd probably just think that herb was LOUD. Jah feel?

Its current owners, Erin Wallace Ghedi and Jim Ghedi, purchased the Magnolia Hotel in 2013. As soon as renovations began, so did the hauntings. According to a local psychic, thirteen ghosts occupy the hotel.

Ah, *Thirteen Ghosts*. Great horrible movie.

The spirits of traveling salesmen, abandoned lovers, and child residents can be glimpsed at windows or in mirrors. You can smell James Campbell's cigar smoke and hear his boots on the hardwood floors. Upstairs, a Madame Rosebud's perfume hangs in the air. An unoccupied rocking chair rocks.

KIND OF REMINDS ME OF A BUZZFEED LIST: "13 GHOSTS THAT DEFINITELY HAUNT THE MAGNOLIA HOTEL—YOU WON'T BELIEVE THE LACK OF PHOTOGRAPHIC EVIDENCE!"

You can take the man out of Buzzfeed, but you can't take the Buzzfeed out of the man.

The Tragic Tap Dancer
of Green Mountain Inn

Stowe, Vermont

NEW CONTENDER FOR BEST CHAPTER TITLE. LET'S FUCKING GOOOOOOO.

Tough to top the tap to this title.

Thirty-four years before President Gerald Rudolph Ford pardoned Richard Milhous Nixon for his involvement in Watergate, the sexy, young, part-time model (Gerry not Tricky Dicky) was doing a sexy ski photo shoot at Green Mountain Inn that would be featured in *Look* magazine.

I'VE JUST LOOKED UP THE PHOTOS AND CAN CONFIRM THAT GERALD FORD WAS A HUNK. LOOKS LIKE HE SHOULD BE CHASING JAMES BOND THROUGH THE ALPS.

An absolute fuckin' unit.

Since 1833, the building has seen all kinds of snowstorms and operated in all kinds of capacities.

Shane and I once almost stranded the entire *Unsolved* crew in a whiteout because we got lost in the sauce perusing craft beer at a local liquor store.

First it was a residence, which owner Peter C. Lovejoy traded for a 350-acre farm. Stillman Churchill, the second owner, added a double front porch, a dance hall, and two brick wings, then lost the whole shebang in a mortgage foreclosure to W.H.H. Bingham. He renamed it and opened it as a hotel to serve the summer tourists taking in the seasonal verdancy of Mount Mansfield, the highest peak in Vermont. A couple more owners later, in 1893, it got its current name.

TBH, THIS PLACE SOUNDS SICK AS HELL.

God, imagine being rich enough to trade land like Pokémon cards.

POTUS Ford died in 2006, but his is not the spirit whose footsteps can currently be heard on the inn's roof—that's Boots Berry, a former horseman who was born in the third-floor's servants' quarters, Room 302, in 1840. The son of a chambermaid and horseman, he made a name for himself by rescuing a stagecoach when its horses bolted down Main Street. From then on, everywhere he went, Stowe townsfolk were eager to buy him a drink. Sounds wonderful, except that he became an alcoholic, got fired, hit the road, and did something stupid enough to land him in a New Orleans jail. There

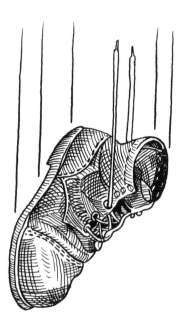

he learned to tap dance and earned the nickname Boots—which apparently is pithier though less accurate than Tap Dancing Shoes.

HEY, I LOVE EVERYTHING ABOUT BOOTS BERRY. WHY ARE WE NOT CELEBRATING HIM MORE? THE PUBLICATION OF THIS BOOK WILL HAVE BEEN WORTH IT IF ONLY TO BRING RENEWED ATTENTION TO THIS MAN.

That's a top ten *Unsolved* ghoul name in my eyes.

By 1902, he made his way back to the place of his birth. Somehow, a little girl got stranded on the inn's roof. Boots, ever the hero and perhaps hoping to get back into the town's good graces, climbed up on the roof to save her. Which he did. Then he fell to his death.

THAT IS *SO* BOOTS!

You either die falling off a rooftop or live long enough to see yourself become the villain.

A decade later, some Swedish immigrants introduced the town to a funny mode of transport called skiing. Today, skiers and snowboarders come from far and wide to strap boards to their feet and careen down mountains by day and drink hot toddies in front of roaring fires by night. At the Green Mountain Inn, guests report hearing the sound of tap dancing on the roof.

THAT'S IT?! IT'S A ROOF! THERE'S PROBABLY CHESTNUTS PLUNKIN' OFF OF IT ALL NIGHT! HONESTLY SOUNDS LOVELY. I'M BOOKIN' A ROOM.

You're just in it for the hot toddies. I'm in.

The Ghostly Guests
of the Golden Lamb Inn

Lebanon, Ohio

Had Darwin Awards been a thing when Charles Darwin was alive, the man himself would have honored Clement L. Vallandingham. An Ohioan congressman and attorney, Vallandingham accidentally shot himself in the abdomen while preparing the defense of an accused murderer—he was demonstrating how the victim probably accidentally shot himself. Whoops!

SUCCESS!

A commitment you just don't see nowadays.

Other people who've died at the inn: papa of Civil War general William T. Sherman and Ohio Supreme Court Justice Charles R. Sherman, who left his family destitute. Most of his eleven children had to be put up for adoption. Eliza Clay, the young daughter of Kentucky senator Henry Clay, fell ill and died at the inn and was buried nearby, far from home in Lexington. Sarah Stubbs didn't die at the Golden Lamb, though she haunts it. She moved to the inn at the age of five, when her father died and her uncle and hotel manager took custody. By all accounts, she had a nice childhood there, so nice, in fact, that when she died at seventy-nine, she reverted to the age of that trauma and took up ghostly residence. Today her room on the fourth floor is a museum.

. . . WHAT? SO SHE DIED AND THEN BECAME A LITTLE GIRL AGAIN? LIKE A POSTMORTEM BENJAMIN BUTTON? IS THAT ALLOWED? CAN I BE A BABY WHEN I DIE? I THINK IT'D BE COOL TO BE SWADDLED AND CARRIED AROUND BY ADULT GHOSTS. GIVE MY GAMS A REST AFTER A LIFETIME OF LUGGING THIS AWFUL HUMAN VESSEL AROUND.

Don't you mean Benjamin Bootton?

Opened in 1803 by Jonas Seaman, the establishment got its name from its original signage, which had the image of a golden lamb for those who couldn't read.

Oh wow, signage must've been tough back in the days of widespread illiteracy.

The signature dish for the past ninety years, however, is spring chicken, the recipe that got into the hands of a fellow by the name of Colonel Sanders, though whether he used it for his fried chicken franchise is up for debate.

A Popeyes man, myself. They didn't pay me for that. It's just true. But if you're reading this, Popeyes, I'll take a lifetime of free biscuits if you're offerin'.

Many notables have stayed there in the past 215-plus years, from sharpshooter Annie Oakley to sharp singer Kesha, and a bunch of presidents, too.

Feel like Kesha should have gotten top billing here, but I'll let it slide. Kesha always gets top billing.

The wandering of Clement, Charles, Eliza, and Sarah is the inn's main mode of haunting, and the ghosts tend to be pretty mellow. Except, perhaps, the five-year-old ghost of Sarah Stubbs—one guest claimed that he heard a child's laughter after tripping and falling in his room.

I WONDER IF KESHA WILL HAUNT THIS PLACE IF SHE EVER DIES.

Maybe! Speaking of Timber, if we ever visit this place, there'll be plenty of fodder for ghost children to laugh, as Shane falls all the time. I blame the top-heaviness of it all.

The Creepy Clowns of the Clown Motel

Tonopah, Nevada

NOBODY NEEDED TO BE INFORMED THIS WAS IN NEVADA. JUST AS HUMANS ARE BORN WITH THE INNATE FEAR OF THE WOLF'S CLENCHED FANGS, WE ARE ALSO IMBUED WITH THE COSMIC KNOWLEDGE THAT IF A CLOWN MOTEL EXISTS, IT EXISTS IN NEVADA.

Disagree. I would have guessed Florida.

A fire in the local Belmont Mine killed Clarence David, who had a clown collection. He was buried in Tonopah Cemetery, and a few decades later, his children, Leona and Leroy, opened a motel next door to dear old dad's gravesite and decorated it with his 150 clowns.

This is actually very sweet and wholesome, excluding the fact that the dad collected clowns. Which is undeniably weird.

Since 1985, the collection has grown to over two thousand clowns, plus "thirty-one rooms featuring two to three eclectic pieces of clown art" (according to the motel website). Some of these rooms have themes, like *It* and *Friday the 13th* and *The Exorcist*.

TRULY DID NOT EXPECT THE STORY OF A CLOWN MOTEL TO OPEN WITH A FIRE IN A MINE. WE'RE REALLY PILING ON SOME ELDRITCH LORE HERE. HAVING SAID THAT, IT SOUNDS LIKE THEY'VE CURATED A VERY EROTIC ATMOSPHERE, AND I'M CURIOUS TO KNOW MORE.

> Yeah, it's certainly niche. Btw, I do want to single out the themed paintings. They're basically making clown art like those very funny Big Dogs T-shirts. Do those still exist?

The neighboring cemetery is the cherry on top. Founded in 1901, it officially closed in 1911 because mine tailings—water, crushed rock, additives, miscellaneous minerals—kept washing over the three hundred or so graves, but during that decade, plenty of local color was interred within. Respected Sheriff Thomas Logan was shot outside a brothel in only his nightshirt. George "Devil" Davis, political leader and the first Black man in town, was shot in the back by his wife.

> It's always the ones you love most.

Bina Verrault, the head of a New York "love syndicate"—i.e., she seduced suitors into giving her lots of jewels, to the tune of $2.5 million in today's money—was on the run from the law when she fell ill and died from acute alcoholism in 1908. Hero Big Bill Murphy died while rescuing miners from the Belmont Mine fire of 1911. Fifty-six people died in a plague between January and April of 1905, likely from pneumonia.

> $2.5 MILLION! SOUNDS LIKE A BUSY WOMAN.

> Yeah, she probably spent half of that on dry cleaning.

Jim Butler, the town's founder, is not buried there. A favorite legend is that the rancher was throwing a rock at a stubborn donkey in May of 1900 and realized the stone was extra heavy; it was laced with silver.

> Donkeys do be stubborn.

In 1901, the mines around the town produced nearly $750,000 worth of minerals, totaling $121 million for the twenty years of its peak run. By the time the 1942 fire killed coulrophile Clarence David, the town was already drying up, though its location between Reno and Las Vegas off US Route 95 and its renown as the "Scariest Motel in America" have kept it alive.

> WAIT, DID THIS GUY FUCK CLOWNS? IS THAT WHAT THIS ROTTEN BOOK JUST INSINUATED?

> Lol, wait! Seriously though, you can't just sneak that in there and expect no follow-up questions.

It will come as no surprise that a clown motel next to an Old West cemetery is haunted. A life-size mannequin moving on its own has been caught on film. Shadowy figures have been seen; strange voices have been heard. Also, there are clowns.

> No surprise here, but I also detest clowns. Something very unnerving about a permanent smile.

The Hidden Door
of the DeSoto House Hotel

Galena, Illinois

Since 1855, the DeSoto House Hotel has boomed and busted along with its little port town on the Mississippi River. It started out big, serving the crowds disembarking from the steamboats chugalugging up and down the river.

As you now know, I love a steamboat.

Billed as the "largest hotel in the west" (according to the hotel website), it had 225 guest rooms, room for three hundred hungry guests in the dining hall, a saloon, separate gentlemen's and ladies' parlors, and even a bowling alley. President Abraham Lincoln gave a speech from his room's balcony on July 23, 1856, followed by a series of other important dudes giving various speeches and hosting various events. A reception for hometown hero Ulysses S. Grant was held there after he returned from the war.

GORGEOUS TOWN, GALENA. TUCKED IN THE WESTERN HILLS OF ILLINOIS. I'VE ACTUALLY DINED AT THIS HOTEL. HAD A BURGER THERE. IMAGINE MY SHOCK WHEN THE WAITER WAS A G-G-G-GHOST! JUST KIDDING. BUT ALL INCREDIBLY FUNNY JOKES ASIDE, I DID EAT A BURGER THERE.

Insufferable.

Then, only four years after its grand opening, a fire devastated the building, and only ten years later, a boiler exploded in the basement, a misfortune from which the hotel struggled to recover. Then the local lead mines closed, but not before clogging the river with sludge and the railroads overtook the steamboats. The top two floors were removed in 1880 for structural reasons. The flood of 1915 didn't help matters, nor did the even worse flood of 1937. Eventually, the DeSoto House Hotel was downgraded to a hotel-slash-boardinghouse, until its mayor-driven restoration in 1986.

I KNOW YOU'RE ALL READING THIS FOR THE MORBID STUFF, BUT JUST ACKNOWLEDGE FOR A MOMENT THAT IT'S ALSO NICE TO READ ABOUT THE HISTORY OF AN OLD BUILDING. WHO NEEDS BLOOD AND GUTS WHEN YOU'VE GOT EXHILARATING DETAILS LIKE A FAULTY BOILER AND STRUCTURAL IRREGULARITIES?!

Nothing gets Shane hot and bothered like a structural irregularity.

Of its many spirits, the most famous is the Lady in Black. For more than a hundred years, there have been reports of sightings of this full-body apparition walking down the stairs into the lobby and vanishing into a wall.

Lots of ladies in black or ladies in white. Ladies get very monochromatic in the afterlife, apparently. If I ever turn into a ghost, I'm wearing that bright orange suit/top hat combo from Dumb and Dumber. I'll dazzle.

In 2011, yet another flood damaged that very same wall, and when contractors began the repairs on the plaster, they discovered a doorway.

Oh shit! This is good!

Who is this woman? No one knows. She keeps company with other specters, who tend to stand creepily at the foot of beds and gaze forlornly out of windows before disappearing. The second and third floors tend to be the most active. The cigar smoke of those powerful, long-dead men still lingers in the air.

WHAT'S BEHIND THE DOOR?! THIS WRETCHED BOOK HAS ONCE AGAIN LEFT MY MIND REELING!

The Dead of Fairmont Hotel

Deadwood, South Dakota

Long before HBO's potty-mouth Al Swearengen said, "In life, you have to do a lot of things you don't fucking want to do. Many times, that's what the fuck life is: one vile fucking task after another," the area around Black Hills in western South Dakota was a battleground. For generations, the Chippewa, Lakota and Dakota Sioux, Mandan, Hidatsa, and Cheyenne tribes came into conflict over land and then, as white settlers pushed west, diminishing territory.

> Classic white settler behavior. Funny guys they were. Stealing all that land. A riot!

In 1874, Lieutenant Colonel George A. Custer led a group of 1,200 men to explore the region, ostensibly to find a good spot for a military fort, but really to see if the rumors of minerals in the region were true. In August, a prospector discovered gold, and as for treaties with the Native Americans? All bets were off. Chief Sitting Bull, who had distrusted the Fort Laramie Treaty and refused to sign, had been right.

> Impossible for me to read "prospector" and not immediately picture Skinny Pete from *Toy Story 2*. Feels like anytime I see a photo of a prospector, he looks exactly like that. Did all prospectors do their prospectin' in that same uniform? Was there a national prospecting conference where this was agreed upon?

An early mining operation was founded in a gulch full of dead trees, and soon thousands arrived to seek their fortunes. Like other mining towns, Deadwood tended to attract roughriders and risk takers, folks who maybe didn't care all that much about law and order; plus, technically, the entire town was illegal due to the aforementioned treaty. Wild Bill and Calamity Jane were two such characters; they're both buried at Mount Moriah Cemetery. Given the avarice and violence that seemed to accompany gold rushers, it's no wonder the entire town is believed to be haunted.

I WOULDN'T LAST A DAY IN DEADWOOD. I'D BE SHOT BUYING SOAP.

No argument here. You'd be a (large) dead man walking.

In 1878, smallpox swept through, and by 1879, most of the good stuff had dried up. Then a fire did what fires do. Those who stuck around were extra fierce. A railroad line came to town in 1888, and ten years later the Fairmont Hotel's brothel and saloon opened to serve them. Beyond the regular mishigas that comes with drinking and sex work, there was allegedly one suicide and one murder-accidental suicide. A working girl named Margaret Broadwater supposedly drank herself stupid and jumped out of a third-floor window in 1907. Her sad specter slams doors on the first floor.

Interesting that she wouldn't haunt the third floor. But truthfully, I have no idea why ghosts haunt certain areas. Some go back home to haunt a place they liked. I really hope the afterlife is CYOH: choose your own haunt.

A sex worker's boyfriend got jealous and attempted to shoot his girlfriend but shot her client instead, then accidentally shot himself. Now Mister Toxic Masculinity aggressively haunts the unoccupied third floor.

This is now the second time in this book that someone has accidentally shot themselves. Seems impossible. I guess a ricochet scenario makes sense.

There's also a little boy ghost, perhaps the son of a sex employee who succumbed to one of the poxes. Jack McCall, the bad guy who shot Wild Bill in the head at Saloon #10 next door, hangs around, having fun as he did in days of yore.

AS MUCH AS I LOVE HISTORY AND HBO, I THINK I'M GONNA PASS ON ADDING THIS TO MY LIST OF MUST-SEE DESTINATIONS. IT'S JUST AN OLD TOWN FULL OF PEOPLE WHO DIED COVERED IN PIG SHIT. PROBABLY DOESN'T EVEN HAVE A CHIPOTLE.

That's how Wild Bill died?!

The Female Stranger of Gadsby's Tavern

Alexandria, Virginia

On the weathered tabletop tombstone in St. Paul's Cemetery are the words "To the memory of a female stranger whose mortal sufferings terminated on the 14th day of October, 1816 / Aged 23 years and 8 months / This stone is placed here by her disconsolate Husband in whose arms she sighed out her latest breath, and who, under God, did his utmost to soothe the cold dead ear of death."

> WHITE KNIGHT MUCH, BRO? LMAO.
>
> Such a nasty thing to say. What a lovely inscription. Big fan of "mortal sufferings terminated" as a sub for "died."

Such an elaborate gravestone wasn't cheap—it was estimated that the new widower paid around $1,500. Either his Bank of England note bounced or he skipped town before paying back his lender, but either way, he was impossible to trace, and purposefully so. The couple was an unknown entity when they arrived in the Old City port and checked into Room 8 of the Gadsby's Tavern. She was dressed from top to toe in black as though in mourning and already deathly ill. On her deathbed, Female Stranger extracted an oath from all who'd attended her to never reveal her and her husband's identities. When the defrauded party went to look them up on the Gadsby's Tavern ledger, he found that their names had been scratched out.

YOU DON'T HAVE TO KEEP CALLING HER FEMALE STRANGER. JUST GIVE HER A NICKNAME!
LIKE, I DUNNO, THE UNKNOWN WOMAN!

To be fair, it's what the stolen gravestone said.

Who was the Female Stranger? No one knows, though theories abound. Was she Theodosia Burr Alston, the daughter of former VP Aaron Burr, MIA since 1813? Was she a con artist on the run? A Juliet-style star-crossed lover?

HONESTLY, WHO CARES?

I do. I'll have a look at the case file and have this wrapped up before lunch.

Whoever she was, today Female Stranger haunts Gadsby's Tavern, established in 1796 by John Gadsby in two buildings—a tavern built in 1785 and the four-story City Tavern built in 1792. At time of purchase, it was a successful enterprise, with fourteen sleeping rooms, multiple dining rooms, and an elegant ballroom; and he set about further fancying it up with the unpaid help of enslaved people. The US Capitol had just been set in nearby Washington DC, and the venue was perfect for George Washington's Birthnight Ball in 1798 and 1799. President John Adams downed a pint there in 1800, and President Thomas Jefferson held his inaugural ball there in 1801.

MUST BE NICE TO HAVE BALLS.

They're overrated. Kinda just in the way sometimes.

Gadsby moved on to other enterprises in 1808, but his name stayed, as did the ghost of the woman who died there a few years later. An attractive apparition in nineteenth-century garb has been spotted at costume balls, but when she is followed to Room 8, she vanishes, leaving a lit candle in her place.

DON'T CALL THE APPARITIONS ATTRACTIVE.

"Dude, I just saw a ghost . . . she was a total smokeshow."

The Lingering Lincolns
of the Equinox Golf Resort & Spa

Manchester Village, Vermont

The Equinox once hosted a campaign speech, that of Teddy Roosevelt, in the summer of 1912. Many years earlier, revolutionaries used the place to plot and scheme, eventually seizing it from its first owner, William Marsh, who'd made the mistake of declaring allegiance to the British during the Revolutionary War. There was a turnover in ownership over the next few decades, and in 1839, one owner thought to himself, *What this place needs is more fluted columns.*

> DID THIS GUY GO ON TO FOUND THE CHEESECAKE FACTORY?
>
> GOT 'EM!

Other presidents who stayed at the green-shuttered hotel included Ulysses S. Grant, William Howard Taft, and Benjamin Harrison. Abraham Lincoln was slotted to stay in the summer of 1865 but instead got assassinated.

> MAN, ULYSSES S. GRANT IS ALL UP IN THESE STORIES. IS HE THE MOST GHOST-FRIENDLY PRESIDENT WE'VE EVER HAD? I KNOW HE WAS NO STRANGER TO SPIRITS, HEY-O! (NOTED ALCOHOLIC UNFORTUNATELY.)
>
> The Civil War was tough.

It is thought that the more than 250-year-old establishment's two primary ghosts, a woman and a child, are those of First Lady Mary Todd Lincoln and one of her sons. Of her four sons, there are two age-appropriate possibilities, both of whom died before Mary's first visit. Edward died of tuberculosis at age four, in 1850, and beloved Willie died of typhoid fever in 1862. Three years after that terrible loss, Mary took her youngest son, Tad, who would die a few years later at the age of eighteen, and her oldest son, Robert, the only Lincoln child to grow into full-fledged adulthood, to the resort for a vacation. It is theorized that the place provided such a sweet balm for Mama Lincoln's aching heart that, in the afterlife, she returned with one of her young dearly departeds.

Wonder how the four boys sorted out who had to spend their entire afterlife shacked up with their mom.

Lone Lincoln grownup Robert must have accrued some fond memories there, too, for he built his summer estate down the road. His daughter, Mary Lincoln Isham, lived in the historic 1811 House that is now part of the corporate-owned Equinox estate, which also includes the main resort, the Orvis Suites, and the Marsh Tavern, all of which appear to have various degrees of haunting. Guests report that, upon returning to their rooms after a yoga class or a "Vermont glow" facial or a day on the links, various items have been moved around their rooms. Others claim to hear whispers, to be awakened in the night when the light inexplicably goes on, and to see shadowy movement out of the corners of their eyes.

I know I'm a big ol' scaredy cat, but nothing is frightening me after whatever a "Vermont glow" facial is. Sounds delightful.

BERNIE SANDERS SLATHERS YOUR FACE IN MAPLE SYRUP AND THEN A BEAVER LICKS IT OFF.

I'll take it!

The Spirits of the Palmer House Hotel

Sauk Centre, Minnesota

The site upon which the Palmer House Hotel now stands has always been a nerve center for the city of Sauk Centre. Formerly the Sauk Centre House, some say it was a straightforward restaurant and hotel, while others claim it was a tavern and brothel. If it's like pretty much everyplace everywhere throughout all of history, it was probably both. On June 5, 1900, the mayor himself gave members of the Old Settlers Association keys to the city while banqueting there. Then, on June 26, it burned to the ground. There is no clear consensus as to whether anyone lost their life in the fire.

> THIS IS USUALLY SOMEWHAT EASY TO DETERMINE, RIGHT? LOOK FOR HOT PILES OF BONES.
>
> Probably was a big tangled mess of wood. Though after said wood is moved eventually, yeah, you'd think you would have found some bones if there were any at all.

The following year, Ralph and Christena Palmer bought the land and constructed a luxury late Queen Anne–style hotel outfitted with the day's modern amenities, like electricity and a shared bathroom on every floor.

I wish I could travel back in time to watch the reaction of the first person to take a dump on a modern toilet. Must have been a real magical moment. Surprised there hasn't been a movie made about that. Especially since they made a movie about that lady who invented that fancy mop.

Sauk Centre native and Nobel Prize winner Sinclair Lewis grew up just blocks from the hotel and reportedly used its rooms to work; his 1920 satirical novel, *Main Street*, caused scandal when locals recognized themselves in some of his characters; the hotel itself, located on the corner of Main Street and Sinclair Lewis Avenue, is featured as Minniemashie House.

Very bold to accuse a writer of basing a character off you. Even if I read a book by someone I knew that had a character that loved basketball, popcorn, cinema, and Disneyland but hated ghosts, I'd still feel like it was too presumptuous to accuse the author of aping me.

The Palmer House Hotel got a makeover in 1993, but despite its new fanciness— free Wi-Fi plus a bathroom in every room—the ghosts of yesteryear remain. One regular is a little boy who is rumored to have died of the flu early in the Palmers's tenure. He likes to bounce a ball down the halls and occasionally sits on the stairs going up to the third floor.

NEXT TIME SOMEBODY SEES THAT KID, THEY SHOULD DO HIM A FAVOR AND CHUCK HIS BALL INTO THE LIGHT. SEND HIS ASS TO VALHALLA.

Sweet of you!

There also seems to be an apparition, or many apparitions, who entertain themselves by spontaneously flipping light switches, flushing toilets, and moving stuff around— furniture in Room 17, silverware in the dining room, remote controls throughout. Room 11 is always cold.

IT...KIND OF JUST SOUNDS LIKE A POORLY MANAGED HOTEL.

"Yeah, we don't have hot water, or Netflix on the telly, but ya know, not much you can do about those ghosts. They hate streaming."

Those staying below Room 18 report hearing footsteps, even when no one is checked into the rooms above them, and footsteps are often heard on the stairs. Other strange incidents include random knocking, unusually loud slamming doors, disembodied whispers, shortness of breath, and the feeling of being watched by someone standing in the corner.

Have had this happen to me in New Orleans. Didn't sleep a wink. Scary. And annoying.

I SLEPT LIKE A LITTLE, TINY, SLEEPY BABY.

The Soldier Specters of
Lightner Farmhouse Bed & Breakfast

Gettysburg, Pennsylvania

I n 1736, William Penn and family bought the land now known as Adams County from the Iroquois Indians. And everyone lived happily ever after.

An actual legit transaction? This sounds, dare I say, not horrible?

Actually, twenty years later, the French and the Wabanaki Confederacy teamed up against the British and the Iroquois Confederacy to fight about imperial rule, and settlers along the Maryland/Pennsylvania border got caught in the crossfire. Many people proceeded to die horrible deaths.

Never mind.

VERY AMERICAN THING TO DO, DIE A HORRIBLE DEATH. EVEN TODAY!

Once the Seven Years War ended, the area saw an era of peace and prosperity. To celebrate, Samuel Gettys opened a bar. His son established the town of—you guessed it—Gettysburg. By 1860, there were ten roads leading into the bustling mecca of industry, which had grown to 2,400 citizens. In 1862, Isaac and Barbara Lightner began construction of a fancy Federal-style house befitting Isaac's fancy position as sheriff of Adams County. The couple certainly did not imagine that their beautiful home would soon become a stinky field hospital. But then General Lee and his seventy-five thousand troops and General Meade and his ninety-five thousand troops marched along those convenient roads into town for a blood-soaked meet.

God, imagine you've just toiled for months and months on remodeling your brand-new kitchen and living room. You're stoked to have a certified rager to celebrate, and then the Civil War takes a dump on your home. Hate to see it. I'd like to think they got in several solid game nights beforehand, though.

The Lightner residence just so happened to be two miles from the battlefield. George W. New, Union 1st Corps surgeon of the Indiana Seventh Infantry, and Elmina Spencer, nurse of the 147th New York Infantry, annexed the house to be used to treat the new injuries brought about by the latest craze in warfare technology.

Gotta be a pain in the ass to scrub that blood off the new kitchen tiles. Especially if it gets stuck in the grout. That's checkmate usually.

Instead of breaking bones, as did the short-range muskets and round lead balls of yore, the new conical Minie ball and more accurate, longer-range muskets splintered bones and damaged tissue so thoroughly that infection was common. Often the best chance of survival was amputation. Soon the pretty Lightner lawns were covered by thousands of wounded young men, moaning and grinding their teeth and waiting their turn for treatment or death—or treatment then death.

ANNOYING TO HAVE YOUR WHOLE DINING ROOM FILLED WITH GAUNT, PERFORATED MEN LEAKING ROTTEN BLOOD. PASS THE GRAVY, I GUESS.

And again, the tiles! Not enough 409 in the world to salvage 'em!

In an impromptu operating room in the parlor, the dedicated staff lopped off limbs and tossed them out the window onto the pile of amputated appendages outside. We can only hope that Surgeon New had a decent supply of ether.

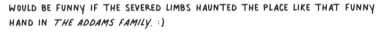

WOULD BE FUNNY IF THE SEVERED LIMBS HAUNTED THE PLACE LIKE THAT FUNNY HAND IN *THE ADDAMS FAMILY*. :)

Wonder if they called something out as a warning before tossing arms out the window. Working this makeshift hospital seems bad enough, let alone getting blindly bitchslapped by a rogue disembodied hand on your smoke break outside.

More than fifty thousand husbands, sons, and brothers were killed or maimed during the three-day battle. As the Lightner Farmhouse B&B's website says, "Come for the history, stay for the hospitality!" Today, guests have reported being awakened by the sound of something heavy being dragged across the floor, and there have been sightings of ghostly blue- and gray-coated soldiers roaming the grounds and bearded apparitions peeking out windows. For more paranormal activity, mosey on down to Gettysburg National Military Park.

All jokes aside, I highly recommend you visit Gettysburg and especially this park. Quite the historical journey they have down there. Also, a great cigar shop in town.

Redrum at the Stanley Hotel

Estes Park, Colorado

In a departure from haunted norms, the Stanley doesn't have a list of murder and mayhem as long as a skeleton's arm. Rather, in 1974, Stephen King, while asleep in Room 217, had a nightmare, which inspired his bestselling novel *The Shining*, which inspired the controversial Stanley Kubrick movie, which inspired a whole lot more nightmares.

> Gonna use this opportunity to suggest that everyone watch the trailer for *Maximum Overdrive*, specifically the one with Stephen King talking to the camera. It's batshit and always good for a laugh. In fact, I'm gonna give it another view right now. Holy smokes, I never knew that movie featured a young Gus Fring!

In 1903, F.O. and Flora Stanley visited a resort in the Rocky Mountains to take the clean-air cure, as recommended by the steam-car inventor's doctor to alleviate his consumption. And it worked! The couple fell in love with the area and soon bought land in Estes Park. They first built a summer "cottage"—a three-story, 5,240-square-foot home called Rockside. It was nice, but they yearned for the more cosmopolitan company they were used to, so they built a Colonial Revival hotel, offering one hundred rooms to classy folks like John Philip Sousa, Molly Brown, and Theodore Roosevelt.

Though the hotel had the highest-end amenities, a true accomplishment for a venue located in mountain wilderness, it lacked central heating and so closed as the weather turned cool. After F.O.'s death in 1940, owner turnover led to the hotel's decline. By the time Stephen King and his wife were the last guests at the end of the '74 season, it was fairly rundown. The author spent the weekend wandering the halls alone, and from that the idea of a psychic child and an alcoholic off-season caretaker losing his marbles was born.

IT'S GOT VIBES. I'LL SAY THAT. DEFINITELY WORTH A VISIT. THESE INTERJECTIONS DON'T ALL HAVE TO BE NASTY LITTLE QUIPS. RYAN, WE HAD A BLAST THERE, DIDN'T WE?

Great hotel, ornate, and vibes off the fuckin' charts. I enjoyed my time. Could also see how one would lose their mind in there.

Some say the ghost of F.O. visits the billiard room and bar and the ghost of Flora plays the piano in the Concert Hall. Not because they're angry or sad, but because they loved the place so dang much.

These seem like my kind of ghosts. They have my respect.

The two hold hands as they ascend the grand staircase, nicknamed "the vortex" because of its concentration of paranormal energy. The ghost of a chambermaid named Elizabeth, who was injured in a 1911 explosion caused by a gas leak, tidies up the room in which King stayed—Room 217—and makes her disapproval of unmarried people sharing a bed known by acute coldness.

This chambermaid sounds like the same group of prudes who didn't want Lucy and Ricky to share a bed.

Ghostly children laugh and play on the fourth floor, and a ghostly cowboy appears at the corner of the bed in Room 428. A little boy ghost called Billy peeks around corners in the former icehouse. Ghost pets roam the grounds.

SEEMS LIKE THERE'S AN INORDINATE NUMBER OF GHOST BOYS NAMED BILLY OUT THERE, BUT I GUESS IT WAS A PRETTY TRENDY NAME FOR A WHILE. IN A HUNDRED YEARS, PEOPLE WILL PROBABLY BE HAUNTED BY COUNTLESS AIDENS, JAYDENS, BRAIDENS, AND KAYDENS.

These regulars are mostly benign. But the hotel has become something of a spirit hangout, and there are other angrier or sadder ghosts around, ones who met unhappy ends. Redrum, anyone?

No thanks!

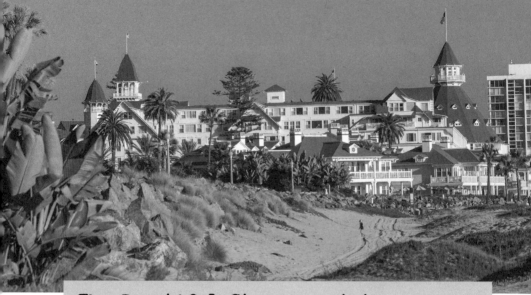

The Beautiful Stranger at the Hotel del Coronado

San Diego, California

OH HELL YEAH, BUST OUT THE SUNSCREEN AND THE SPEEDOS, BABY. GHOUL BOYS HITTIN' THAT BEACH. NOTHIN' BUT SUNSHINE AND GOOD VIBES, MON FRÈRE.

I do love me some SD.

Just four years after the beachside resort opened to sun worshippers in bathing costumes and sixty-six years before Marilyn Monroe cast her transcendent glow on Coronado Beach in *Some Like It Hot*, the luxurious Hotel del Coronado was briefly made famous by a tragic suicide.

THESE ARE NOT GOOD VIBES, MON FRÈRE.

You jinxed it, man. Went too far with the Speedos.

WE ALWAYS DO.

The body of a pretty young woman in her mid-twenties was found dead by gunshot wound in an exterior staircase leading to the beach. She'd checked into the hotel and signed the register "Lottie A. Bernard, Detroit," and she'd told hotel employees that she was waiting for a brother, Dr. Anderson of Minneapolis. After five days, he had yet to show, and some assumed that she'd been stood up by a secret lover.

I DON'T THINK PEOPLE SHOULD BRING GUNS TO THE BEACH. THERE. I SAID IT. HOT DOGS? SURE. RIDGED POTATO CHIPS AND A SUITABLE DIP? ABSOLUTELY. A GLOCK? YOU DON'T UNDERSTAND WHAT THE BEACH IS FOR.

> While we're making rules, here's another one: When you come upon a dead body, don't say, "Oh, she's pretty."

The coroner ruled it a suicide, and soon it became clear that she'd given a fake name—a real person by the name of Lottie A. Bernard was alive and well in Detroit. The coroner then received a letter suggesting this person had represented herself as Josie Brown elsewhere, and a young man she'd claimed to be her brother had visited her there. With the identity of the suicide up in the air, the newspapers began referring to her as "the beautiful stranger."

> IS THIS WHAT THAT MADONNA SONG FROM *AUSTIN POWERS 2* IS ABOUT?

> Words right out of my mouth. Let's get back to this mystery lady.

Then a wealthy local turned in a trunk labeled "Mrs. Kate Morgan" to the police. Inside were several photographs of what were presumed to be an uncle, a husband, and four children; a lock of blonde hair; a marriage certificate dated December 30, 1885; and a letter of recommendation. There was also a photograph of Mrs. Morgan, which, according to a nasty article in the *Los Angeles Herald* from December 10, 1892, didn't match the complimentary description given by hotel staff. It read, "The photograph does not denote the appearance of a woman accustomed to stopping at first-class hotels as a guest, or one who wears lace shawls; neither does it show her to be pretty, and the features certainly are not those of a highly educated woman."

> HOW THE HELL WAS THE HOTEL STAFF DESCRIBING THIS WOMAN? "OH MY GOD, SHE WAS SOOOOOOO HOT. SHE DEFINITELY LOOKED LIKE THE KIND OF WOMAN WHO WEARS LACE SHAWLS IF YA KNOW WHAT I MEAN. ANYWAY, YES, WE FOUND HER BLEEDING ON THE STAIRS OUT BACK."

> Lol, seriously, what kind of Zuckerberg "Hot or Not" hotel staff worked there?!

It was determined that the deceased was in fact Kate Morgan, though what she was doing at the Del and the reasons for her suicide are unknown. Today she haunts her former room, as well as the hotel grounds, where guests report seeing the apparition of a beautiful woman. There have been so many occurrences of disembodied shadows, moving furniture, cold spots, slamming doors, and electronics turning on and off that in 1992 the hotel brought in a parapsychologist to conduct a year-long 24/7 paranormal investigation. He interviewed eleven hundred people and conducted ten thousand hours of monitoring, and concluded that a "significant percentage" of the data showed paranormal phenomena.

> OH MY GOD, CONGRATS TO THAT PARAPSYCHOLOGIST FOR HOPPING ON BOARD THAT GRAVY TRAIN. TEN THOUSAND HOURS? ONLY TO CONCLUDE: YEP, SEEMS HAUNTED. HILARIOUS.

> Yeah, I'm of the opinion that if you constantly monitor a haunted location for one year and have no video or photo evidence, it's probably not haunted.

The Heartbreaking Faceoff
of the Peter Shields Inn

Cape May, New Jersey

Cape May, located at the very most southern tip of New Jersey where Delaware Bay meets the North Atlantic Ocean, claims to be America's original seaside resort town.

| BOLD claim, New Jersey.

First noticed by white people in 1609, Anglo settlers purchased the land from the Kechemeche Indians of the Lenni-Lenape tribe in the 1630s and turned it into a locus of fishing and whaling. Prosperity ensued, and by the mid-1700s, the area was known for its sea-based leisure activities and seafood-based cuisine. In the decades before the turn of the twentieth century, however, a terrible fire and the ascension of other chichi destinations like Newport and Atlantic City were starting to take its toll on the town's prospects.

| NOTICING A LOT OF FIRES IN THESE STORIES. HAVEN'T THESE PEOPLE EVER HEARD OF
| WATER? WORKS LIKE A CHARM.

| Agreed. Fires seem to be as common as Wi-Fi going down. Which, by the way, cycling
| power is usually the fix. For the Wi-Fi. Not the fires. As my colleague pointed out,
| that's gonna be water.

Enter Peter Shields. The wealthy Pittsburgher joined a group of developers hell-bent on returning Cape May to its former glory and was soon appointed president of the Cape May Real Estate Company.

| This name screams polos, shorts, and boat shoes.

He then began the construction of his grand summer Georgian-Revival cottage, which was completed four years later, in 1907. In 1908, Peter's fifteen-year-old son, Earle, accidentally shot himself in the face while hunting marsh hens.

| WAS IT LIKE . . . A . . . PRANK GUN?

| Now the third person in this book to accidentally shoot themselves. Starting to
| think guns are bad.

It was a gruesome injury—the bullet broke his jaw and blew out his eyeballs before lodging itself in his brain. He was rushed to the Cape May Yacht Club and attended by every doctor in town to no avail. His parents were at his side when he passed to the other side.

FOLKS, YIKES.

WELP that was quite the image.

Or did he? The Shields family left the area in 1912, after the Cape May Real Estate Company declared bankruptcy. Now the Peter Shields Inn and Restaurant offers nine gorgeous guest rooms, afternoon wine-and-cheese plates, expansive ocean views, a beachside wedding venue, Zagat-recommended dining—and ghosts.

God I wish Zagat reviewed hauntings.

Those who've met Earle say that he's a sad ghost, not an angry one. Most believe that he feels guilty for causing his mother so much grief, for leaving his short life and his friends behind, and for defying his father's veto of the trip that led to his untimely death.

I MEAN, I FEEL FOR THE GUY, BUT . . . WAS THE . . . HEN ON HIS . . . FACE, OR . . . ?

They say eyes are the window into the soul, so, respectfully, how do we know he's sad?

Whatever the case, it is said that Earle waits for the return of his family more than one hundred years after their departure. He can be found hanging around the stairway, the third floor, the attic, or in what used to be the home's cellar. Sometimes other ghosts keep him company. Windows and doors open on their own. The wine-and-cheese plates mysteriously disappear.

WELL, I HOPE HE FINDS HIS EYES.

At least he's eating well.

The Glowing Ghosts
of the Elms Hotel & Spa

Excelsior Springs, Missouri

Unlike other health spas in the country (Arkansas's Crescent, we're looking at you), the Elms Hotel & Spa didn't attract a charlatan who capitalized on the infirm's vulnerability like a vulture on carrion. Were the springs' healing properties exaggerated? Hard to say. In 1880, the city itself was a wheat field until farmer Travis Mellion used the reddish waters of the Siloam Spring, an offshoot of the Fishing River, to treat his daughter's tuberculosis.

THEY WERE JUST SORT OF TRYING ANYTHING BACK THEN, HUH? WATER THAT DON'T LOOK LIKE IT OUGHT TO? TRY IT ON YOUR DAUGHTER'S BUM LUNGS!

Penicillin was discovered by accident.

Apparently, a few weeks of bathing and drinking the stuff cured her, and so Civil War vet Frederick Kuglar took a gander at a gunshot wound that had yet to heal. The waters cured him, too. With that, houses popped up like mushrooms hither and yon, two hundred of them within a year, and health seekers arrived in droves to camp out along the more than forty newly discovered water wells and springs. The Elms Hotel opened in 1888.

THIS HAPPENED TO ME ONCE. EXCEPT INSTEAD OF A GUNSHOT WOUND IT WAS A BIG-ASS SCRAPE ON MY SHIN. AND INSTEAD OF THE CIVIL WAR IT WAS JUST ME TRIPPING OVER A ROCK IN GRIFFITH PARK, BECAUSE I WAS DISTRACTED ARGUING ABOUT WHY I THOUGHT *TOMORROWLAND* WAS A PRETTY BAD MOVIE, STRUCTURALLY AND OTHERWISE. THE SCRAPE ACTUALLY HEALED PRETTY QUICKLY, TOO, SO I GUESS IT'S NOT ALL THAT SIMILAR. HEY, HAS BRAD BIRD LOST HIS FASTBALL?

As mentioned earlier, Shane falls a lot. Also, they got me. I'm fully in on this magic water now. Booking a flight.

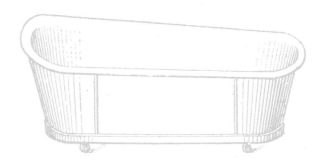

Ten years later, a fire destroyed the wooden building. Ten years after that, the second Elms was constructed. Two years after that, in 1910, Elms Jr. burned. This would be enough for some to stick a fork in it and call it done. But not Elms! A third hotel, made of limestone, opened in 1912. As with pretty much any older venue—hotel, bar, restaurant, you-name-it—the hotel and spa claims that the likes of Al Capone, "Pretty Boy" Floyd, and Bugs Moran stayed as guests during the 1930s, boozing it up with the governor of Missouri. Presidential nominee Harry S. Truman, born in Lamar, Missouri, got the full spa treatment in 1948 and was positively glowing in his election victory photo in the *Chicago Tribune*.

FOR A HOTEL BUILT EXCLUSIVELY FOR ITS PROXIMITY TO A NATURAL WATER SOURCE, THIS PLACE SURE DOES CATCH ON FIRE A LOT.

Hahaha.

Oddly enough, there are no scary deaths at the hotel on record, no immolations during either fire—though there are rumors of staff deaths that went unreported—nor Wild West hangings nor jilted-bride suicides nor romantic wastings away while clutching blood-soaked hankies. Yet an apparition in a 1920s uniform gives the housekeeping staff cleaning and spiritual advice, and the presence of a Prohibition-era gambler has been experienced in the lap pool area. Perhaps the ghosts are people who so enjoyed the soaks and scrubs that they never wanted to leave.

Or perhaps that magic water had a price.

NOT TAKING SPIRITUAL ADVICE FROM SOME IDIOT GHOST WHO DOOMED THEMSELVES TO HAUNT THE EARTHLY REALM FOR ALL OF ETERNITY.

EERIE INSTITUTIONS

The Haunted Halls
of Waverly Hills Sanitorium

Louisville, Kentucky

THE LADS HAVE BEEN HERE. I'LL GIVE THIS PLACE CREDIT: IT IS DAUNTING. PRIOR TO
INVESTIGATING THIS PLACE, WE HAD ONLY BEEN TO SMALL OR RELATIVELY DOMESTIC
LOCALES. WAVERLY IS A DUMMY THICC NIGHTMARE BUILDING WHERE LONG HALLS OF
EMPTY ROOMS STRETCH INTO DARKNESS. AND IT'S A LOT OF WALKING, SO BRING A
LITTLE BAG OF CHEX MIX OR SOMETHING.

This place is hell on earth.

For the most part, stories about Waverly Hills Sanitorium are not horrifying or grotesque. There are no tales of mad doctors or sadistic nurses or snake oil salesmen. But a lot of people died there for one simple reason: tuberculosis. TB was seriously bad news in the twentieth century and probably for a few millennia before that—archeologists discovered TB in the remains of a mother and child buried nine thousand years ago in Atlit Yam, a city now under water off the coast of Israel. It is estimated to have caused around 25 percent of all deaths from the 1600s to the 1800s; it was also known as consumption and the white plague, because victims became pale and emaciated as the malady consumed them.

ONE OF THE UNDISPUTED CHAMPS OF KILLING THE SHIT OUT OF HUMANS.

It's like the mosquito of the plague world.

Robert Koch's discovery of the mycobacterium tuberculosis in 1882 put an end to the vampire panics of New England and the theory that TB was hereditary, but antibiotics weren't available until the 1950s. Before then, the only treatment was quarantine and, for those who could afford it, healthy living.

"Well, Mr. Johnson, I regret to inform you that you have tuberculosis. I'm going to prescribe you a nice weekly jog."

The first American sanitorium opened in 1875 in Asheville, North Carolina; Waverly Hills Sanitorium opened on July 26, 1910. It was five stories tall and, since it needed to be self-sufficient, surrounded by farmland for raising livestock and growing crops. It was built atop a hill for two reasons: 1) so that up to five hundred patients could get fresh air and quiet; and 2) a five hundred–foot tunnel going downhill was easier to traverse while wheeling dead bodies out of sight of the living. Loads of spirits hang out in the body chute.

How many people died within the walls of Waverly Hills? Unknown. Once the blessed arrival of antibiotics tamped down tuberculosis, Waverly Hills Sanitorium closed its doors in 1961. Yet it is considered one of the most haunted places in the world. Visitors claim to hear children's laughter and slamming doors and to see faces and shadow people in empty rooms. There is heightened activity in the first-floor morgue, for obvious reasons, as well as the fifth floor, where patients with infection of the brain received electroshock therapy.

Room 502 is the most active, with two alleged suicides along with all that zapping. In 1932, a nurse jumped from the balcony, or maybe she was pushed. Four years earlier, Nurse Mary Hillenburg hung herself in the hallway. An apparition in a white doctor's coat has been seen entering a treatment room on the fourth floor, and a full-bodied apparition has been seen in the waiting room. On the third floor, a little boy named Timmy plays with a blue rubber ball.

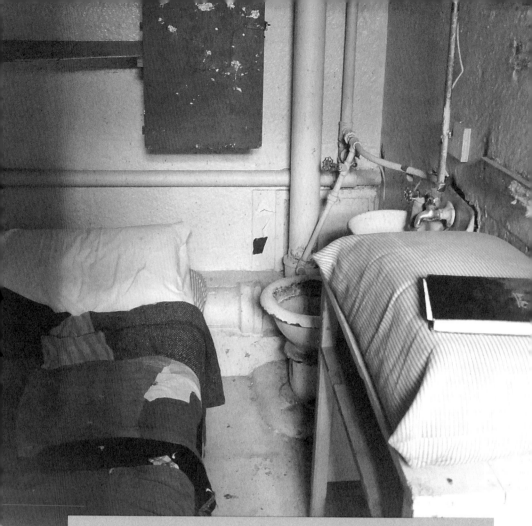

The Angry Apparitions
of Wyoming Frontier Prison

Rawlins, Wyoming

From 1901 to 1981, around 235 people at Old Penn died from the usual prison-related causes: violence, disease, insanity, poor conditions. There was no hot water until 1978, and the heating system wasn't great. The temperature during Wyoming winters routinely dropped below freezing, and at least two people froze to death.

I'M GONNA BE HONEST—THIS ALL SOUNDS PRETTY BAD!

Nothing about the name Frontier Prison screams a good time.

Many of the total 13,500 convicts were locked in the dungeon or in solitary confinement, or they got handcuffed to the "punishment pole" and whipped with rubber hoses. When not being punished, they were crowded into cells or put to work making brooms, shirts, military-grade blankets, or license plates.

Well, this certainly sounds awful. Side note: How many brooms could they have possibly needed at this joint?

THE... THE BROOMS AREN'T FOR THEM. THEY SHIP THOSE THINGS OUT. YOU THINK THEY'RE JUST MAKING NOVELTY LICENSE PLATES FOR THE PRISONERS TO HANG IN THEIR CELLS? LIKE **MURDRR1**?

Ah. That makes sense.

The high-desert prison hosted fourteen executions by portable gallows, indoor gallows, hydrocyanic acid gas in the in-house gas chamber, and lethal injection, depending on the era. Tom Horn was hanged in 1903, and ever since, his guilt in the murder of a fourteen-year-old son of a sheep rancher has been questioned. What hasn't been questioned is whether the hit man was hired by the Wyoming Cattlemen's Association to kill a whole lot of troublemaking ranchers. His execution took seventeen minutes; the Julian gallows, named for James Julian, was designed to be DIY using water weight and so had the advantage of avoiding the executioner's fee. One disadvantage was that it took a while.

WHAT IF I DON'T REALLY WANT TO KNOW ABOUT ANY OF THIS?

Didn't think I'd learn about a DIY gallows, but here we are.

A behatted ghost who could be Horn has been seen in the "death house," though the building wasn't added until 1916. Or it could be Mark Hopkinson, who hired a hit man to torture and murder someone in Wyoming while serving time in California; he was lethally injected in 1992. Famous for his vindictiveness, he chose to use his final statement to call the special prosecutor "a lying, manipulating piece of shit." (Fun fact: One murderer who did not get executed was Annie Bruce, one of only eleven women who were incarcerated during the prison's history. She poisoned her father with a strychnine-laced pie and was the first woman ever convicted of murder in the state, in 1907.) Today you can be one of the fifteen thousand visitors who get freaked out annually.

CAN WE LEARN ABOUT LUXURY HOTELS AGAIN? REMEMBER THAT CHAPTER ABOUT THE FLOATING MCDONALD'S?

Poisoning someone with pie is just cruel. The humane thing to do would be to use cake instead. Because cake blows.

I THINK I'D RATHER DIE EATING PIE, THOUGH. THAT SOUNDS NICE.

Wouldn't everyone?

The Horrors of Pennhurst
State School & Hospital

Spring City, Pennsylvania

BABY, THIS PLACE IS GROSS.

Easily one of the most heinous and disgusting places we've visited.

For what it's worth, we wish that people were nicer to each other, especially to those who might need extra support. Alas, that's not the world we live in, nor was it the world of 1908, the year that Pennhurst State School and Hospital began receiving people with epilepsy or intellectual disabilities, whom they labeled "feebleminded." All patients were called "children" regardless of age, and the parents of actual children with disabilities were told that Pennhurst would be a safe environment.

Awful history aside, this place is truly gnarly. Two post-hunt showers still didn't feel like enough.

This was a lie, according to a 1968 documentary called *Suffer the Little Children*, a 1974 class-action lawsuit, and a 1999 memoir by former resident Roland Johnson.

Overcrowding, understaffing, and underfunding led to atrocious living conditions. Residents were restrained for hours on end, threatened and physically abused, and controlled through overadministration of medication. In the documentary, Dr. Fear—yes, that's his real name—admitted to asking one of his staff members to punish a resident by giving them the most painful injection that would not cause damage.

Do you think being named Fear predestined this dude to a life of being a piece of shit? Also, just odd to me that a person named Fear would choose to be a doctor.

Terry Lee Halderman, the plaintiff in the class-action lawsuit, reportedly suffered about forty injuries, including cracked teeth, a broken jaw, and a fractured finger. Her suit described the state facility thusly: "Conditions at Pennhurst are not only dangerous, with the residents often physically abused or drugged by staff members, but inadequate . . . Indeed, the court found that the physical, intellectual, and emotional skills of some residents have deteriorated at Pennhurst." Halderman won, resulting in the school's closure in 1978.

I'D BE HAPPY TO RETURN TO MOST PLACES WE'VE INVESTIGATED OVER THE YEARS, BUT THIS IS ONE OF THE FEW THAT I'M HAPPY TO AVOID. IT WASN'T, YOU KNOW, FUN.

I'm never going back.

One theory is that those who experienced pain are more likely to remain, making Pennhurst a primo paranormal zone. Underground tunnels that link its twenty buildings have much activity, as does the former dormitory on the third floor of the Mayflower Building. There have been reports of a shadow man by the name of Fisher caught on camera in the common room. A little boy named Howie likes to play with a toy airplane, and an angry nurse, perhaps the one working under Dr. Fear, likes to stab people with a needle.

ROT IN PISS, DR. FEAR.

The Demon Priest of Mission San Francisco Solano

Sonoma, California

We had late-night Taco Bell after this investigation. Good times.

IF YOU GO TO SONOMA, YOU *MUST* TRY THE TACO BELL.

In 1542, Spain claimed the land that would be California. Of course, this land wasn't technically available, given that there were an estimated three hundred thousand people already living there. The land itself, with its treacherous mountain ranges and deserts, served to isolate Indigenous groups from one another, and the dry climate encouraged a hunter-gatherer lifestyle, making division of real estate moot. These factors resulted in a relatively peaceful region, with small clans going about their business.

MISSIONS WERE NEW TO ME WHEN I MOVED TO CALIFORNIA. NOT A LOT OF OLD SPANISH MISSIONS IN ILLINOIS. ALL WE HAVE IS THAT BIG METAL BEAN, WHICH HAS BEEN THERE SINCE THE DAWN OF TIME.

I'll admit that the Bean, although strange and pointless, is wholesome.

IT WAS PUT THERE BY GOD.

Such is the state in which missionaries found the locals, whose souls they quickly set about "saving."

Oh, I'm sure they felt very saved.

Friars attracted the Native Americans with gifts and promises, then baptized them, a ritual that formally tied them to the compound. At that point, if a "neophyte" left the mission, they were considered a runaway and duly rounded up and punished. Then they were forced to work the land, and the usual horror of human nature mixed with religion mixed with power followed: family separation, imprisonment, slavery, torture.

YEAH, JESUS JUST LOVED THAT SHIT.

Particularly Old Testament Jesus. Homeboy was a straight-up savage.

I THINK YOU'RE CONFUSING HIM WITH HIS DAD AGAIN.

I kinda just skimmed the bible tbh.

The first official mission was founded in 1769 and the last, the San Francisco Solano Mission, in July 1823. Founder Padre José Altimira was known for going above and beyond in terms of cruelty. A rebellion broke out two years into his tenure—that's how terrible he was. It is believed to be Altimira's apparition—or his demon—seen in the chapel.

THIS GUY SOUNDS VAGUELY BAD, BUT IT SOUNDS LIKE HE VAGUELY GOT WHAT WAS COMING TO HIM!

During the eleven years in operation, thirteen hundred members of the Coast Miwok, Pomo, Suisunes, Wappo, and Patwin tribes were baptized—and close to one thousand Native Americans died. The exact location of their graves is unknown, but historians believe that the cemetery or cemeteries were adjacent to one or both of the mission churches. A plaque with the Christian names of over nine hundred neophytes, including two hundred children, memorializes the deceased.

WHO NEEDS GHOSTS WHEN YOU CAN BE JUST AS UNSETTLED BY THE ABJECT HORROR OF THE ACTIONS OF HUMAN BEINGS?

In any comparison, humans are always the scariest. Even in zombie movies.

Along with the padre, other priest apparitions have been encountered in what has come to be called the "priest's quarters," not because priests lived there but because that's where their ghosts seem to hang out. In the courtyard rambles an apparition of a bear thought to somehow be related to the Bear Flag Party, who kidnapped the general in charge, hunkered down in the barracks, and declared an Independent Republic of California for twenty-five days. At the Whipping Tree, screams and sobs can be heard.

WE DIDN'T SEE THE GHOST BEAR WHEN WE WERE THERE, AND I'M STILL PISSED AS SHIT.

Totally forgot about the ghost bear. But glad it didn't make an appearance. Literally my worst nightmare as it combines two of my greatest fears.

The Terrors of Yuma Territorial Prison

Yuma, Arizona

The Yuma Territorial Prison was either great or terrible, depending on whom you ask.

If you're asking me, it's terrible. Packed to the gills with bats.

MORE BATS THAN YOU'RE USED TO SEEING ANYWHERE AT ALL!

Locals called it the "country club on the Colorado" because of its view of the Colorado River and its superior amenities. Open from 1876 to 1909, it had Yuma's only three flush toilets, plus three showers and two bathtubs, forced ventilation, electricity, and a prison band. Madora Ingalls, the wife of a superintendent who served two stints in the 1880s, brought in two thousand books, creating the largest library in the territory at the time. She also manned the Lowell battery gun during escape attempts.

SWEET OF HER! BRINGING IN BOOKS! TO A REPREHENSIBLE INSTITUTION!

Hard to read when you're distracted by the flapping wings of hordes of bats.

Inmates, meanwhile, describe the prison as "impossible to endure, more impossible to escape," though twenty-six people did manage to escape.

Sounds like that unsinkable boat. The *Titanic*, I think it was called.

Temperatures could reach 118 degrees in the summer. Fractious prisoners were stripped down to their undies and shackled inside the Dark Cell—a ten-foot by ten-foot lightless iron cage carved into the hillside—for months at a time. It was dubbed the Snake Den because an especially mean guard liked to drop scorpions and snakes down the vent.

CAN'T BE DOING THAT.

I've been in there. Not a snake to be seen. But there were definitely bats. About fifty-two of them from my count.

Of the 3,069 total prisoners, including twenty-nine women, many infamous outlaws served their time at Yuma. Nine Mormon leaders were convicted of polygamy under the Edmunds Act of 1882 and incarcerated, including William Jordan Flake, who later moved to Snowflake to live with his two wives and twenty children.

FUN FACT: NO TWO OF MR. FLAKE'S WIVES WERE THE SAME.

Nor his twenty children.

After killing a bunch of people in Tombstone, including O.K. Corral shootout survivor Billy Claiborne, "Buckskin Frank" Leslie was finally convicted of murder after shooting his girlfriend while drunk. Wyatt Earp supposedly said he was "the only man who could compare to Doc Holliday's blinding speed and accuracy with a six gun." Elena Estrada served seven years for stabbing her cheating boyfriend and then cutting open his chest, ripping out his heart, and, in what some might consider overkill, throwing it in his face.

Gotta stay faithful, folks.

Only 112 prisoners died, the majority from tuberculosis and other "natural causes." Eight were shot during escape attempts, six killed themselves, five died in work accidents, two were murdered, and one was executed by the county. The unpopular John Ryan died by suicide in cell 14, where visitors feel cold and see a glowing apparition with shining eyes. Of course, the most feared spot, then and now, is the Snake Den. Male visitors report getting punched and female visitors get pinched, while the sounds of cursing and moaning echo in the darkness.

THE GHOST SNAKES PUNCHED PEOPLE?? GOD, ONE OF THE SCARIEST THINGS I CAN IMAGINE IS A SNAKE WHOSE TAIL IS JUST A BIG-ASS FIST. I HOPE GMOs DON'T EVER LEAD TO THAT, BUT AT THE RATE WE'RE GOING, IT FEELS INEVITABLE. HAVING SAID THAT, I DON'T REALLY KNOW WHAT GMOs ARE.

Neither do I. But I do know that this horrible den is full of horrible bats. Half a star. Will not return.

The Burning Boss of Sloss Furnace

Birmingham, Alabama

Colonel James Withers Sloss knew an opportunity when he saw one. The nation was rebuilding after the Civil War, and the ground around Jones Valley in central Alabama just so happened to have iron ore, limestone, and coal in abundance.

> It's been a while since I played Settlers of Catan. Might have to brush the dust off that bad boy.

After making a fortune in coke and coal, he founded Sloss Furnace Company in 1880, commissioning two blast furnaces that were sixty feet high and eighteen feet in diameter, two blowers, ten boilers, and a labyrinth of pipes. This equipment heated the raw materials to upwards of 1,400 degrees until they became molten, then collected the pure iron and slagged off the impure slag.

> IMAGINE THIS GUY IN HIS OWN *NARCOS* SPINOFF. ANYWAY, COKE IS A MINERAL, READERS. NOT COCAINE.

> Good to clear that up. Also, I got a bad feeling about these blast furnaces.

From the get-go, Jim Crow segregated the operation, from drinking fountains and bathrooms to pay and division of labor. Management considered Black employees expendable, often assigning them the most dangerous work. The first deaths on record were those of two Black workmen named Aleck King and Bob Mayfield, who were dislodging "clinkers," caked-on ore and coke, from the blast furnace interior. A chunk dropped into the fire below, releasing a plume of noxious gas that overwhelmed them so that they, too, fell.

> HAVING SHARED HOTEL ROOMS WITH RYAN BERGARA, I, TOO, HAVE BEEN OVERWHELMED BY PLUMES OF NOXIOUS GAS.

> Just marking my territory.

It is unknown just how many deaths and accidents there were over the years, because casualties weren't always reported. On top of that, reality and rumor have blurred. There are tales of death by suicide, like the time an employee jumped into the blast furnace known as Big Alice. An unnamed, unmarried pregnant woman took her life the same way, though how she got into the factory and up to the top of the furnace is up for debate. Eight men fell eighty-five feet when scaffolding collapsed under them; two died on impact. Two men drowned in an open water tank in the late 1800s. Another guy suffocated on poisoned gas. One man was crushed by gears in the diesel shed. Another burned when molten iron was accidentally poured on him.

> WOULD LOVE TO SEE THIS *UNDERCOVER BOSS* EPISODE.

In 1887, supervising foundryman Theophilus Calvin Jowers fell into a vat of molten iron—only his head, bowels, and hip bones were recovered. Some believe this story inspired that of James "Slag" Wormwood, the foreman on the graveyard shift who, according to legend, relentlessly drove his employees. Forty-seven workers died and many others were permanently disabled on his watch, including six workers who were blinded in an explosion in 1888. In 1906, Slag lost his footing and fell into the hellfire of Big Alice, where he melted into the slag that was his namesake.

> Feels like half of OSHA's standards and practices came from peeking at this joint's case file.

> THANK GOODNESS. SEEMS TO HAVE PUT A STOP TO PEOPLE GETTING THE T-1000 TREATMENT ON THE REG.

> Regardless of whether or not Slag fell into this pit, it seems definitive that he was a total dick.

Allegedly, a ghost with badly burned skin continues to yell at those who enter his domain, pushing a night watchman and telling him to "get back to work" in 1926. Three supervisors were directed to "push some steel" before being locked in a small boiler room and losing consciousness in 1947. Others sense a malevolent entity throughout the grounds. Is this ol' Slaggy? Or is it an alloy of the spirits who, in life, worked in the pits of hell?

> Pushin' steel at 24 Hour Fitness is my religion.

The Unbelievable Horrors
of Old City Jail

Charleston, South Carolina

IF PARANORMAL TRAUMA HAS FRACTURED THE SOUL OF RYAN BERGARA, THEN I THINK IT'S SAFE TO SAY THAT THIS LOCATION IS ONE OF HIS HORCRUXES. THE MAN'S BRAIN HAS NOT BEEN THE SAME SINCE VISITING HERE.

What's crazy is that I barely even remember this individual investigation. Just scattered images here and there.

YOU WENT FULL JOKER. AND NOT EVEN LEDGER. JOAQUIN, DUDE. JOAQUIN.

Estimates of the death toll in Old Jail vary wildly, with numbers as high as fourteen thousand. More conservative estimates, based on death records, puts it in the hundreds range, with most inmates dying from disease or Civil War wounds. There were, however, a number of hangings on the premises.

I'm starting to think the Civil War wasn't a lot of fun!

LOTTA BLEEDING.

Before the original four-story building and two-story octagonal tower were erected in 1802, the land served as a public cemetery. It had many other goodly neighbors during its time: an asylum, most of Charleston's hospitals, and a workhouse where enslaved people who had fallen ill were forced to work. In 1822, after a series of escapes and escape attempts, an architect was brought in to add solitary confinement cells and other fortifications, like iron cladding on death row.

When you go to school for architecture, are there, like, specialized classes for building prisons? Or is it just all the bad architects are forced to build shitty things like prisons and Walmarts?

During its 137-year operation, many men, women, and children suffered the unsanitary and inhumane conditions. In the antebellum era, free Black sailors who happened to land in Charleston Harbor were sometimes locked up for no reason, and during the Civil War, captured Black Union soldiers were essentially treated as run-away slaves rather than prisoners of war, including the all-black 54th Massachusetts Regiment, as depicted in the 1989 Oscar winner *Glory*. One POW said the jail was "a dirty, filthy place unfit for human beings to live in."

Jesus, and that's coming from a guy who lived on the move during the Civil fucking War.

Jeremiah is believed to be the ghost of a nine-year-old boy who haunts the old morgue and occasionally tries to hold the hands of visitors. Perhaps his body was taken there after he succumbed to cholera. It is said that another blue death victim sat in the 1820s wheelchair that is now parked on a landing, dropping the temperature and bumping into the legs of passersby. Death row and a room in which guards tortured prisoners are especially active.

RYAN SAW CAR HEADLIGHTS PASS A WINDOW HERE AND ALMOST PASSED OUT.

Definitely not headlights, my dude.

One specter is believed to be that of Lavinia Fisher, the first female serial killer in America. Held from 1819 to 1820, she and her husband, John, killed twenty to thirty men, or so the legend goes, with some estimates as high as 120. Allegedly, the beautiful Lavinia seduced guests at the couple's inn, put oleander in their tea, then pulled a lever that dropped them into a chamber below, where John dismembered them.

COOL SYSTEM. OBVIOUSLY I CONDEMN THEIR ACTIONS, BUT AT LEAST THEY DID SOME *13 DEAD END DRIVE* STUFF.

Yeah, these were two despicable humans. But clearly they were made for each other.

No bodies were found, and the lovebirds were convicted of highway robbery and not murder. At the time, the law prohibited the hanging of married women, so the jailers hanged John first. Lavinia had foreseen this possibility, so she showed up to her scheduled hanging in a wedding dress, hoping to seduce someone into a Hail Mary marriage. She was to be disappointed and chose to jump from her stand after shouting, "If you have a message you want to send to hell, give it to me; I'll carry it." Apparently, Satan himself refused her entry, so she walks the jail to this day, screaming and leaving her signature three scratches on visitors.

WE'VE HANDILY DEBUNKED THE EXISTENCE OF THIS GHOST. WE OFFERED UP OUR BELLY BUTTONS TO HER. SHE DIDN'T OBLIGE. NO WAY SHE'S REAL.

Again, an awful human. But pretty baller last words.

The Shadowy Spirits
of Rolling Hills Asylum

East Bethany, New York

ANOTHER PLACE WE'VE BUSTED GHOULS. QUITE POSSIBLY ONE OF THE COLDEST LOCATIONS WE'VE EVER BEEN. WIND SO FRIGID MY TESTICLES RETREATED FULLY INTO MY BODY. HAVEN'T SEEN THEM SINCE. THANKS, ROLLING HILLS.

So that's what happened to your balls. Explains earlier.

I n keeping with tradition carried over from across the pond, early American settlers took a fairly punitive approach to dealing with the poor. The Poor Laws were administered by local authorities, who were, for the most part, a bit on the privileged side of the spectrum, and who had the power to decide who deserved financial aid and who deserved to be sent to the poorhouse. The unworthy often included orphans, the physically disabled, the elderly, widows and unwed mothers, the "lazy" or "shiftless," and people whom the modern zeitgeist would consider mentally ill. Along with criminals, these varietals of poor were housed together, a hellacious version of America's melting pot.

GREAT START. WHAT A LIGHTHEARTED SECTION OF THIS BOOK. AMERICA'S INSTITUTIONS ARE A VERITABLE HOOT.

Best country in the world.

Rolling Hills Asylum—formerly the Genesee County Poor Farm—was one such government-run facility. Opened on January 1, 1827, the massive fifty-three thousand-square-foot building admitted the poor of all stripes, from unspecified vagrants to fifteen-year-old paraplegics to immigrants to senior citizens. Those who could were put to work cooking, cleaning, and raising livestock and growing crops on the poorhouse's two hundred acres. Criminals and convicts made coffins in the asylum's woodshop. Before its closure in 1974, Rolling Hills Asylum was converted into a nursing home. There were 1,700 documented deaths during its 147 years in operation; the current owner thinks there are likely three times as many, since record keeping has been spotty. Where are the bodies buried? If they're on the premises, the grass has long since grown over the graves.

SURE, THAT *SEEMS* LIKE A LOT OF DEATHS . . . I DON'T REALLY HAVE A FOLLOW-UP HERE. THAT SEEMS LIKE A LOT OF DEATHS.

I'm no horticulturist, but it's my understanding that grass grows quite slowly. So if your excuse for losing track of deaths is because the grass grew over the graves, it's quite likely that your establishment is run by shitheads.

PRETTY SURE GRASS GROWS FAST. DON'T QUIT YOUR GHOUL JOB.

Again, not a horticulturist

Today, most of the many, many spirits in the asylum are believed to be nice. Nurse Emma appears when visitors call for help and responds in both English and German. Roy Crouse, a 7.5-foot gentleman with gigantism, loves opera music and once killed a rat for the owner—his massive bloody fingerprints can still be seen on the wall outside the infirmary. Young Elizabeth, her blonde hair in pigtails, waits in the chapel for her father or a father figure, and prankster Jeff runs and skips in the tunnel; children play with toys in the east-wing basement Christmas Room, where they would go to sit on Santa's knee in auld lang syne.

HAPPY GHOSTS! THAT'S A NICE CHANGE OF PACE! I GUESS IF I HAD A CHRISTMAS ROOM, I'D BE A PRETTY HAPPY GUY, TOO. I HAVEN'T SAT ON SANTA'S LAP IN AGES. THEY DON'T LET ADULTS DO THAT. WHAT'S THE BIG DEAL? LEMME GET ON THAT LAP. I WON'T DO ANYTHING WEIRD.

And seeing as how you stopped looking like a child at age three, I'm guessing you missed out on a fair share of opportunities. Really sad. I've been sitting on Santa's lap for years. Don't know why they let me.

Less friendly specters include grumpy Steve and the Screaming Lady, thought to be the first resident of the poorhouse, who arrived as a little girl and lived there for fifty-six years.

I'D LIKE TO KNOW MORE ABOUT THIS SCREAMING LADY, BUT I HAVE A HUNCH I CAN PIECE TOGETHER THE DETAILS.

Some believe she is simply trying to communicate and, out of frustration at not being understood, screams her freaking transparent head off, sometimes for up to twenty minutes. Others believe she is re-experiencing her murder.

NEVER FUN.

Both are bad, but I'm going to choose to believe the former.

In the most active area, the hallway leading to the infirmary in the east wing, shadow people peep out of doorways, roam the hallways, and creepily crawl along the floor. An odd room houses a portal or vortex—visitors experiencing nausea or headaches mean the portal is open.

ANOTHER CASE OF PEOPLE JUST SAYING THINGS.

I get the feeling you were lied to a lot as a kid.

The Skeletal Specters of the
Institute of Natural Therapeutics

Olalla, Washington

Dr. Linda Hazzard's faith in her work never wavered, even when she was convicted of manslaughter.

DATELINE–ASS WAY TO INTRO THIS PLACE.

Lol.

Claire Williamson's death was a result of inflamed ovaries and a uterus that had dropped against the spine, the fasting specialist claimed, and it was pure coincidence that she'd succumbed to the inevitable while in care. The young woman weighed fifty pounds when she died. Claire's was not the first fasting-cure death, and it would not be the last. Her sister, Dorothea, nearly followed her into the afterlife in a rudimentary cabin at Wilderness Heights, in the rainforest of Washington, in 1911. The two wealthy Williamsons, with nothing to do and all the resources in the world to do it, had made health-seeking their primary vocation, and they had come to Seattle to undergo the fasting cure with the charismatic Hazzard. Three months later, one sister was dead, the other nearly so—and the unlicensed Hazzard and her convicted bigamist husband, Sam, were a whole lot richer.

IT SOUNDS LIKE DR. LINDA IS A REAL *HAZARD* TO HER PATIENTS. HAHA! BUT FOR REAL, SHE SOUNDS LIKE A MONSTER.

Aptly named in my opinion!

During Hazzard's trial, a pattern of starvation extortion was revealed. In the small rural town of Olalla, residents reported living skeletons lurching along the road from what they called Starvation Heights to the grocery store, sometimes to get the exercise that was part of their regimen, sometimes to beg for food or rescue. These patients ingested only two cups of tomato or asparagus broth a day for weeks at a time, endured hours-long enemas, and underwent walloping osteopathic massages.

THIS IS ALSO RYAN'S FITNESS ROUTINE WHEN HE HAS TO GET BACK IN SHAPE FOR GHOST HUNTING. JUST THE HOURS-LONG ENEMAS, THOUGH. HE SAYS IT "GETS THE GHOULS OUT." READER, YOU CANNOT FATHOM HOW MUCH MONEY HE'S SPENT ON RUBBER HOSE.

I prefer using a strong bidet. This regimen also functions as a twofer in ghost-hunting prep, as I do my best thinking while sitting on the john.

Once thoroughly starved, they were induced to change their wills in Hazzard's favor, grant her power of attorney, and bequeath her their land, furs, and jewels. At least fifteen patients died on Hazzard's watch, though rumor has it that many more went uncounted. Hazzard performed DIY autopsies in the bathroom, and she and a local funeral home had a special arrangement that meant patients—and their medical files—occasionally disappeared without a trace. There was also an incinerator conveniently located near a ravine on the property.

This lady sucks.

After serving her prison sentence, Hazzard opened a new practice in New Zealand, then returned to Olalla to finish building a grand sanitarium in which to do more of the same. The Institute of Natural Therapeutics burned down in 1935, but she continued to occupy the house. Three years later, Hazzard set out to prove her methods once and for all and cured herself to death.

I GUESS, AT THE VERY LEAST, SHE BELIEVED IN HER METHODS. YOU'D THINK SHE'D MEDITATE ON HER TRACK RECORD AND REALIZE THAT SHE WAS ABOUT TO K-WORD HER OWN ASS.

Or at the very least take a look at her nametag and re-evaluate professions.

With such tortured departures, it's no surprise that ghosts remain at Starvation Heights. Paranormal investigators have reported dark energy, and a muffled recording picked up a voice saying, "Help me," and another saying, "Dig us up." An amateur paranormalist heard another say, "Feed them."

Never going here.

The Captive Spirits of Eastern State Penitentiary

Philadelphia, Pennsylvania

THE MOST HAUNTING PLACE WE'VE EVER BEEN.

I still give the nod to Waverly. Though this is also the place where you nearly pooped your pants mid-hunt. So I guess that edges it out in your rankings.

IT WASN'T MY FAULT!

In 1787, Benjamin Franklin and friends formed the Philadelphia Society for Alleviating the Misery of Public Prisons. Bad behavior, they argued, springs forth from bad environment, and therefore prison reform would beget rehabilitation. Moved by Quaker ideology, they concluded that penitence was the special sauce, and the key ingredients were discipline, labor, and complete solitude—hence "penitentiary."

LOOK, OUR FLIGHT TO PENNSYLVANIA GOT DELAYED. WE LANDED AT LIKE 4 P.M. AND HAD TO SHOOT THAT SAME NIGHT. EVERYBODY NEEDED TO EAT IN A PINCH. AS LUCK WOULD HAVE IT, THERE WAS A HOT DOG STAND IN BAGGAGE CLAIM. THERE WERE ONLY A FEW LINKS SITTING ON THE HEATER SO, BEING A PAL, I LET EVERYBODY ELSE TAKE THEIR PICK. BY THE TIME I GOT TO THE REGISTER, THEY ONLY HAD SPICY HOT DOGS LEFT. I GOT TWO, SLATHERED THEM IN MUSTARD, AND ATE THEM IN THE CAR ON THE WAY TO

THE LOCATION. EVERYTHING WAS FINE FOR A WHILE. BUT THEN MY STOMACH STARTED EMITTING LONG, STRANGE BUBBLING TONES. IT SOUNDED LIKE HYDROTHERMAL VENTS ERUPTING IN THE DEEP OCEAN. BEFORE LONG, MY FOREHEAD WAS DRENCHED IN A COLD SWEAT AND, VERY RESPONSIBLY, I TOOK SPORADIC BREAKS TO EXCUSE MYSELF TO THE RESTROOM. BUT EVERY TIME MY ASS GRACED THE SEAT, NOTHIN'. STOPPED UP, WHICH WAS RICH BECAUSE EVERY MOMENT I *WASN'T* IN THE BATHROOM, I TRULY FELT LIKE I WAS ON THE VERGE OF FOAMING MY PANTS TO THE BRIM. ANYWAY, SOMEHOW I MADE IT THROUGH THIS SHOOT WITHOUT ANY FECAL TRAGEDIES OCCURRING, BUT IT WAS PRETTY TOUCH AND GO. I EVENTUALLY PUT THE WORK IN AND GOT IT ALL OUT ONCE WE GOT BACK TO THE HOTEL, BUT THAT I WAS ABLE TO ENDURE AN ENTIRE EPISODE WITHOUT DESTROYING MY PANTALOONS SPEAKS TO MY UNPARALLELED PROFESSIONALISM.

I love how your excuse for eating TWO baggage claim hot dogs is because you let others take their pick of the other dogs. Which, while undeniably gentlemanlike, still offers no explanation for why you CHOSE to eat the TWO remaining baggage claim links. Play shitty games, win shitty prizes. I'm honestly sad you didn't grease your pants. Would have undeniably been a top five *Unsolved* moment caught on camera.

IT WOULD HAVE BEEN GOOD CONTENT. I CAN ADMIT THAT.

Eastern State Penitentiary welcomed its first penitents in 1829, though construction wasn't completed until 1836. It was actually pretty cush, with running water, heating, and flush toilets. A Bible in every room, vaulted ceilings, and a strict policy of silence were meant to inspire reverence and reflection. Each cell had a single source of light in the ceiling, known as the Eye of God. Prisoners had minimal interaction with guards—in theory—and no contact with other inmates, and they were often forced to wear masks and hoods while outside their cells, including during bath time.

> I KNOW IT PROBABLY WASN'T "NICE," BUT BATH TIME SOUNDS LOVELY.
>
> Compared to other prisons and facilities in this book, this place sounds like the Ritz.

In 1942, Charles Dickens toured the prison and noted that solitude wasn't all that it was cracked up to be. Not sure if Benji Franklin would have approved of the torture: inmates dunked in water and hung up on a wall outside during winter, bound to a "mad chair," silenced by an iron gag, and locked in the Hole for days on end.

> Okay, so maybe I went a little far on the Ritz comparison. More like a Ramada.

Also, there seemed to be a little problem with rampant insanity and tuberculosis, a highly contagious airborne bacteria that killed indiscriminately, including the prison's youngest inmate, eleven-year-old arsonist Mary Ash.

> ARSONIST MARY ASH IS BEGGIN' FOR SOME JOKES HERE, AND I WILL NOT GIVE HER THE SATISFACTION.

That, plus other diseases, suicide, and the occasional homicide made up the over one thousand entries in the death ledger. The rules relaxed as isolation rehab fell out of favor, and the prisoner population soared from the original 250 to 1,700 in 1926. A series of riots and the prison's gradual deterioration over the following decades led to its closure in 1971. For twenty-three lonely years, the grounds sat abandoned.

Today, the prison is open to the public, and it is a well-known hot spot for paranormal activity. Tour guides, John Q. Public, and professional ghost hunters have reported a range of occult occurrences, from shadowy figures roaming the cell blocks to doors that open on their own. Voices and maniacal laughter echo down cold, dark passageways, and screaming and crying can be heard in the infirmary. On death row, the damned still whisper.

> MY PANTS WERE ALSO WHISPERING THAT NIGHT.
>
> And screaming and crying.

The Stately Ghosts of the National Building Museum

Washington, DC

Almost one hundred years after the National Building Museum was built, a renovation prompted the repair of some of its floors.

Imagine building a building museum.

INCEPTION—ASS MUSEUM.

Workers were surprised to discover women's and men's shoes from the 1880s under the floors in the corner spaces created by the arched ceilings below. And it was clear that these shoes hadn't been lost or overlooked; they had been placed with intention.

ONE OF THE REASONS I'D LOVE TO OWN A HOME IS JUST TO LEAVE FREAKY SHIT BEHIND FOR FUTURE OWNERS. MAYBE SCRATCH A BABADOOK OR TWO INTO THE WALLS OR MAKE A DOLL OUT OF MY OWN HAIR AND SET IT UNDER THE FLOORBOARD. TREATS.

Oh, I love that. I'd wedge fake skulls in the walls. And then I'd hide some beef jerky next to them somehow out of sight. Jerky takes about two or so years to go bad, so by year two they'd likely start smelling a "strange odor" coming from their walls.

Investigation revealed that the original builders had been following an old European tradition. Shoes—still holding the shape of their owners' feet—stand as sentinels to ward off evil spirits. But why would this building, with its grand Roman-palace-inspired design, need protection?

THROUGHOUT ITS HISTORY, WAS THE BUILDING EVER—EVEN BRIEFLY—A DSW? SOMEBODY SHOULD CHECK THE RECORD. EVEN IF IT WAS ONLY A DSW FOR A YEAR OR TWO, THAT PLACE IS GONNA BE LOUSY WITH LEFTOVER SHOES.

Completed in 1887, the building formerly known as the Pension Building was used by the US Pension Bureau to serve the Union soldiers, nurses, and widows who had been impacted by the Civil War. It was architect and US Army Quartermaster General Montgomery C. Meigs's cumulative masterpiece, with a great hall featuring soaring ceilings and Corinthian columns. These columns were the site of a strange haunting—the day after Buffalo Bill died, in January 1917, the shape of a human head and a buffalo appeared, followed by the shape of a skull. Eventually, the columns were painted over.

ALL DUE RESPECT—SOUNDS MADE UP.

Had no idea that Buffalo Bill's nickname came from the fact that he was prolific at murdering buffalo.

A 1,200-foot-long frieze on the exterior depicts soldiers marching into battle, and the walls are made of more than 15 million red bricks, earning it the pejorative Old Red Barn, an insult to Meigs's life's work. It was within these walls that James Tanner, a veteran who had lost his feet in the war, worked his day job—his real vocation was lecturing on the assassination of Abraham Lincoln. Two decades earlier, he had been called in to the Petersen House in the wee hours of the morning of April 15, 1865, to transcribe the testimony of witnesses to the assassination as Lincoln lay dying in a nearby bedroom. Forever after, Tanner was intent on spreading the truth, work he apparently continues to this day.

WHAT TRUTH WAS HE PRESERVING, EXACTLY? WERE THERE DOUBTS AS TO WHETHER OR NOT THE BIG GUY TOOK A SLUG TO THE DOME? THERE'S A SOGGY PILLOW ACROSS THE STREET FROM FORD'S THEATRE THAT SEEMS TO SETTLE THE MATTER.

Yeah, I'd say in the event of an assassination, its success and who did it are the two main details. Anything after that, not really debate-worthy.

The ghost believed to be Tanner is not a friendly ghost. In 1972, a guard came upon him and ran screaming from the building.

SOUNDS TO ME LIKE THE GUARD IS THE RUDE ONE HERE.

Can't blame the guard for running away from a spirit that's screaming about Lincoln getting shot in the head (in accurate detail).

Other postbellum specters include a Lady in White and a soldier riding horseback down the halls—some believe this is General Meigs, returned to defend his building's honor.

NOT TO POKE HOLES, BUT HOW DOES A GHOST HORSE WORK? DOES THE HORSE ALSO HAVE UNFINISHED BUSINESS? OR IS IT JUST CURSED TO WANDER THE EARTH TETHERED TO THE DAMNED SOUL OF SOME A-HOLE WHO SLAPPED ITS ASS AND FED IT SUGAR CUBES? SUCKS TO BE A HORSE.

Hate to admit it, but this is a good point.

SHANIAC NATION, RISE UP.

The Phantom Prisoners
of Ohio State Reformatory

Mansfield, Ohio

From the road leading to the prison to the windowless "chair room," the Ohio State Reformatory provides ample opportunity for haunting. The two hundred fifty thousand-square-foot Gothic fortress, nicknamed Dracula's Castle, was originally designed for the spiritual rehabilitation, education, and life-skill development of first-time offenders back in the mid-1880s.

Wouldn't mind living in a place called Dracula's Castle.

SOUNDS LIKE A THEMED HOTEL IN VEGAS. NOW I REALLY WISH IT WAS.

As tends to happen with big stone structures built to involuntarily contain people, however, the reformatory evolved beyond the founders' initial intentions, giving way to the realities of the criminal justice system. (They probably also hadn't imagined becoming "Hollywood's favorite prison" for its use in *The Shawshank Redemption*.) The first 150 inmates took up residence on September 15, 1896, and over time, the population ballooned, filling up the West Cell Block and the East Cell Block, the world's largest freestanding steel cell block, a six-tier, six hundred–cell monstrosity completed in 1910. During the reformatory's ninety-four years in operation, 154,000 inmates would enter its gates.

THEY WERE REALLY FEELIN' THEMSELVES WHEN THEY BUILT THIS GIANT MONSTROSITY OF HUMAN MISERY.

Can confirm that this is the largest freestanding steel cell block in the world. I haven't researched any competitors. I just know that when I was there, I uttered, "That's a big-ass jail."

AN ASS JAIL?

But not everyone would leave. A cemetery outside the fence boasts 215 graves, most containing those who died of contagious diseases like consumption and influenza. The combination of overcrowding, isolation, untreated mental illness, and general sadism led to rampant violence as well. Prison guard Frank Hanger was attacked when trying to stop an attempted escape in 1932; he died from an iron-bar head injury, and two of the inmates involved were sentenced to death.

Head injury sounds bad. Iron-bar head injury sounds REAL bad.

THAT'LL GIVE YA THE VISION™.

An inmate allegedly hanged himself in the showers, another hanged himself in the Hole. Two inmates went into a cell together one night, but only one emerged come morning—the body of the other was found stuffed under the bunk. Twenty-two-year-old James Lockheart doused himself in turpentine and set himself on fire in his cell. Helen Glattke, the warden's wife, was mysteriously shot in the lung in 1950; the warden died of a heart attack nine years later. From 1897 to 1963, 315 people, including three women, died in the warm embrace of Old Sparky.

I'M NOT PICKING UP A LOT OF ~GOOD VIBES~ FROM THIS PLACE.

Yeah, definitely not a lot of "reform" happening at a place where people are setting themselves on fire.

These deaths, in turn, led to unhappy souls unwilling or unable to exit the mortal plane. Though they have long since served their time, many prisoners remain, their spirits trapped in the cells or showers or basement that trapped them in life.

As far as hauntings go, getting trapped in an everlasting shower doesn't sound half bad. I always feel guilty taking long showers here on this mortal coil.

Visitors claim to feel cold spots and pressure on their backs or arms and even the sensation of being watched, or breath on the backs of their necks. People have claimed to see an inmate alight in the East Cell Block and to smell Mrs. Glattke's rose-scented perfume in the family's quarters. Some feel claustrophobic while inside the Hole.

PEOPLE FEEL CLAUSTROPHOBIC IN THE HOLE, YOU SAY? THAT'S GHOSTS. DO THEY FEEL A CHILL IN THE WALK-IN FREEZER? OR EXPERIENCE MYSTERIOUS SWEATS IN THE BOILER ROOM? ALSO GHOSTS. WON'T SOMEONE PUT A STOP TO THESE CEASELESS UNEXPLAINED FRIGHTS?!

Counterpoint: Seeing a phantom lit on fire is pretty unexplainable.

The Bloody Trail
in the AI Engineering Building

College Station, Texas

Do animals have ghosts?

> **DO SONGS HAVE DREAMS? DO WHISPERS WALTZ 'NEATH THE HARVEST MOON?**
>
> Not even the same train of thought.
>
> **DO TRAINS HAVE THOUGHTS?**
>
> Unbelievable.

If so, the AI Engineering Building—formerly known as the Animal Industries Building—would have an infinitude of pig, cow, and lamb apparitions clip-clopping its halls. For simplicity's sake, however, we'll focus on human ghosts. In this instance, he goes by the name of Roy Lee Simms.

> **WHAT WERE THEY STUDYING HERE? WHAT HAPPENS WHEN YOU STICK A KNIFE IN THE THROAT OF EVERY ANIMAL YOU SEE?**
>
> Maybe they're just trying to see if they can make a horse like really, really small. You know, for like, 1G or something.
>
> **WHOA.**

The Animal Industries Building opened its doors in 1931. It is a beautiful Classic Revival building,

> **AN ABSOLUTELY BREATHTAKING FEAT OF DESIGN, SOON TO BE SPATTERED WITH LAYERS UPON LAYERS OF ANIMAL VISCERA.**
>
> Lol. Jesus, man.

with intricate cow-and-horse-themed friezes, ornate iron gates, and pretty tile floor motifs.

> **I HOPE TO ONE DAY UTTER THESE EXACT WORDS IN MY *ARCHITECTURAL DIGEST* HOME TOUR.**
>
> If you have cow-and-horse-themed friezes, I'm never coming over again. It's fuckin' weird.

Today it is used by the nuclear engineering department, but it was originally designed for the animal science department, with the meat laboratory located in the basement, beneath the main lecture hall. This is Roy's favorite haunt and the locale of his death in 1959.

OH YEAH, I'LL BET ROY ABSOLUTELY LOVES TO HANG AROUND THE MEAT ROOM WHERE HE DIED. IT'S ALL ANY OF US CAN HOPE FOR IN THE AFTERLIFE. A NICE, COZY MEAT ROOM TO CHILL IN FOR ALL OF ETERNITY.

You really gotta figure out your jerky addiction. It's starting to get concerning.

IT'S MEAT YOU CAN PUT IN YOUR POCKET!

By that point, he had been working for the university for twenty-one years, first as an employee in the campus dining hall, and then, after a stint in the navy during World War II, as meat locker room foreman. It was in this role that he accidentally killed himself. It happened one early morning a couple weeks before Thanksgiving.

THE TWO-WEEK WINDOW BEFORE THANKSGIVING IS, BAR NONE, ONE OF THE WORST TIMES TO EAT IT. YOU'RE GETTING ALL HYPED FOR THAT FOUR-DAY WEEKEND, AND WHAT DO YOU GET INSTEAD? ETERNAL NOTHINGNESS. MAYBE IT'S JUST ME, BUT I'D RATHER EAT TURKEY THAN BE DEAD FOREVER.

Never been a fan of Thanksgiving, and not even 'cause of relatives. I love my family, but I just think the food is pretty bland.

WELL, IF YOU'RE LUCKY, THIS NOVEMBER MAYBE SOMEBODY WILL FUCKING OFF YOU.

God willing!

Roy was momentarily alone in the lab, butchering a slab of bacon by cutting the belly away from the skin, pulling the knife toward himself.

WHAT THE HELL ARE THEY DOING IN THIS LAB? MAKIN' BLTs?

Damn a BLT sounds good as hell right now.

MMM, TASTY-ASS MAYO SLATHERED ALL OVER HOT HOG. I'M DROOLIN'.

His hand slipped, and the tool sliced into his leg, opening his femoral artery.

THE FIRST RULE OF KNIVES IS TO LARGELY REFRAIN FROM SLASHING YOUR FEMORAL ARTERY.

Not the artery you want to unwrap.

Rumor has it that Roy, crazed with the kind of animal fear that precedes death, crawled toward the nearby freight elevator, leaving a spreading red trail on the floor behind him. It was there that he bled out, dying just minutes later. His assistant returned to find a grisly scene, human blood leading from the butchered pig to the butchered man.

YOU KNOW PIG GHOST WAS JUST LOVIN' THIS WHOLE SCENE.

Lol. Just high fivin' all the ghost cows.

Now, more than sixty years since, Roy wanders the hallways of the AI Building, his footsteps ricocheting off those pretty tile floors.

SECOND TIME THESE FLOORS HAVE BEEN DESCRIBED THIS WAY. I GOTTA GET SOME EYES ON THESE FLOORS. THEY SOUND SEXY AS HELL.

I do love a well-done tile floor; easy to wipe blood off them, too. Unless, as mentioned before, it gets in the grout.

WHAT?

By all accounts, he was a friendly person in life, and those who believe in his continued tenure assume that he is friendly in death. Still, he slams doors, flickers lights, moves equipment and implements in the meat lab, and screams as he must have decades ago.

FRIENDLY PEOPLE DO THIS KIND OF STUFF ALL THE TIME, YEAH.

Yeah, this sounds just like Casper, the other friendly ghost.

CASPER AND HIS BEST FRIEND, THE ANGRY SCREAMING MEAT GHOST.

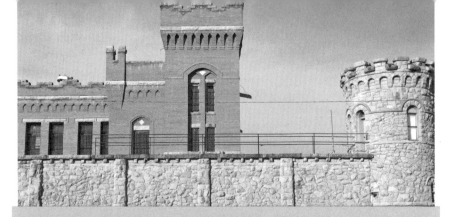

The Sinister Presences
of Old Montana Prison

Deer Lodge, Montana

I've always wanted to go to Montana. Seems like such a pleasant place.

IT'S COVERED IN ANTLERS.

Before Montana became a territory in 1864, locals did justice the Wild West way—hangings and other impromptu executions swiftly enacted by a hotheaded and well-armed vigilante committee.

Well, it seems pleasant nowadays.

Once it was recognized as a political entity, however, the federal government got involved in an effort to elevate the area to a kind of civility. Hence the construction of the Old Montana Prison, which opened for business in 1871 and operated for more than one hundred years.

WELL, EVERY OTHER PRISON DISCUSSED IN THIS BOOK HAS BEEN A HORROR SHOW OF HUMAN RIGHTS VIOLATIONS, BUT MAYBE THIS ONE WILL BE DIFFERENT!

Maybe all the natural beauty chilled some of these folks out!

Building a prison and housing prisoners is expensive, and from the get-go, the prison was overcrowded and underfunded. When Montana became a state in 1889, the feds relinquished oversight to the local government; prisoners had to get permission from state authorities to grow mustaches.

ACTUALLY SICK AND TWISTED. IT'S ONE OF THE GREAT JOYS OF LIFE, GROWING AND CARING FOR A BEAUTIFUL MUSTACHE.

Have to agree that when it comes to psychological torture, this is not only humane but very creative.

New warden Frank Conley hired out convicts to raise money to be used to renovate the facility. The prison was expanded in 1896 through the elbow grease of the incarcerated, who fashioned 1.2 million bricks by hand, some while wearing cement shoes, in order to build twenty-four-foot-high walls.

A curious choice to trust the dudes you're incarcerating to build the chambers of their incarceration.

In most ways, the prison is standard: dank basement showers, steel mesh cages, iron shackles, a narrow passageway with heavy doors that clang shut to announce solitary confinement. The interior is a hopeless gray.

AS OPPOSED TO THOSE PRISONS YOU SO OFTEN SEE WITH BREATHTAKING MAUVE ACCENT WALLS.

There are areas designated for more ornery prisoners: East Siberia and West Siberia. For the really ornery, there were the Hole and the Black Box cells, which featured a peephole's worth of light and a diet of bread and water. After ten days, a doctor would examine the prisoner and, if deemed healthy enough, would readmit him to the Hole.

"NICE AND HEALTHY! WELP, BACK TO THE HOLE WITH YA!"

Obviously, this is unjust and inhumane, but a breadstick and water diet doesn't sound half bad. Especially if they're Olive Garden breadsticks. Though, I imagine the bread served here could be used to bludgeon someone to death.

I DON'T ACTUALLY GET THE HYPE FOR OLIVE GARDEN BREADSTICKS. I THINK THEY PALE IN COMPARISON TO LITTLE CAESAR'S CRAZY BREAD. EVEN PIZZA HUT IS PUTTING THEM TO SHAME. I MAY HAVE EATEN TOO MANY BREADSTICKS IN MY LIFE.

Another bonus feature: walls that extended four feet below ground to prevent tunneling. This didn't stop the attempts of convicts George Rock and William Hayes, who killed Deputy Warden John Robinson and stabbed Warden Frank Conley so many times as to require 103 stitches.

PROUD OF ROCK AND HAYES FOR STANDING UP FOR THEMSELVES. VIA STABBING.

The two men were hanged in the prison yard. Another unsuccessful escape attempt in 1959 resulted in a three-day riot that led to the death of another deputy warden and the murder-suicide of the two ringleaders at the top floor of the tower.

Prison breaks are only fun when they work.

The galloping gallows—so named because they were built to be easily disassembled and relocated, per the state's capital punishment needs—is now on display in the old W.A. Clark Theater, erected by convicts in 1912. Unsurprisingly, visitors experience a feeling of dread when entering the prison, and some have reported a sinister presence in the Hole. Passageways echo with whispers and footsteps. It is cold.

OKAY. BUY A SPACE HEATER?

Montana cold is probably brutal.

The Guilty Ghost of the Calcasieu Courthouse

Lake Charles, Louisiana

Toni Jo Henry, née Annie Beatrice McQuiston, was just a pretty young gal in love when she planned a Valentine's Day rendezvous with her new husband, Claude "Cowboy" Henry, in 1940. Except that he was locked up for killing a police officer during a bar fight. "I'll get you out, Cowboy! Don't worry!" she'd promised at his trial.

> Very sweet. "Cowboy" as a nickname absolutely stinks. But only if Claude is, in fact, a cattle driver. If Claude is an accountant, however, suddenly "Cowboy" is badass. 'Cause now I'm wondering why an accountant has earned that moniker? "Claude must be a wild guy!" I'd say to myself. That make sense?

> I HAVE LITTLE DOUBT THAT THIS IS A NICKNAME HE FULLY BESTOWED UPON HIMSELF WHILE STARING IN THE MIRROR ONE FRIDAY NIGHT. CRINGE AS HELL. IT'S CERTAINLY NOT SOMETHING THAT I, SHANE "MONDO HOG" MADEJ, WOULD EVER DO.

And so, with a newly released ex-offender by the name of Finnon Burks, Toni set out for Huntsville Prison, stealing weaponry on the way. She thumbed a ride from an unlucky salesman named Joseph P. Calloway and then, with Burks, took his wallet, forced him into the trunk, and after a few miles, made him crawl naked over barbed wire into a deserted field. There someone shot him between the eyes.

Jesus, even Jigsaw gave his victims a chance to survive. Yes, the window was small, but there was a window!

I GUESS THE WINDOW WAS THE FLEETING MOMENT WHERE HE HAD TO DECIDE WHETHER OR NOT TO GIVE A RIDE TO A HITCHHIKER CARRYING A SACK FULL OF WEAPONS.

Local police were at a loss until Toni Jo's uncle, state police inspector George McQuiston, brought her in. "I've come to give myself up," she told them. At her trial, she claimed that Burks pulled the trigger; both were found guilty of murder and sentenced to death by electrocution.

Looks like she's gonna have to cancel that sweet Valentine's Day rez.

CUT TO AN EMPTY TABLE, A GLISTENING BAKED ALASKA MELTING IN THE CANDLELIGHT, A POINTLESS WAITER ON THE VERGE OF SOBBING.

Newspapers dubbed the twenty-six-year-old self-proclaimed streetwalker and dope fiend Tiger Girl and the Meanest Woman in Louisiana, and she wasn't shy about telling them her thoughts and feelings right up until the very end. Her victim didn't haunt her, she told an *Evening Star* reporter six days before her date with Old Sparky, adding, "I never think of him." The next day, Cowboy broke out of prison but didn't make it very far. "Hurry up and get that zoot suit off and walk out the front door like a man so your mother will be proud of you," she apparently said to him during their last phone call, after he'd been caught hiding out in a hotel in Beaumont. "Go straight, and try to make something of your life." Spoiler alert: He did not go straight, and he was shot to death three years later. Whether he was wearing a zoot suit is unknown.

This lady is the worst but also metal af.

VERY RICH OF HER TO OFFER LIFE ADVICE. IT'S GENUINELY IRRESPONSIBLE FOR A REPREHENSIBLE PERSON TO OFFER SOUND WISDOM.

Today, the first and only white woman in Louisiana to get the electric chair haunts the courthouse where her fatal sentence was laid down. State employees have reported hearing screams, footsteps, and slamming doors throughout the building, and they blame the guilty ghost for the inexplicable disarray of office supplies. The smell of burnt hair pervades.

Burnt hair is legitimately nauseating. I once singed off my eyelashes trying to blow out trick candles (hate those), and it really ruined my birthday party.

LIFE IS A RICH PAGEANT.

DEVILISH DRINKERIES

The Hollywood Ghosts
of the Legendary Viper Room

Los Angeles, California

WELL, WE'VE BEEN HERE! IT'S A BAR IN HOLLYWOOD, WHICH, AS NEIGHBORHOODS GO, IS NOT AS GLAMOROUS AS YOU'D THINK.

More than one celebrity friend warned River Phoenix away from drugs, the tonic and the undoing of many a child star. But the preternaturally talented young actor, who had won an Academy Award for his role in *Running on Empty* at the age of seventeen, died of a cocaine and heroin overdose on the sidewalk outside 8852 Sunset Boulevard on October 31, 1993. He was only twenty-three.

At that time, the Viper Room was the height of cool. Owned by Johnny Depp and Anthony Fox, it was the spot where famous people could grab a drink or two without getting hassled by fans or paparazzi. Christina Applegate, Sean Penn, Tim Burton, David Arquette, Norman Reedus, Shannen Doherty, Tori Spelling, and Drew Barrymore, among others, were regulars.

Assuming the ghoul boys were excluded from this list of celebs solely because we aren't regulars?

But the address wasn't always so cool. The building, built in 1921, was originally a grocery store, until the Cotton Club took over in the 1940s to cater to the Hollywood party scene. From there it would become the Greenwich Village Inn, the Rue Angel, the Last Call, and the Melody Room, the last of which was home to cabaret acts and the gangsters who watched them.

Living in the time of the mob must have been scary as hell. Just imagine sippin' an old-fashioned, staring facedown into your glass, hoping you don't look at the wrong dude the wrong way.

It is rumored that Mickey Cohen and Bugsy Siegel were patrons (though good ol' Bugs died in 1947, three years before the Melody Room became the Melody Room. Perhaps he was the venue's first ghost?). In 1973, the name changed yet again to the understated Filthy McNasty's.

Will become a regular here if they rebrand to this.

Twenty years later, and Joaquin—then known as Leaf—Phoenix was frantically calling 911 to get help for his brother. The coroner's report showed a fatal cocktail of heroin, cocaine, valium, marijuana, and cold medicine in the young man's bloodstream. According to employees, River's spirit remains at the club. A voice believed to be his has been heard saying his name and "I get confused." A bartender claimed that occasionally when she answered the office phone, a man would say, "Hi, it's me" before the line went dead.

GHOSTS AIN'T CALLING ANYBODY. IF THEY WERE, THE PHONE COMPANIES WOULD HAVE FOUND A WAY TO BILL THEM.

Boo-st Mobile.

Whether this is River or former owner Anthony Fox is unclear. What's also unclear is whether Fox is alive or dead. He disappeared in December 2001, shortly before he was scheduled to testify against Depp and four others in a lawsuit over millions of dollars of profits. Some believe that he is buried under a dirt floor in a small room behind the downstairs lounge.

RYAN ACTUALLY WEASELED HIS MOLE RATLIKE BODY INTO THAT LITTLE ROOM. DID YOU SEE A BODY DOWN THERE, BERGOOZE?

Didn't have my digging paraphernalia on me at the time. Also, it was too gross to take note of anything.

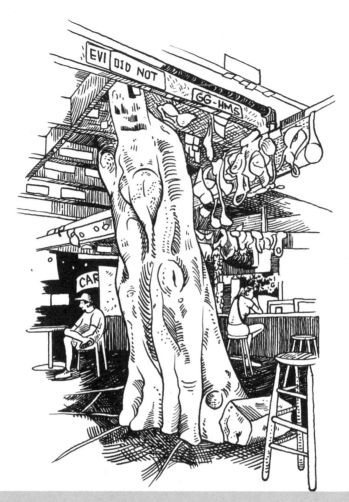

The Hanging Tree at Captain Tony's Saloon

Key West, Florida

Before Jimmy Buffett memorialized the shoes-optional, bra-festooned bar in "Last Mango in Paris," Captain Tony's Saloon was a morgue in Margaritaville. There followed a stint as a cigar factory, a bordello, and a gay bar frequented by sailors before the navy put a quash on it.

> WOULD BE PRETTY COOL IF IT WERE ALL THOSE THINGS AT ONCE. SMOKE, DRINK, AND SMOOCH TILL YOU DIE, THEN GET YOUR BODY EMBALMED BEHIND THE BAR.
>
> A true one-stop shop.

Joe Russell bought it in 1933 and named it Sloppy Joe's Bar per the recommendation of Ernest Hemingway, who drank Teacher's scotch and soda and wrote *To Have and Have Not* there. Captain Tony Tarracino, son of a bootlegger and puppeteer, and a gun-runner, gambler, boat captain, mayor, and father of thirteen by eight different women, took ownership in 1958.

> THAT IS SOME KINDA LIVIN'! WHAT STORIES HE MUST HAVE!
>
> Sounds like Tony was a little more sloppy than Joe, imo.

In the middle of the Key West landmark and national treasure is a hanging tree, where reportedly seventeen people, mostly pirates, met their maker at the end of a rope. One non-pirate remains—the Lady in Blue—who stabbed her husband and children to death and now haunts in a bloody blue dress.

> WE HAVE GOT TO COME UP WITH A BETTER WAY OF DESCRIBING FEMALE GHOSTS. LADY IN WHITE, LADY IN BLACK, LADY IN BLUE. THEIR EYES ARE UP *HERE*, FELLAS!

Another killer is Elvira Drew, whose grave marker was discovered with anonymous human bones—possibly leftover from the locale's morgue days—during construction. Some say she caught her husband canoodling and killed their baby out of spite; others say she killed her abusive husband in self-defense.

> Fingers crossed for the latter, so he got what was coming.

In what is now the pool room, a body of unknown identity that was set loose during the 1865 category 2 hurricane is allegedly buried. It is perhaps one of these spirits who locks the stalls in the ladies' restroom, opens and closes doors, and says scary things like "Don't leave." Papa Hemingway is said to stop in every now and then for a seat on his designated stool.

> BATHROOM GHOSTS ARE JUST SHORTHAND FOR "WE'VE GOT SOME REAL PERVS WORKING HERE."
>
> Or just proof that there's Taco Bell in the afterlife.

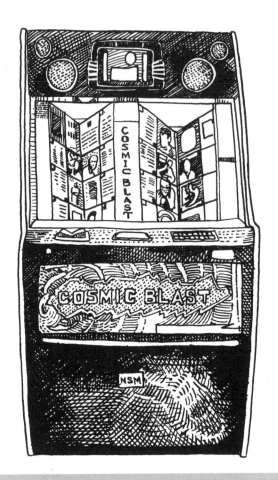

The Haunted Jukebox of Earnestine & Hazel's

Memphis, Tennessee

Like most stories about earlier eras in these good ol' United States of America, the tale of the building that now houses Earnestine & Hazel's self-proclaimed dive bar is a little bit awkward. It was originally a church, built in the late 1800s. Abe Plough was barely out of short pants when he started peddling "healing oils" in the late 1930s. Eventually, he opened a pharmacy at 351 South Main Street to sell hair straighteners and bleach cream. He made a bundle of monies and gave the building to hairdressing-slash-madaming sisters Earnestine Mitchell and Hazel Jones. They turned it into a jazz café-slash-saloon-slash-brothel, while Mitchell's husband, Sunbeam, opened Club Paradise, where soul, jazz, and Motown legends from Tina Turner to Chuck Berry, Sam Cook to B.B. King performed.

What a time to be alive.

Afterward, musicians and crew would head over to Earnestine & Hazel's for a late-night nosh and to "find action from women upstairs" (according to the bar's website). Allegedly, this setup was the inspiration for the Rolling Stones's song "Brown Sugar." Allegedly, Ray Charles used one of the rooms to do heroin.

SO FAR, IT SOUNDS ALRIGHT. EVEN THE HEROIN THING. LOOK, IT'S BEEN ESTABLISHED ON THE SHOW THAT BEING EXPOSED TO HEROIN AGAINST MY WILL IS ONE OF MY GREAT FEARS, BUT IN THE EARLY TWENTIETH CENTURY, IT WAS BASICALLY LIKE COCA-COLA. IT WAS HOT! IT WAS THE THING TO DO!

I can't believe you make fun of me for being scared of ghosts.

The nationwide recession hit Memphis especially hard, turning it into a ghost town in the 1970s, and the venue changed hands over the next few decades. Russell George bought the place in 1993 and, after bringing it back to life via open mic nights and the Soul Burger, killed himself in his office there in 2013. Out of this flux come rumors of the kinds of deaths—suicides, drug overdoses, murders—that are par for the course for bordello/music joints, lucky thirteen in total. The jukebox is haunted in Big Brother Alexa-style, somehow overhearing the conversation of drinkers at the bar and playing related songs. According to one longtime bartender and manager named Karen Brownlee, the juke spontaneously played "I Feel Good" on the day that James Brown died.

I know I'm the ghost guy here, but having "I feel Good" play on a jukebox seems like a fairly pedestrian daily occurrence.

And the piano upstairs occasionally plays sans pianist.

How did we not lead with this?!

A sex worker who died by suicide in a bathtub haunts the second-floor bathroom, and footsteps and voices on the floors above are often heard. Sightings of apparitions of what are believed to be johns and ladies of the night have been reported. Photos of orbs abound.

HONESTLY, CONSIDERING THE PLACE HAS BEEN AROUND AS LONG AS IT HAS, I THINK IT'S UNFAIR TO LET THESE UNFORTUNATE INCIDENTS MAR ITS REPUTATION. SOUNDS LIKE A COOL LITTLE DIVE WITH SOME FASCINATING HISTORY. I SAY WE STOP BY NEXT TIME WE'RE IN MEMPHIS AND TOSS BACK SOME FOAM UNTIL WE'RE SEEING ORBS LEFT AND RIGHT.

I'll investigate any place with brew on tap and a jukebox.

The Ghosts and Demons
of Bobby Mackey's Music World

Wilder, Kentucky

THE BIRTHPLACE OF ONE OF THE GREAT MEMES OF OUR TIME. NOW THIS IS WHAT I
CALL HISTORY.

A dark horse contender for one of the coldest places we've ever investigated. It was
FRIGID. People be dancin' in this place for warmth.

Bobby Mackey's famous portal to hell is located in a well in the basement, where the former slaughterhouse used to drain animal blood in the 1850s. This well, claimed Bobby Mackey himself in an interview, connected to a tunnel that further drained the blood into nearby Licking River. Much has changed since then, though the portal reportedly stays the same. Allegedly, occultists took over the building from the meatpackers in the 1890s, as it was the perfect place to worship the devil and sacrifice animals (see blood draining above).

I suppose there aren't many joints that classify as "turnkey" for occultists.

In fact, the *Chicago Tribune* reported a heinous crime therein, calling it "the most sensational murder of the nineties." As in, the 1890s. A headless body was found at midnight on the road between two nearby farms, and by tracing the size three shoe, it was identified as twentysomething Sunday school teacher Pearl Bryan. She had a bellyful of cocaine and a five-month-old fetus. One theory is that her boyfriend, Scott Jackson, and friend, Alonzo Walling, both dental students, had decided to apply their medical training to a DIY abortion followed by a DIY decapitation. Her head was never found, and some believe that it was used by occultists in some kind of ritual or simply tossed in the well. This made the demons happy. Jackson and Whaling were hanged together on March 20, 1897.

I WAS SO PREOCCUPIED THINKING ABOUT MY EARTH-SHATTERING MEME THAT I FORGOT
THIS PLACE WAS CHOCK-FULL OF EXTREMELY DEPRESSING HISTORY. LET ME GET US BACK
TO A GOOD PLACE: HEY THERE, DEMONS! IT'S ME, THE GUY TRYING TO FORGET THE
DETAILS OF THE ABOVE PARAGRAPH!

In the 1920s, the building exchanged black candles for banjos as the Bluegrass Inn and possibly used the tunnel/portal to smuggle liquor during Prohibition. In the following decades, it operated as a gambling hall and nightclub called the Primrose Club and then the Latin Quarter. Legend has it that a dancer named Johanna killed herself in the dressing room, which was located in the basement at the time. Another version paints her as the daughter of one of the gangster casino owners and posits that she killed herself and her daddy after she got knocked up and he took a hit out on her boyfriend, a singer named Robert Randall. Whatever the case, she is one of the locale's star ghosts.

WHY ARE THE DETAILS ON THIS SO FUZZY? IT WAS THE 1920S, AND WE'RE SPEAKING OF IT LIKE AN ANCIENT SUMERIAN LEGEND.

I was thinking the same thing. But I suppose the mob has a way of fuzzin' things.

Authorities closed the establishment after a bunch of fatal shootings in 1978, and country singer Bobby Mackey bought the building that same year.

A *BUNCH*? WHAT HAPPENED IN 1978?!

Bobby don't give a shit, he just wants to party.

His wife, who has been pushed down the stairs and screamed at by an apparition she believes to be Alonzo Walling, refuses to enter the club. Today, a sign warns that management is not responsible for any actions of ghosts/spirits on the premises.

Love a sign or a waiver that essentially says, "You really shouldn't come in here, but we really hope you do."

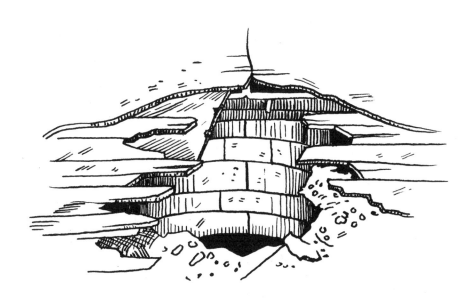

The Soiled Doves
of the Red Onion Saloon

Skagway, Alaska

During the Klondike Gold Rush, thousands of people made the treacherous journey to Alaska and Canadian Yukon Territory. Many didn't realize, however, that Skagway, at the tip of Chilkoot Inlet, was just a pit stop. Those who had the funds stocked up on the required year's worth of supplies and continued the five hundred miles up the White Pass Trail, nicknamed Dead Horse Trail for the carcasses that lined its muddy lane.

> AGAIN, SUCKS TO BE A HORSE.
>
> Even for the most famous of horses. I wouldn't even think about trading my life for Seabiscuit's.
>
> I'LL BUY YOU A BIG FLOWERY WREATH TO HANG AROUND YOUR NECK IF YOU'RE JONESIN' FOR HORSE LIFE.

Some who couldn't afford the next leg of the journey bought a steamship ticket and sailed back the way they came. Others got stuck in the brand-new boomtown. To service the transient population, entrepreneurs established a bounty of saloons and brothels, which provided jobs for those who were trying to save up to get out. Different jobs paid different wages: A dishwasher could earn 10 cents a day, a hotel cleaner 25 cents, while a sex worker, in towns that were 80 percent male, could earn $1 to $5 per trick. The lives of those who earned a living on their backs were not always glamorous, but neither were the lives of those who panned in the harshest conditions, dreams of gold spinning in their heads.

> RYAN AND I OFTEN HAVE DREAMS OF GOLD SPINNING IN OUR HEADS, BUT WE'RE NOT TALKIN' THE SHINY STUFF. WE'RE DREAMIN' OF PILES AND PILES OF PERFECT, FLUFFY, GOLDEN POPCORN, LIGHTLY DRIZZLED WITH THE FINEST BUTTER AND TENDERLY SPRINKLED WITH SALTY GOODNESS.
>
> Ain't nothing better.

Many visitors had one last hurrah at the Red Onion Saloon, which welcomed its first clients in 1898. The ground floor was the saloon proper where, along with booze, stampeders could find the infamous ten dolls that represented the good-time girls on shift. If a doll was lying flat on its back, the sex worker was occupied with another guest. If the doll was sitting upright, the sex worker was available for hire.

I SUPPOSE THAT'S KIND OF A NEAT SYSTEM. IT'S LIKE WHEN YOU GO TO A COFFEE SHOP AND THEY'VE GOT A PEN FOR SIGNING RECEIPTS SITTING IN A LITTLE FLOWER POT FULL OF COFFEE BEANS. AND TO REALLY SELL THE ILLUSION, THERE'S A LITTLE FLOWER ON THE END OF THE PEN. ONE OF LIFE'S GREAT PLEASURES, SEEING A FLOWER PEN.

Would be really funny if those dolls actively updated positions, kinda like some bewitched *Potter*like sex trackers. Doesn't seem to be the case, unfortunately.

The ladies operated out of the ten bedrooms, or "cribs," on the second floor. It is here that a ghost named Lydia resides. One story is that she was left in Skagway by a lover who promised to return with a pocketful of gold and marry her. Another is that she was simply trying to get to Dawson City up north and ran out of cash. Either way, she became a soiled dove.

ANYBODY WHO'S BEEN IN THIS TOWN FOR MORE THAN FIVE MINUTES SURELY ISN'T PLACING MUCH STOCK IN SOMEBODY MAKING CLAIMS OF RETURNING WITH POCKETS FULL OF GOLD. THEY'VE WITNESSED THE ONGOING PARADE OF LOSERS TRUCK THROUGH MAIN STREET INTO THEM THAR HILLS.

You ever think about how weird it is that people lost their collective shit over shiny rocks for a couple of decades? I guess contemporary money is pretty stupid, too. It's alllll an illusion, maaaaan.

YEAH, IT'S DUMB AS HELL. IF YOU DON'T WANT YOURS, YOU CAN JUST VENMO IT TO ME.

There have been many sightings of Lydia hanging from a rafter. She has a mark on her cheek, a common branding done by madams or pimps when a sex worker contracted a VD, like syphilis. Such a designation meant the end of a career—and, for someone who'd already hit bottom—suicide might have seemed the only option. The employees of the modern-day brothel museum have worked to welcome Lydia as part of the Red Onion crew. She can be found walking the halls, trailing the scent of perfume in her wake, and her dainty footsteps can be heard on the stairs. The moistness of the establishment's potted plant soil is attributed to Lydia, watered by an unseen hand.

WHAT A LOAD OF HORSESHIT.

I've once mentioned on the show that I'd love to haunt a place but in a very helpful way. Folding clothes. Refilling the Brita. Seems like Lydia feels the same. OR guests are getting piss drunk on the reg and then pissin' in that plant.

The Loads of Spirits
at the Holly Hotel

Holly, Michigan

After the second fire ravaged the place, the Holly Hotel officially became a drinkery that annually memorializes anti-alcohol activist Carry Nation's visit with cheap drinks.

GET DUNKED ON, CARRY NATION!

That's like any sports arena memorializing you!

Built by John Hirst in 1891, the brick three-story hotel accommodated passengers arriving by train to the city. It was deluxe, with upscale furnishings, multicourse dinners served on fine china, and even electric lights and furnace heating. Gentlemen could get their hair done in the basement barbershop.

CHECKING THIS PLACE OUT ON YELP. LOOKS COZY AS FUCK.

Just once, I'd like a nice meal served on fine china.

Not everyone who stopped in for a sip at the bar was a gentleman, however, and some of the patrons took it outside, sealing the energy of obnoxiousness and violence to the place forevermore. Locals called the street Battle Alley. Some were probably fed up with all that intemperance and so welcomed Carry Nation—along with her signature Bible and hatchet—to town on August 29, 1908. She and her pro-temperance avengers stormed the Holly Hotel bar, hitting drinkers with their umbrellas and smashing whiskey bottles left and right. The proprietor had her arrested.

BOOOOOOO, CARRY NATION AND YOUR GANG OF UPTIGHT LOSERS, BOOOOOOOO, I SAY.

Always carrying a Bible is strange enough, but A HATCHET in addition? What kind of person needs both? Was she a vampire hunter?

The hotel and bar burned down in 1913 and was rebuilt, only to deteriorate over the next decades into a boardinghouse and pizza parlor. Then, in a message-from-the-universe-style coincidence, it burned again *to the hour* sixty-five years after the first fire.

I CAN'T BELIEVE THAT DURING OUR TENURE ON *UNSOLVED* WE NEVER ONCE INVESTIGATED A HAUNTED PIZZA PARLOR. SOMEONE MUST HAVE DIED AT A HUT OR A WING STREET AT SOME POINT. I JUST WANT MORE ON-SITE PIZZA DURING OUR INVESTIGATIONS IN GENERAL.

Admittedly, an oversight on my part.

Norman Gauthier, a ghost hunter before it was cool,

ALL THANKS TO THE PARANORMAL BAD BOYS.

declared the hotel "loaded with spirits" in 1989.

Norm sounding like a used car salesman here: "Oh yeah, this place, loaded with spirits. Packed to the brim. Can't even get a word in. Anyway, that'll be one hundo for an overnight session."

OG owner Mr. Hirst has been seen in a frock coat and top hat, smoking a cigar and expressing ghostly censure of noise making in his fine establishment.

Dude fixed his place up, and now he has a-holes like Shane and me stomping through his living room with a spirit box. Sad.

His rat terrier, Leona, has been heard barking and running up and down the halls. A footless apparition of a Native American man has been seen in the dining room. Guests have seen former hostess Nora Kane in the bar and back hallway, and claim to have smelled her floral perfume and heard her playing the piano or singing. She's even asked people standing near the piano to play her a tune.

"HI, I'M A GHOST. DO YOU KNOW 'TIMBER' BY KESHA?"

Based on her black attire in the portrait hanging in the lobby, some wonder if she lost someone special and if the ghost of a little girl in the kitchen is her daughter. The child loves to tinker with the meat cleaver.

SOUNDS LIKE A GREAT KID.

Wonder how she died.

The Terminal Terminal
of Kells Irish Restaurant & Pub

Seattle, Washington

Edgar Ray Butterworth and his five sons moved their mortuary, established in 1888, into the five-story Beaux Arts building on First Avenue in 1903. In this thriving logging town next to the Puget Sound, lots of people had been dying of the usual causes—epidemics, harsh living, violence—without a good system for disposal. Mr. Butterworth essentially had a monopoly on death, hence his ability to commission the flashy new space.

> A RELIABLE INDUSTRY. ESPECIALLY FOR THE ERA.
>
> Everybody dies, sure. But I really hope when I die, they refrain from calling the burial the "disposal."

For two decades, a majority of Seattle's deceased stopped in at this Butterworth & Sons location before heading to the cemetery. Lauded as "the most complete undertaking establishment in the west" by the *Seattle Republican*, it had "one of the nicest chapels in the United States" and "an unusual and unique . . . cold storage vault." The paper also noted, "The nature of the location is such that with basement and sub-basement, ample space is afforded for stable and carriage room for horses and hearses." Black

coaches transported the bodies of men, white coaches carried women and children. Where they parked is where Kells is today.

ARE WE FAMOUS ENOUGH GHOST HUNTERS THAT UPON OUR PASSING OUR BODIES COULD BE TOURED AROUND THE COUNTRY IN A HORSE-DRAWN HEARSE? PROP OUR EMBALMED BODIES UP FOR MEET AND GREETS. WE'D MAKE STACKS.

In case there's any doubt at how much I would like to not do the above, let me make this clear . . . please never do this to my body. Cremate the shit out of me.

HE'S BEING SARCASTIC. CHECK TICKETMASTER IN THE DAYS AFTER OUR OBITUARIES.

The Irish restaurant and pub boasts a farm-to-table Irish menu, with whiskey and beer galore, Ballycastle sausage rolls, corned beef and cabbage, a variety of pastries, bangers and mash, and the "Danny Boy special."

FAR AS I CAN TELL, THE ONLY THING SCARY ABOUT THIS PLACE IS WHAT'S GONNA HAPPEN WHEN TWO NASTY LITTLE PIGGIES LIKE US STRAP SOME BIBS ON AND START PACKING OUR GREASY LITTLE MOUTHS FULL OF IRISH BREAKFAST. ALSO, I THINK I HEARD MY UPSTAIRS NEIGHBOR GETTING A DANNY BOY SPECIAL LAST NIGHT AROUND 2 A.M.

Never been a corned beef guy. The name itself doesn't even sound appetizing, tbh.

BUDDY, YOU'RE MISSIN' OUT.

During its interior construction, a plumber found some piles of ash under the floorboards, perhaps the leftovers from Butterworth's crematorium. Candles light and glasses break spontaneously, and voices can be heard. The presences of many unseen entities have been felt. Owner Karen McAleese reported a sighting of a tall man with thin hands in a suit jacket. The apparition of a red-haired girl is often spotted—she appears on the stairs or in the main room when traditional Irish music is playing. A bodiless fellow called Sammy is frequently caught grinning at patrons in the back wall mirror's reflection.

I ALWAYS CHECK OUT WHEN WE START LISTING GHOSTS. TALL MAN, WENDY FROM WENDY'S, CHESHIRE CAT. GOT IT. NEXT.

You don't like rigor mortis roll call?

The Spirits of Slippery Noodle Inn

Indianapolis, Indiana

WELL, NOW THIS SOUNDS LIKE OUR KIND OF ESTABLISHMENT! RYAN'S PRETTY SLIPPERY (HE'S SLICK LIKE AN OTTER) AND I'M AS NOODLY AS THEY GET.

Like a human water weenie. Remember those? Too dated of a ref?

In operation since 1850, the former stables and inn is the oldest continually operating building in the state and a nationally lauded blues bar since the Yeagy family took over in 1963. There had been a turnover in ownership during the decades before that, and you can bet your sweet bippy that the joint had seen all kinds of shenanigans. One owner even killed himself in the basement.

UH, PRETTY FLEXIBLE DEFINITION OF SHENANIGANS HERE.

Yeah, not exactly a whoopie cushion on Grandpa's favorite chair.

Like most old buildings, it was supposedly one of the good guys, a way station on the Underground Railroad, and a small room in the basement supposedly sheltered enslaved people seeking freedom. Unsurprisingly, one of the ghosts is a former runaway, an apparition affectionately called "George in the basement." For the gray years of Prohibition, the basement was used as an illegal distillery and at some point as a slaughterhouse—rusty old meat hooks add that *je ne sais quoi* to its décor.

MEAT HOOKS GET A BAD RAP. HOW ELSE YA GONNA HANG YOUR MEAT, EINSTEIN?

One little ol' *Leatherface* movie, and suddenly they're the villain. The power of cinema prevails. Oh, I guess they hang people by them in mob films, too. Yeah, I guess I get it.

Two slugs lodged in the ceiling of the back room attest to gang action, perhaps that of local John Herbert Dillinger, whose gang killed ten men, robbed a bunch of banks and police arsenals, and thrice broke out of jail in a giddy ten-month spree during 1933 and 1934.

Still wild to me that people actually liked mobsters.

The Brady gang—so ruthless and reckless that they "would make Dillinger look like a piker"—is also thought to have patronized the joint, before Alfred Brady was gunned down in 1937 in Bangor, Maine. Upstairs, in what used to be the brothel, one client stabbed another during a fight over a sex worker, then left the bloody knife on the bar. This homicide precipitated the bordello's closure in 1953, and that area is regularly haunted by a soiled dove specter who slaps dudes in the face. She might be Sara, a former madame in an old-timey blue dress, who got murdered by a customer.

GETTING BIG "M'LADY" VIBES FROM THIS "SOILED DOVE" TERMINOLOGY. ALSO, ALL JOKES ASIDE, WOULD LOVE TO GET SLAPPED BY A GHOST. WOULD MAKE FOR GREAT INTERNET.

I'd love for you to get slapped, too. Flexible on the ghost part.

Those stabbings are only a couple of the rumored thirteen deaths at the old bar, and allegedly human bones have been found on site. A depression in the basement floor was prayed over, then paved over without further digging. Doors slam, footsteps thump, cold spots are cold.

"COLD SPOTS ARE COLD." THIS FUCKING BOOK.

Where'd the bones go? Doesn't make sense that bones were allegedly found. Either they were or they weren't. Bones aren't exactly something you come across and then throw in the garbage. They usually go somewhere, you know? Like, say, a police station or, I dunno, a cemetery.

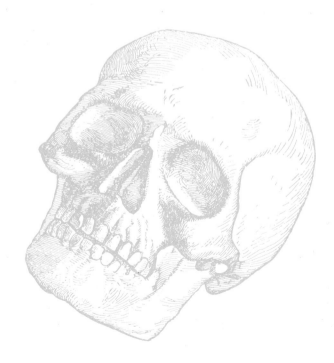

The Shadowy and the Vague at the Horse You Came In On Saloon

Baltimore, Maryland

"The boundaries which divide Life from Death are at best shadowy and vague. Who shall say where the one ends, and where the other begins?" wrote Edgar Allan Poe in his short story, "The Premature Burial," published in 1844.

> THE POOPING OF THE PANTS IS USUALLY A PRETTY NOTICEABLE THRESHOLD.
>
> Welp, two sentences in, and we're already talking about pinching a loaf in your pants.

Five years later, he would be dead, following his cousin and wife, Virginia, to the grave. What he did in the last days of his life is unknown, but the Horse You Came In On Saloon claims that it was there that Poe imbibed for the very last time.

> THE HORSE YOU CAME IN ON. "ON" BEING THE OPERATIVE WORD HERE. (IS THIS JOKE TOO DISGUSTING? I THINK IT GRACEFULLY TOES THE LINE.)
>
> If this bar has neon signage, you're really banking on "in" and "on" both being lit or dead.

On October 3, 1849, he was found wandering a few blocks away in a state of semi-consciousness. He died four days later at Washington University Hospital, having never recovered his senses.

> PROBABLY KIND OF CALMING TO BE GAZONKED OUT OF YOUR GOURD AT THE TIME OF YOUR PASSING.
>
> By all accounts he was the king of tipsy town.

Though "congestion of the brain" was listed in a local newspaper, the cause of death continues to be debated. Was it alcohol poisoning, carbon monoxide poisoning, heavy metal poisoning? What about the common flu, a brain tumor, rabies?

> CONGESTION OF THE BRAIN? THAT'S EXACTLY WHAT I HAD AFTER WATCHING *TENET* ON TOO MANY EDIBLES.
>
> Lol, I think the papers didn't want to print that Poe was fuggin' smashed.
>
> MAYBE, YEAH. I CAN'T BELIEVE I GOT TO TALK ABOUT *TENET* IN THIS BOOK.

Whether or not he did in fact drink his final drink at the Horse, as locals called it, he did die nearby, as did many, many other patrons, given that the bar opened in 1775.

> Weird for a bar's claim to fame to be, "Hi, welcome to the Horse. Our cocktails killed Edgar Allen Poe. Anyways, what you folks drinkin' tonight?"

It is one of America's oldest saloons, with one claim to fame being that it somehow managed to continue operation during Prohibition. Located in Fell's Point, one of Baltimore's oldest neighborhoods, one block up from the Bond Street Wharf on the Patapsco River, it has been visited by countless sailors, merchants, and shipbuilders over its centuries-long tenure. With so many people passing through, and with the boundaries between life and death being so shadowy and vague, it's no wonder that the tavern has high energy levels.

> JUST WANT TO NOTE: THE BOUNDARIES ARE NOT VAGUE. IT'S A PRETTY BINARY THING. ASK ANY LIVING PERSON: THEY'RE ALIVE.
>
> And yet we talk to dead people all the time, my tall friend.
>
> ANYBODY CAN TALK TO ANYTHING. GO TALK TO A DOG TURD AND SEE WHAT HAPPENS.

The sight of inexplicable white orbs is a common occurrence.

> THEY USUALLY JUST SHOW UP IN PHOTOS, BUT I WOULD GENUINELY LOVE TO SEE AN ORB. CAN YOU IMAGINE? BIG, JUICY, GLOWIN'-ASS ORB JUST FLOATIN' ON BY LIKE A FAT-ASS GUPPY? MAN, I'D JUMP OUTTA MY SKIN.
>
> Don't think that's how that works.

Patrons have reported seeing Poe's ghost inside the bar and weaving drunkenly along the cobblestones of Thames Street, heading toward the Wharf Rat brewery, one block north on Ann Street.

> THIS ISN'T SUPER COMPELLING TO ME BECAUSE I ASSUME THAT ANY DRUNKEN PERSON STUMBLING ACROSS THE COBBLESTONE STREETS OUTSIDE A PLACE CALLED THE WHARF RAT JUST LOOKS LIKE A GHOST BY DEFAULT.
>
> Fair, any image of us stumbling out of a bar is equally haunting. Especially you. Like watching an unleveled ladder constantly on the edge of toppling over.

Some believe ol' Eddy is responsible for everything from the breaking of steins to the sound of footsteps. One night, a glass mug set atop the bar randomly shattered—just as it had in the exact same spot the night before.

> OUR SWEET, GENTLE EDWARD AIN'T OUT HERE BREAKIN' STEINS. NO WAY A TENDER LITTLE GOTH LIKE HIM IS CAUSIN' A RUCKUS.
>
> You never know, the dude partied.

Usually the horror writer's continued patronage is benign, however, and the Horse bartenders customarily leave out a cognac, his favorite drink, at closing time. The glass is found empty in the morning.

> OH YEAH, SURE. A "GHOST" (WINK) MUST HAVE DRANK (WINK WINK) THE COGNAC (WINK, WINK, WIIINK). I'M BEING SARCASTIC. A PERSON DRANK IT.
>
> How dare you. A spirit drinking a spirit is POEtry.

Shaker's Cigar Bar

Milwaukee, Wisconsin

In 1894, Schlitz Brewing Company, the creators of "the beer that made Milwaukee famous," opened a cooperage in what is now Shaker's Cigar Bar. When Prohibition hit, the infamous Capone brothers took it over and turned it into the kind of place they'd want to visit on their way up to Al's house on Cranberry Lake.

| Is this . . . wholesome?

The speakeasy was located on the main floor, and the brothel occupied the second and third floors.

Ah, guess not.

YOU WANT SOMETHING WHOLESOME? AL CAPONE SENT A BARREL OF BOOZE TO MY GREAT GRANDPARENTS' WEDDING. TRUE STORY. A WONDERFUL, PERFECT MAN.

What?

The current owner bought the place in 1986. While exploring the basement with a ground-penetrating radar, as one does, he allegedly found two skeletons of human remains in the back corner of the building. When he reported his discovery to the police, they told him in so many words, finders keepers. He left the remains where they lay underneath the concrete and brought in spiritual mediums, who determined that the bodies belonged to two young gentlemen, perhaps aspiring politicians, whom the gangsters saw fit to dispatch.

I've read a lot about mob history, and it always astounds me how much access they had to concrete and contractors in general. From all accounts, aside from the fact that they're hiding murdered bodies, they did beautiful work.

THIS IS WHY I'VE ALWAYS BEEN VERY, VERY SUSPICIOUS OF THE PROPERTY BROTHERS.

Another body, allegedly found on the third floor during renovation in 2001, is that of an underage sex worker who was strangled to death by a lover in 1929. Said lover burned her body in the fireplace. The murder victim also hangs around, and she apparently has an affinity for male visitors, touching their hair and various body parts and even giving a ghost's version of hugs. There have supposedly been eight deaths within the building, and rumor has it that Jeffrey Dahmer, the serial killer known as the Milwaukee Cannibal, occasionally stopped in. Did he pick up one of his seventeen victims at Shaker's?

Let it be known that Jeffrey Dahmer popularized takeout before the pandemic made it mainstream. If that joke is in bad taste, I'm sorry.

[DISAPPOINTMENT IN THE FORM OF A VAST OCEAN OF SILENCE.]

Today, the bar is all about cigars and paranormal happenings. Apparitions are regularly seen within the smoky setting, and an overwhelming sense of sadness has made more than one spiritual medium cry. Things move around, including a safe that weighs over five hundred pounds. Temperatures drop, and doors slam or spontaneously lock.

God, the thought of investigating while smokin' a fat stogie is appealing.

SMOKING IS OBVIOUSLY GOD-AWFUL FOR YOUR HEALTH AND A GROSS HABIT ALL AROUND, BUT I'VE ALWAYS LOVED THE IDEA OF US CHAIN-SMOKING CIGARETTES THROUGH EVERY EPISODE OF *UNSOLVED*. SOMETHING ABOUT IT JUST FEELS AESTHETICALLY APPROPRIATE.

NAUTICAL
NIGHTMARES

The Haunting Shadows
of the St. Augustine Lighthouse

St. Augustine, Florida

BEEN HERE! HELL OF A TALL THING. LOTTA STAIRS. THEY NEED TO INSTALL ONE OF THOSE HANDY LITTLE CHAIRS THAT SHUTTLES THE ELDERLY FROM FLOOR TO FLOOR.

While they're at it, some AC in there would be nice, too. Felt like stepping inside of a Coke can left in the Florida sun.

Juan Ponce de León claimed the land one hundred miles north of Orlando for the Spanish crown in 1513. The area, like much of the United States, was rife with conflict between Indigenous peoples and European colonizers. One bright spot in this particular area's history, however, came about in 1738, when the Spanish government commissioned a nearby settlement called Gracia Real de Santa Teresa de Mosé, or Fort Mosé, to be sanctuary for Africans fleeing slavery from English colonies in the Carolinas. All the refugees had to do to get in was pledge allegiance to Spain and convert to Catholicism, which more than one hundred people did, making it the first free Black community in the region.

THE CLOSEST THING I HAVE TO RELIGION IN MY LIFE IS MY AFFECTION FOR THE PERFECT MOTION PICTURE *SPEED RACER*.

Your second favorite film after *Jurassic World*.

Based on a map of Sir Francis Drake's plundering of the settlement, it is deduced that some sort of watchtower or lighthouse has kept tabs on the northern end of Anastasia Island since at least 1586. Still, accidents happened. The HMS *Industry* sank off the coast in 1763, and sixteen British ships fell victim to a nor'easter in 1782. Keeper Joseph Andrew fell off scaffolding and "struck the roof of the oil room about thirty feet below, whence he glanced off and struck the stone wall which encloses the Light House, and thence to the ground—a stone pavement."

YAHTZEE!

During the construction of a new lighthouse five hundred yards southwest of the original, Eliza and Mary Pittee, two of the superintendent's children, and an unnamed child were pinned underwater by a supply cart. Keeper William Harn died of consumption. One keeper or assistant supposedly hanged himself in the basement of the keeper's house. Smokey, a cat who survived being strapped to a kitty-size parachute and thrown off the tower, died of old age. Countless birds, confused by the beacon, crashed into the tower.

BIGGEST TWIST IN THIS BOOK IS SMOKEY THE CAT DYING OF OLD AGE.

Funniest conspiracy theory on the internet is still the idea that birds don't exist. The main piece of evidence being, if birds ACTUALLY are real, you'd think we'd see more dead ones on the reg. Which, come to think of it, it's not like they're burying their dead, I suppose. I imagine a fair amount of birds just have a heart attack on their flight to work. Huh. Do I believe this one?

FUNNY STORY: I ACTUALLY HAD A WONDERFUL LITTLE BIRD IN MY YOUTH! A RED-LORED AMAZON. HE CAUGHT A COLD AND DIED. DURING HIS FINAL MOMENTS, I CRADLED HIS FEATHERY LITTLE BODY IN MY ARMS AND TOLD HIM I LOVED HIM. I GUESS THIS STORY ISN'T ACTUALLY THAT FUNNY.

Is this the one you ate?

As they say, time equals tragedy equals ghosts, so no wonder the oldest continually inhabited settlement in the United States is haunted. Of course, the souls lost at sea are all over the place. Human pinball Joseph Andreu is there, as well as an apparition of his wife, Maria Mestre de los Dolores Andreu, who replaced him in 1860, becoming the US's first official female lighthouse keeper and one of the first Hispanic employees.

A rare pleasant fact!

GREAT JOB, THIS ONE LIGHTHOUSE!

People have reported seeing a little girl—in a red dress, or with a bow in her hair, or in a lace dress—in or nearby the keeper's house and hearing the sounds of children at play. A tour guide claimed to find a child's footprints in the keeper's house. The sound of consumptive coughing has been heard in the keeper's bedroom.

We actually picked this up on our investigation!

A tall, cranky guy who hates tourists has been encountered in the basement. Quacks and caws can be heard in the wind.

THIS LAST SENTENCE IS JUST A FUN FACT THAT APPLIES TO MOST PLACES IN THE WORLD.

You're just upset this book called you cranky.

The Mournful Cries
of Eldred Rock Lighthouse

Haines, Alaska

In 1898, buddies S.W. Mix, Ed Fenley, and Perry Wiley discovered gold on Porcupine Creek, which was a whole lot closer to the coast than the Yukon, where a little gold rush known as the Klondike was taking place. Word spread, and fifty new buddies arrived to uncover around $50,000 worth of precious metal along the Porcupine and its tributaries over the next year.

Would be crazy to find gold. A thing the ghoul boys definitely know nothing about.

Not everyone was so lucky. The Lynn Canal, which connects the Gulf of Alaska to the Chilkat and Chilkoot Inlets to the shores of Haines and Skagway, is all kinds of treacherous. The *Clara Nevada*, packed with miners, booty, and illegal dynamite bound for Seattle, exploded after running aground on Eldred Rock in February 1898.

HAD TO BE A SIGHT. I LOVE TO SEE STUFF BLOW UP. OBVIOUSLY NOT WHEN PEOPLE ARE INJURED. BUT YOU EVER JUST STAY UP TILL SUNRISE WATCHING VIDEOS OF GIANT EXPLOSIONS? OR TORNADOS? OR THAT TIME THEY ACCIDENTALLY SET OFF EVERY FOURTH OF JULY FIREWORK AT ONCE IN SAN DIEGO?

Can confirm that the SD fireworks video is very, very funny.

Out of seventy-five casualties, only one burned body was recovered and none of the 850 pounds of gold. Four people survived.

Four survived this?! That's some Bruce Willis *Unbreakable* shit right there.

This accident was the final straw that convinced congress to establish a lighthouse on teeny-tiny Eldred Rock Island. The construction of the lighthouse was delayed by weather, shining its first beacon on June 1, 1906. The three keepers—head keeper Nils Peter Adamson and two assistants—shared the living space and manned the light and foghorns.

LIGHTHOUSE LIVING IN GENERAL SEEMS APPEALING. COLD, SLIPPERY, LOTS OF BIG SOCKS, TINNED FISH, AND BAD ALCOHOL. THE DIGNIFIED HONOR OF MANNING A FOGHORN. YOU AND YOUR WET PALS CACKLING THE DAYS AWAY AS YOUR COLLECTIVE SANITY SLIPS AWAY IN THE MIST.

You have a very strange definition of appealing.

Surely some tragedies were avoided because of the lighthouse's fifteen-mile beam, but not all. Between 1878 and 1915, there were eighty-seven shipwrecks along Alaska's coast.

THAT SHAKES OUT TO A LITTLE OVER TWO SHIPWRECKS PER YEAR. I GOTTA SAY, IF I'M THE LIGHTHOUSE KEEPER, I DON'T LIKE WHAT I'M SEEING UP THERE ON THE SCOREBOARD.

Maybe they just liked watching shipwrecks. Best seats in the house if so.

It is unknown just how many passengers and crew lost their lives or how many spirits haunt the icy waters strewn with gold dust and dead dreams. Then there's the lightkeepers themselves. The elements and isolation chipped away at keepers' sanity—there were sightings of sea monsters and the ghosts of murdered Aleuts, as well as random acts of violence and, of course, accidents and their fallout.

RYAN, PICTURE IT: WE'RE MANNING A LIGHTHOUSE TOGETHER. A COUPLE WICKIES IN OUR FINE-ASS PEACOATS, TOILING AWAY, HOLLERIN' ABOUT WIND AND KEROSENE. WHICH ONE OF US IS THE FIRST TO CRACK?

If there's a DVD shelf with only *Speed Racer* on it. One hundred percent me.

OH MY GOD, THIS SOUNDS LIKE HEAVEN.

In February 1910, Assistant Keepers Scottie Currie and John Selander set out by boat for the Point Sherman Lighthouse. They did not return, though their launch was found a few days later. For thirty days, Adamson surveilled Lynn Canal; for thirty nights, insomnia brought him to his bedroom window, where he stood and called out his trusted assistants' names. Some believe that the wind still carries their screams and the sound of Keeper Adamson's cries.

SOUNDS LIKE THOSE GUYS DIED.

The Lost Souls of the USS *Yorktown*

Mount Pleasant, South Carolina

HUGE-ASS SHIP. COULD BARELY PAY ATTENTION TO THE GHOSTS ON IT BECAUSE I JUST KEPT THINKING, "THIS IS A HUGE-ASS SHIP."

As huge as it was hot, I sweated from places I didn't even think possible aboard this hell hog.

On the morning of December 7, 1941, Japanese fighter planes killed more than twenty-four hundred Americans at Pearl Harbor. Just six days earlier, construction of a massive aircraft carrier had begun, and now that the United States was fully embroiled in the war, builders rushed to complete the job. A mere seventeen months later, First Lady Eleanor Roosevelt christened the ship USS *Yorktown*. The USS *Yorktown* could carry 2,600 men and one hundred aircraft.

And on the night we were there, it carried six dipshits. Very funny.

In August 1943, it saw its maiden combat in a raid on isolated atoll Minami-Tori-shima. For the next two years, it fought the Japanese navy, including a successful mission sinking the *Yamato*, one of the largest battleships ever built. It would also see failure and fire—on March 18, 1945, a Japanese dive bomber unleashed a bomb on the starboard side of the bridge, killing three instantly and wounding eighteen. Two more died the next day.

WAR, BABY.

Stoked I didn't grow up in this era.

The ship would receive eleven battle stars and the nickname *Fighting Lady*. During the Cold War and the Vietnam War, it acted as an antisubmarine aircraft carrier, winning five more battle stars. It had the honor of recovering the crew of *Apollo 8*, the first manned mission to orbit the moon, in 1968.

It also has 4.5 stars on Yelp!

GONNA GUESS THAT MISSING HALF STAR HAS SOMETHING TO DO WITH THE COMPLIMENTARY SWAMP ASS.

In 1975, the aircraft carrier retired in Charleston, South Carolina, to live out its old age as the centerpiece for the Patriots Point Naval & Maritime Museum. And so the hauntings began. In one estimate, 141 brave servicemen lost their lives on the *Fighting Lady*—the entire ship is a hub of paranormal activity, even hosting the largest collective paranormal experience, with eighteen Boy Scouts as witness.

On one foggy evening in 1987, Troop 149 had set up their tents on the flight deck when the troop counselor realized that one boy was missing. The leader found him standing at the rail on the starboard side, where, in the water below, hundreds of soft red lights glowed then rose out of the water and surrounded the nearby USCGC *Comanche*.

NOT IN A MILLION YEARS AM I BUYING THIS. IT TAKES A "GHOST" AN ENORMOUS AMOUNT OF "ENERGY" TO INTERACT WITH OBJECTS IN THE PHYSICAL WORLD, BUT SOMEHOW THIS ONE GOT HIS TRANSLUCENT HANDS ON AN ARMY OF DRONES AND IS OUT HERE CHOREOGRAPHING HIS OWN *FANTASMIC*? FIBS.

Eighteen witnesses.

The specters of uniformed seadogs and glamor boys show up in photos, one reportedly in the cockpit of a SH-3G Sea King helicopter, another standing on the site of a fatal plane crash. The staff use the name Shadow Ed—a cute play on the military term "Enemy Designated"—to cover the numerous shadowy figures on board. "You see them out of the corner of your eye," said one employee. "I don't think they want to hurt you, but they will sure make you hurt yourself trying to get away from them."

SHIP'S BEEN CLEARED. BUBKES.

I thought I saw something in the bowels of this ship. Footage was inconclusive. Still, a fun time.

The Damning Duel
of St. Simons Lighthouse

St. Simons Island, Georgia

The first lighthouse lasted only fifty-two years—fleeing Confederate troops blew it up in 1862 in the hopes that the Union navy would crash their ships.

CONFEDERATE TROOPS ARE BEST KNOWN FOR FLEEING.

Second to losing.

Rebuilt in 1872 by an architect who died of malaria contracted on the island before its completion, it casts a light twenty-three miles out to sea, guiding ships into St. Simons Sound and welcoming vacationers to the Golden Isle for summer retreat.

> Those Golden Isles look as chill as the name would suggest.

For almost eighty years, the two families of the various keepers occupied the two-story Victorian keeper's cottage. Frederick Osborne was the second head keeper of the second lighthouse, taking up his post in 1874 with his wife, Julia, and their son, William. Fred Jr. was born on October 19, 1875, but lived only two years. Daughter Elizabeth was born in February 1880. Assistant Keeper John Stephens and his wife moved in upstairs that same year, and by March the families were getting on each other's nerves.

> A sitcom waiting to happen here.

Either Osborne made a pass at the missus upstairs, or he simply spoke rudely to her when Stephens was on a trip to the mainland. Either way, at 8:30 on a Sunday morning, the two took it outside. Osborne waved around his pistol, and Stephens went inside to get his own weapon, a double-barreled shotgun loaded with buckshot. Things escalated from there, and Stephens shot Osborne four times from the front door at a distance of ninety-eight feet. The head keeper died later that afternoon.

> Definitely a little murder for a sitcom, but I'd still watch it.

> **A DUEL OUTSIDE A LIGHTHOUSE IS ONE OF THE MOST 1800s-ASS THINGS YOU COULD POSSIBLY DO.**

Reportedly, Stephens felt terrible about what had happened but, you know, too little too late. A Brunswick jury ruled the shooting self-defense, and he took over all lighthouse duties until a new keeper arrived.

> Sounds like a real slap on the wrist for the casual crime of blasting a dude to death with a shotgun.

Osborne, who had died so unexpectedly, apparently didn't realize he was dead and so stayed on the job, walking up and down the old spiral staircase, slamming doors, and hanging out in the tower. He once helped a keeper's wife fix a special mechanism on the light that he himself had invented. Incontrovertible evidence of Osborne's continued tenure is the fact that Jinx—the family dog of C.O. Svendendson, lighthouse keeper from 1907 to 1936—definitely seemed scared a lot.

> Poor work-life balance leads to poor work-afterlife balance. Start good habits while you're still kickin', folks.

> **IMAGINE IF WE TRAGICALLY LOST OUR LIVES ON A GHOST HUNT (LIKE IF A BRICK FELL ON OUR HEADS OR WE ACCIDENTALLY SAT ON BICYCLE PUMPS AND POPPED LIKE BALLOONS), BUT DIDN'T REALIZE WE WERE DEAD AND JUST KEPT ON GHOST HUNTING AS GHOSTS!**

> What if that's already happened?

The Ghost Brothers of the USS *Sullivan*

Buffalo, New York

When Thomas Sullivan opened his front door, he was expecting bad news. "Which son?" he asked.

> I can almost see the "walk and talk" from a reporter as I read this.

"All five," the officer replied.

> AS AN OPTIMIST, I'M TRYING TO THINK OF THE BRIGHT SIDE HERE, BUT IT SEEMS LIKE A PRETTY UNFORTUNATE SITUATION.
>
> Just imagining you IRL, boldly saying, "Well, look at the bright side" before realizing you had nothing.
>
> "BULK DISCOUNT ON CASKETS?"
>
> LMFAO.

George, Francis, Joseph, Madison, and Al Sullivan were brothers and besties who joined the war effort after losing a friend at Pearl Harbor. "It wasn't surprising that the boys insisted on staying together in the navy," reported the *Sunday Star* on January 17, 1943. "They were like that all through life." The five young men were stationed on the USS *Juneau* off the coast of Guadalcanal when a Japanese submarine torpedoed their ship, splitting it in two, and it quickly vanished beneath the waves along with most of its seven hundred sailors. Through binoculars, the captain of the nearby USS *Helena* saw only smoke and empty horizon and, to preserve his own crew, decided to skedaddle rather than search for survivors. But 115 men had survived, at least for a little while.

> Wow.

By the time rescue efforts commenced, nearly all the sailors had succumbed to injury, exhaustion, exposure, and shark attacks. According to one of the ten who was rescued eight days after the attack, the eldest Sullivan brother, George, initially survived but soon became delirious and jumped in the water in a futile attempt to swim to shore.

> I CAN'T WAIT FOR THE FUTURE WHEN ALL WARS WILL BE ROBOTS VERSUS ROBOTS AND EVERYBODY CAN JUST CHILL AT HOME WATCHING *FRASIER*.
>
> I still can't believe this war captain looking at war and thinking, "Too spooky. I think I'll turn around."

This calamity led to the enactment of the Sole Survivor Policy in 1948, which protects people from draft or combat duty if they have already lost a relative in military service. Before that, however, President Franklin named a Fletcher-class Destroyer, DD-537, to honor the lost brothers.

SORRY EVERY ONE OF YOUR MANY SONS GOT BLOWN UP AND EATEN BY SHARKS, BUT, HEY, ONCE YOU'RE DONE SOBBING, CHECK OUT THIS BIG-ASS BOAT WITH YOUR NAME ON IT.

A lovely reminder.

The USS *Sullivan* saw combat in World War II, the Korean War, and the Cuban missile crisis, then parked in the Buffalo Naval Park in 1965. That, combined with the tragic energy of its namesake, has led many to believe that it is haunted. George Sullivan seems to be the primary ghost, the theory being that his death was the most tortured and, in his final days, he carried the guilt of not saving his younger brothers.

Gonna choose to believe this is not the reason. Maybe he had some unfinished business, like getting behind the wheel of a muscle car or opening up an ice cream parlor.

This has kept him between realms, and he walks the ship on eternal watch. In death as in life, the brothers stick together; Frankie, Red, Matty, and Al, along with Porgie, as they were called, make their presences known in the form of misty apparitions, male voices and whispers, footsteps, the opening of hatches and locks, and turning on the radar without electricity.

BUT WHICH ONE WAS PORGIE?

Was wondering the same.

WHICH ONE WAS PORGIE, YOU WRETCHED BOOK?

The Lone Spirit of Heceta Head Lighthouse

Florence, Oregon

Light first shined forth from the Heceta Head Lighthouse in 1894. Located within Devil's Elbow State Park, about halfway along the hundred-mile stretch of coastline from Coos Bay to Newport, the powerful beacon illuminated the rowdy Pacific Ocean twenty-one miles out.

> I've always thought the Pacific was the ocean that partied the hardest.

Three lightkeepers and their families worked to keep the light on, but it was hard and lonely living out there in the isolated community of Florence, pop: 300 in 1900. The keeper's house saw a fair amount of turnover, including operation as a World War II military barracks and a satellite campus for Lane Community College. Throughout this time, employees and visitors have reported strange phenomena, and the primary legend is that the daughter of the keeper and spouse drowned—perhaps it is this girl's body that occupies the overgrown, unmarked grave up on the hillside.

> SOMEBODY SHOULDA MARKED IT.
>
> In such a small town, in an even smaller workplace, you'd think they'd at least have an idea of what happened to people.

In 1970, two notable events occurred. On November 12, the Oregon Department of Transportation attempted to dispose of a beached forty-five-foot, eight-ton sperm whale with a half-ton of dynamite.

WAIT! NO JOKE—THIS IS ONE OF MY GO-TO LATE-NIGHT EXPLOSION VIDEOS! THEY RECENTLY REMASTERED IT! I DIDN'T KNOW WE WERE GONNA TALK ABOUT THE WHALE EXPLOSION!

What in the hell do you do with your free time? Lol.

I WATCH VIDEOS OF WHALES EXPLODING. KEEP UP!

Also in 1970, LLC students used a Ouija board to contact the spirit who frequents the old keeper's house and came up with the name Rue. It is unknown whether Rue is the lost little girl or her grieving mother, who it is believed to have returned to the lighthouse after her death to look for her daughter. It is probably not the name of the sperm whale.

PEOPLE GOTTA CHILL ABOUT OUIJA BOARDS. YOU THINK HASBRO'S MANUFACTURING A BOARD GAME THAT LETS THE DEVIL SLIDE INTO YOUR SOUL'S DMS?

I'm actually surprised this is the first Ouija appearance in this book.

Today Rue is a conscientious presence, but in 1975 she scared the bejeezus out of a worker by the name of Jim Anderson. He was cleaning the attic windows and was startled by a reflection. He spun around and there she was, an apparition with silver hair and a black Victorian-style gown. He likely screamed like a baby and refused to return to the attic ever, even when he broke a window. That night, the caretakers reported hearing scraping sounds, and the next day they discovered a neat pile of glass shards. Sometimes Rue moves items around the room or climbs into guests' beds for a cuddle.

If this ghostly child ever attempted to cuddle with me, she's going in a sleeper hold.

DROP HER TRANSLUCENT ASS WITH A STONE COLD STUNNER.

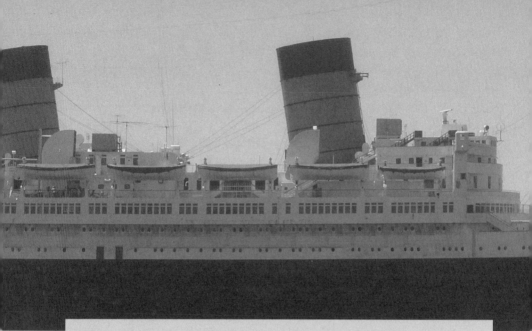

The Haunted Decks of the *Queen Mary*

Long Beach, California

THIS IS WHERE IT ALL HAPPENED. WHERE RYAN BERGARA GOT HIS VISION. THAT
FATEFUL NIGHT WHEN THE AQUAFRESH TWITCHED.

I think the tape speaks for itself.

I n the 1930s, the RMS *Queen Mary* was the height of luxury. Her passengers toasted the end of Prohibition and the Great Depression at the ship's two cocktail bars, waded in its two swimming pools wearing the latest Lastex low-back swimsuits, danced the night away in the grand ballroom, and dined in style in its five dining rooms. There was even a court for mid-oceanic games of squash.

YOU SIMPLY HAVEN'T LIVED UNTIL YOU'VE SQUASHED ON MARY.

Followed up by gettin' smashed on Mary.

Then came World War II, and men exchanged their tuxedos for military uniforms and set sail for the frontlines. The *Queen Mary* was painted gray and eventually nicknamed Grey Ghost for her speed and agility and her ability to outmaneuver Axis U-boats. But not all voyages went smoothly.

Would be kinda cool if people went to war in tuxedos.

In 1942, HMS *Curacao* was escorting the ship from New York to Glasgow, zigzagging ahead of her bow in order to confuse enemy boats. In a fatal breach of communication, the *Queen Mary*'s speed reached three knots faster than the *Curacao*'s and overtook the much smaller ship, splitting it into two pieces that sank one hundred yards apart. The *Queen Mary* had to keep going, calling in the accident to nearby British destroyers, which arrived two hours later. Of the 430 crewmembers on board, only ninety-nine survived.

Following people in moving vehicles is always dangerous imo.

This accident certainly had the highest death toll, but it was not the only tragedy aboard the *Queen Mary*. Captain Sir Edgar Britten bit the dust on October 28, 1936, after having a stroke in his cabin. Senior Second Officer William Stark didn't realize that it was acid not alcohol being stored in an old gin bottle, in 1949.

GRANTED, I'M A DANDY WHO DOESN'T KNOW A JIB FROM A FUTTOCK, BUT I'M REALLY RACKING MY BRAIN TRYING TO FIGURE OUT WHY ANYONE WOULD NEED A BOTTLE OF ACID ON HAND. NOTHING GOOD CAN COME OF THAT. YOU'LL EITHER DRINK IT UP AND DIE OR ACCIDENTALLY SPILL IT ON SOMEONE'S FACE AND CREATE A JOKER.

Yeah, unless you're a high school chemistry teacher, it truly is a head scratcher. And even if you DID need a bottle of acid, surely you'd put it in a well-labeled bottle and not in a bottle that you, ya know, drink from.

STICKERED-UP HYDRO FLASK FULL OF ORGAN-MELTING POISON.

Fireman John Pedder was crushed by an automatic door in 1966. According to an incomplete list in the official logbook, from its maiden voyage in May 1936 to its retirement on December 9, 1967, in Long Beach, California, there were forty-seven deaths on board. But that number doesn't account for deaths unrecorded due to wartime secrecy or deaths covered up due to fear of liability. This may be why three drowned women and a little girl named Jackie haunt the swimming pools.

I can think of worse places to haunt than a pool.

A little boy haunts a passageway where he was rumored to have fallen overboard. A Lady in White dances alone in the Queen's Salon. A specter in a boiler suit wanders the engine room. An Italian prisoner of war named Carlo Giovetti remains captive aboard. A poltergeist cooks up trouble in the kitchen, still angry that the troops threw him in the oven to protest an unsatisfactory meal. A third-class passenger knocks on the door of Room B340.

WEIRD THAT THE TOOTHPASTE INCIDENT ISN'T MENTIONED HERE.

Unbelievable.

The Haunting Music of the Seguin Lighthouse

Georgetown, Maine

The origin and meaning of the name Seguin are up for debate, but the majority agree it means "to make an oral emission," or, more poetically, "place the sea vomits" in Abernaki Indian.

THE LATTER IS PRETTY METAL.

Sounds like directions on a treasure map.

Plans for this seasick lighthouse on the mouth of the River Kennebec were hatched in the mid-1790s. The wooden structure with six oil lanterns gave way to a stone structure with fifteen Argand lamps in 1842, followed by a new and larger tower with a first order Fresnel lens and a new brick keeper's quarters in 1855. A fog whistle replaced the fog bell in 1872, which was replaced by a foghorn in 1907; these warning devices were crucial, given that the area is one of the foggiest locations among all coastal light-houses. According to the local papers, people were excited and not at all bored by these developments.

> I'VE BEEN TO MAINE. I CAN SEE WHY THEY WERE EXCITED.
>
> Oh damn, lick your wounds, Maine!

Even with the evolving technology, however, shipwrecks and boating accidents still occurred, as did encounters with sea monsters. Wars, too, like the War of 1812 and the battle between HMS *Boxer* and USS *Enterprise*—both captains died in the skirmish—added their own brand of death and destruction.

> Feels like lighthouses are just giant odorless candles.
>
> BEING GENUINE HERE: YOU ARE SOMETIMES A POET.

Those who lived on the isolated Seguin Island had to be self-sufficient, and in the mid-1800s, all work and no play made Jack a dull boy. As legend has it, the keeper's wife liked to play the piano, but either her repertoire was limited or the close quarters were getting to her, too. Whatever the case, she played the same tune over and over and over again, the same notes repeated one after the other as the ceaseless fog suffocated the island. Finally, the keeper lost his cool, took an ax, chopped up the piano, chopped up his wife, and chopped up himself. To this day, passing ships and coast guard personnel have reported hearing that haunting refrain echoing across the water on cold, still nights.

> Guess that's what happens when you only know how to play "Chopsticks."
>
> GONNA NEED MORE DETAILS ON THIS. CHOPPING UP OTHER PEOPLE SEEMS LIKE A BREEZE, BUT TO CHOP UP ONE'S SELF WOULD REQUIRE A GREAT DEAL OF MENTAL FORTITUDE. IT'S LIKE THAT THING THEY SAY ABOUT HUMANS NOT BEING ABLE TO BITE OFF THEIR OWN FINGERS. TRY IT. I DARE YOU. CAN'T BE DONE.
>
> I'll Venmo ya fifty bucks to bite off your fingers.

Other ghosts include a young girl, who allegedly died on the island and was buried near the generator house by her grieving parents. She has been spotted climbing the spiral stairs to the tower. Keepers of the now-automated system have seen her wave and have heard her laugh. They've also bumped into an old guy they call Old Captain, who seems to believe that he's still at work.

> More spirits need work/life balance, I say as I type away late into the night.

The Mysterious Disappearance of Roanoke Colony

Roanoke Island, North Carolina

OH GOD. THIS AGAIN.

You knew this was coming.

The Roanoke Colony is one of the contenders for America's first English settlement. Off the coast of modern-day North Carolina, the sixteen-square-mile island was an early Anglo attempt to make a home in the New World. The local Secotans weren't too keen, however, and so the initial arrivals turned home. But the second try took, at least for a little while, and the first baby of English parentage was born in North America in 1587. Her name was Virginia Dare.

CONGRATS TO THIS LITTLE WHITE GIRL FOR BEING BORN IN A PLACE.

Her granddaddy, John White, was the governor of the new Roanoke Colony and its 120 souls.

The fact that White is the last name of the first governor of perhaps the first American settlement is objectively very funny.

A month after landing, he decided to make a 3,600-mile supply run back to England. This was no trip to Costco, and a Spanish armada delayed his round trip. When he finally returned in 1590, everyone was gone. As in *vanished*. The word CROATOAN carved into a fence post and CRO carved into the tree were the only messages left behind.

Remember when you used to go to the mall and one of your friends would go to the bathroom, and then you'd be like, "Haha let's ditch Greg and watch his reaction?" Always good for a laugh. You remember being a dick to your friends, Shane?

I THINK I WAS USUALLY THE GREG.

Sorry, Dude.

Twice White set out to Croatoan Island, fifty miles to the south, to look for his people, but storms thwarted him both times. White died in Ireland in 1593, having never been reunited with his family.

EXTREMELY POSSIBLE THIS GUY SUCKED AND NOBODY LIKED HIM.

I will say that when we ditched Greg, we always waited the appropriate time before coming back. But we always came back.

There are many theories about what happened to the people of the Lost Colony. They might've been dispatched by the Indigenous peoples who held a grudge after the first settlement's governor killed their king. Maybe they got caught in intertribal crossfire between the Secotans and the Chowanokes. Disease is an obvious possibility, though no mass grave has yet been discovered. Or it may have been simple relocation, a theory supported by the British Museum's 2012 re-examination of a map made by White, which found two hidden four-pointed blue star outlines that might indicate an inland settlement. If that is indeed what he intended, why did he keep it a secret?

Kinda funny that the strongest theory in this mysterious mass disappearance essentially boils down to "Maybe they moved next door?"

Or the colony sought refuge with friendly Indigenous tribes, like the Croatoan Tribe—this theory sparked the legend of Virginia Dare. All grown up, she rejected a mansplainy sorcerer, who turned her into a white doe. Then she got shot by another machismo beau who, unbeknownst to him, hunted the gal-turned-doe he was trying to impress. From her spilled blood blossomed the oldest grapevine in America, known as the Mother Vine. Eventually, these scuppernong grapes were smooshed to make a line of Garrett & Company wines called—you guessed it—Virginia Dare wines.

WHAT IN THE ANIMORPH FUCK ARE YOU TALKING ABOUT?

Hahaha. This is certainly a sequence of English sentences.

Of course, there's always mass alien abduction.

NEVER MIND. GO BACK TO THE ANIMORPH THING.

Now we're cooking with gas. Tell me more.

The answer as to what happened to the Roanoke Colony is still up for grabs. But many claim to feel strange energy and ethereal presences on the north side of the island, where the settlers first came ashore.

Wait, that's it?! Ha, I feel like Batman in *Dark Knight Rises*: "So that's what that feels like."

The Avenging Spirit
of the Nancy Brook Scenic Area

White Mountain National Forest,
New Hampshire

THE MOST HAUNTED THINGS IN SCENIC AREAS TEND TO BE THE PUBLIC RESTROOMS. NOTHING LIKE SITTING ON AN ICY STAINLESS STEEL TOILET SEAT AND POOPING INTO THE INKY STINKY ABYSS OF A PENNYWISE HOLE.

I usually just hold that bad boy in. Or if it came to it, I'm just doing it in the woods.

I POOPED AT A REST STOP ON A ROAD TRIP THIS SUMMER. DIDN'T EVEN PUT TOILET PAPER ON THE SEAT. WAS SORT OF A PERSONAL CHALLENGE.

That's honestly the grossest thing you've ever said.

Nancy Barton fell in love in 1778. As the sixteen-year-old servant of Colonel Joseph Whipple, she had plenty of opportunities to meet men as new hands arrived to work the farm. But it was Jim Swindell who stole her heart—then stole her money. Then she died.

A whole lot of awful squeezed in those two sentences.

The couple had planned to get married and move to Portsmouth to start their life together, but Jim was broke. No problem! Nancy's job included room and board, and so she'd been saving every penny for her dowry. They would use that to relocate, then get some new gigs, make some babies, live happily ever after, et cetera.

Colonel Whipple got wind of their impending nuptials, and he decided he'd rather ruin a servant girl's dreams than lose her industry. So he sent Nancy out to purchase supplies and, while she was away, convinced Jim to take the money and run, perhaps for patriotic reasons—her savings were enough to get him to the Revolutionary War frontlines and buy a new uniform, too. Or maybe Jim was a scoundrel who wasn't as in love with Nancy as she was with him and therefore needed little convincing.

Sounds like two solid dudes.

Nancy returned from her errands to find her fiancé gone, Colonel Whipple gone, and all those pennies gone, too. Putting two and two together, she headed south, determined to catch up with them and teach them a lesson about double betrayal. After a thirty-mile trek through snowy, treacherous Crawford Notch over Cherry Mountain, she came upon the ashes of their campfire next to a whispering brook. By that time, she was soaked to the skin, her feet numb, her fingers useless, her teardrops frozen upon her face.

> Holy shit, this is like the *Revenant!*

Hypothermia made her sleepy, so she laid down for just a short rest. By the time the search party arrived, poor Nancy was frozen. They buried her where she lay.

> WHAT?! THIS IS JUST A SAD STORY ABOUT A LADY? GRANTED, ALL OF THE STORIES IN THIS WRETCHED BOOK ARE DEPRESSING, BUT I WAS ROOTING FOR NANCE!

> Unbelievable! Thought it was two ghosts, one campfire time.

The people of Notchland did not forget Nancy's sad tale, and they named a bunch of spots near her resting place in her honor: Mount Nancy, Nancy Cascades, and Nancy Pond.

> Don't think I'd be crazy about my name going triple crown on account of how sad I was.

In 1931, the town erected a sign that reads: "1778 / Nancy Barton / Died in a snowstorm in pursuit of her faithless lover." The sign now stands in the lobby of the Notchland Inn, where Nancy is said to leave flowers and write on mirrors. In the woods, you can hear her anguished cries.

> IF I EVER DIE A NOTABLE DEATH AND YOU WANT TO COMMEMORATE ME, MAYBE DON'T HAVE THE PLAQUE FOCUS ON WHATEVER DUMBASS WAY I DIED AND INSTEAD CELEBRATE MY LIFE. I'D MUCH PREFER "IN MEMORY OF SHANE, WHO MADE A GREAT BOWL OF POPCORN" INSTEAD OF "IN MEMORY OF SHANE, WHO ACCIDENTALLY SAT ON A BIKE PUMP AND POPPED LIKE A BALLOON."

> I'd be totally fine with, "In memory of Ryan, he was an okay dude."

The Ghost Town of the Vulture Mine

Wickenburg, Arizona

INCREDIBLE LOCALE. I REMEMBER BEING REALLY BLOWN AWAY BY THE SIZE OF IT. I WAS EXPECTING A RINKY-DINK LITTLE LINE OF BUILDINGS LIKE IN AN OLD WESTERN, BUT IT WAS A PRETTY EXPANSIVE PLOT OF LAND. ALSO, I HAVE FOND MEMORIES OF EATING AT THE LOCAL DENNY'S LIKE THREE TIMES IN ONE DAY ON THIS TRIP. I DON'T THINK THE WAITSTAFF CARED FOR OUR SUNNY DISPOSITIONS THERE.

I didn't care for this gross-ass mine.

It may be a generalization to say that people who set off into the desert to battle the elements in search of fortune aren't the best record keepers. That's perhaps why most of what happened in this long-abandoned mine is rumor—they just weren't all that into paperwork.

Hard to write when you have that gold fever!

In 1863, Henry Wickenburg stumbled upon a quartz deposit with gold in the Sonoran Desert and from that discovery built one of Arizona's most successful gold mines. According to legend, he dubbed it Vulture Mine either because of the vultures circling overhead or because he shot a vulture and, when he went to retrieve the game, found a gold nugget beside it.

Whoa! It's like he killed a goomba in *Super Mario!*

LOOT!

During its operation from 1863 to 1942, it produced over 340,000 ounces of gold—the equivalent of $430 million in current value—and 260,000 ounces of silver.

THEY WERE ALSO BAT RICH. MANY, MANY BATS TO BE FOUND HERE. MORE THAN YOU'D THINK. IMAGINE BATS. NOW IMAGINE A LOT OF THEM. THE MOST YOU POSSIBLY CAN. NOW QUADRUPLE IT. GUESS WHAT? YOU'RE NOT EVEN CLOSE. THAT'S HOW MANY BATS.

As we said in the episode, this place had FAR too many bats, imo. To be fair, my metric for "far too many" is one. They're fine creatures, I'm sure. But I'd like to keep the relationship professional.

A city blossomed around the mine as prospectors buzzed into the area. A mess hall, workshop, school, and brothel nourished the whopping five thousand residents. Notorious Jacob Waltz, aka the Lost Dutchman, was allegedly a foreman, though how he kept his job after claiming all that gold he had was from a nearby "secret" mine in the Superstition Mountains is anyone's guess.

Just so you know, anybody who tells you they can't tell you something because "it's a secret" is a liar.

For others, this kind of "high-grading" led to the too-short hanging tree, where instead of thieves breaking their neck from the fall and dying quickly, their toes would drag on the ground, sweet eternal relief taking two minutes to two hours to arrive.

This sounds extremely unpleasant. At that point, I'm taking my chances making a run for it. Worst that happens is they shoot me mid-escape. Sounds much better than this awfulness.

Eighteen miners were corporally punished there, but instead of being collated into a concentrated burial zone, the bodies were scattered around the area. Obviously, the hanging tree is highly active in terms of paranormal activity, compounded by a penniless Henry Wickenburg's suicide by gunshot nearby. Though he'd founded this incredibly lucrative mine, the folks who bought most of his share in 1866 refused to pay the agreed-upon price because, they claimed, he didn't have a clear title. Shoddy paperwork strikes again.

Brutal.

Another active area is the Glory Hole, so named not in reference to an anonymous penis-insertion wall, but because that's where seven human thieves and their twelve burro accomplices were sent on to glory in 1923. Apparently, they'd forgotten the purpose of the stone support pillars and, in an attempt to mine them, caused their collapse. The bodies were left in the rubble.

Penis-insertion wall somehow sounds much more graphic than glory hole. And yet, it's a very efficient title. I have a pretty good idea of what the instructions are, just from the title alone.

The 1890s ushered in a downturn in productivity, and the mine was officially shuttered as World War II broke out. Strange orbs and disembodied voices abound in the dilapidated buildings, including the bordello of Mexican Rita, the assay building that housed the vault and therefore was constantly under siege, and the generator room where, allegedly, a worker got pulled into the machinery and was ground to humanburger. A dark apparition and the sound of children's laughter and the old piano haunt the schoolhouse.

WE WEREN'T ALLOWED IN THE SCHOOLHOUSE WHEN WE VISITED BECAUSE IT WAS FULL OF BEES. I HOPE THEY'VE GOTTEN THEIR BEES UNDER CONTROL SINCE THEN.

I'm just gonna start saying that about places I don't wanna go into. Hard to argue with it.

The Search for the Mysterious Mothman

Point Pleasant, West Virginia

Ah, our old pal. What a guy. Really sculpted ass.

One night in November 1966, Roger and Linda Scarberry and Steve and Mary Mallete were enjoying all that Point Pleasant's lovers' lane had to offer.

Oh, I'm sure they were!

The quiet woods now known as the McClintic Wildlife Management Area had been used to manufacture explosives during World War II, which were stored in concrete igloos dispersed across its eight thousand acres. As the couples drove by the abandoned ammunition plant, amore turned to horror when a huge creature with a ten-foot wingspan descended upon the car, its red eyes beaming. It chased Roger's 1957 Chevy at speeds up to one hundred miles per hour, emitting a noise "similar to a record played at high speed or squeak of a mouse" (according to one witness) until they reached the city limits.

NEW THEORY: HE WANTED TO BE THEIR THIRD. NOT SURE IF ANYBODY'S SEEN THE TOWN'S STUNNINGLY EROTIC MOTHMAN STATUE, BUT HE'S A VERY SEXUAL BEING WHO'S NOT AT ALL SHY ABOUT SHOWING OFF HIS CAKES. SHINIEST CLAPPERS EAST OF THE MISSISSIPPI.

An interesting theory. I also wonder if this was a mood killer or if the excitement begot, ya know, more excitement.

Certain that no one would believe their unbelievable tale, the couples returned to the site of the sighting, where they again saw the creature in a pasture nearby.

"Nine-one-one? Yes, he's still here, and he's bending over and slapping his unusually sculpted ass in our general direction."

"HURRY! WE'RE GETTING EXTREMELY HORNY!"

They headed straight to Mason County Courthouse to file a report, and with Deputy Millard Halstead, they returned to the area yet again. There they saw strange shadows and an unexplained cloud of dust. The sheriff held a press conference in the morning.

God, what a time to be alive.

Afterward, one hundred residents came forward to confess that they, too, had seen the giant flying humanoid, soon dubbed Mothman. To this day, rumors abound, and the town hosts a Mothman Festival every September.

> Very funny that this entire town saw this enormous horrifying winged creature that they feared might do them harm and then collectively decided to throw him his own Coachella.

Visitors can get Mothman droppings at the local coffee shop and Mothman pizza—mushrooms for wings, slices of bell pepper for legs, cherry tomatoes for eyes—at the local pizzeria.

> Novelty aside, this pizza was actually quite good.

The Mothman statue in the center of town has super-defined abdominals and buttocks like two halves of a ripe cantaloupe.

> I'd pay to hear the designer of this statue explain his process. It's like he binge-watched *Too Hot to Handle* and then decided, "Time to get to work on that Mothman statue."
>
> IT PUTS THE JOEL SCHUMACHER NIPPLED BATMAN SUITS TO SHAME. I'M SURPRISED MOTHMAN ISN'T SPORTING A MOOSE KNUCKLE.

Still, no one knows for sure what or who the Mothman is. Some believe that the creature is a bird mutated from the contaminating byproducts of the stored munitions. Others posit that it's an actual bird, like the sandhill crane or a plus-size owl. One cryptologist believes it is actually an unknown variety of owl, which he dubbed Bighoot.

> WE DIDN'T COVER BIGHOOT IN THE MOTHMAN EPISODE, AND I'M SUDDENLY LIVID. WHY WOULD YOU NOT TELL ME ABOUT BIGHOOT, RYAN? BIGHOOT IS NOW MY FAVORITE CRYPTID.
>
> Mainly 'cause I didn't know about it.

Some UFO researchers guess that it's an extraterrestrial, or an ultraterrestrial, a creature from another dimension. It could be an angel come to warn the townsfolk of danger or a demon gleeful to spread misfortune.

> Love this story. Having an absolute blast.

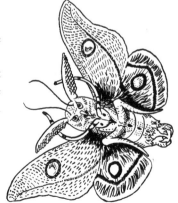

Many inconveniences have been attributed to the creature, from malfunctioning electronics to temporary paralysis to a bridge collapse that killed forty-six people. In 2002, Laura Linney and Richard Gere starred in the movie *The Mothman Prophecies*, based on these unexplained phenomena.

> I THINK IT'S PRETTY DISRESPECTFUL TO PIN THE BRIDGE COLLAPSE ON MOTHMAN. MOTHMAN IS MANY THINGS, BUT A TERRORIST?
>
> Yeah, he's not Bane.

The Night Marchers of Nu'uanu Pali

Oahu, Hawaii

For centuries, the chieftains, or ali'i, of Hawaii, fought for sovereignty over some of the world's most beautiful land. In 1782, Chief Kalani'ōpu'u died, leaving his nephew Kamehameha and his sons, Kiwalao and Keaoua, to fight for rule of the island of Hawaii. Kamehameha won but, unsatisfied, decided he wanted the whole shebang or, rather, he wanted to unite the other islands of Maui, Oahu, Molokai, and Lanai under one rule.

IT'S CLEANER. SURE.

The only thing my brother and I fought over was Mario Kart. But that was settled "on the track," as we say in *Kart*.

But those islands belonged to Chief Kahekili. In 1794, the old chief died before he could be overthrown, and so his son, Kalanikūpule, inherited the feud.

Sounds exciting to inherit a feud.

Kamehameha saw his chance in the transition and rallied his troops to set sail for Oahu. Hundreds of war canoes landed on the island's southern tip, between Waikiki and Waialae, and twelve thousand soldiers stormed the beach, driving Kalanikūpule's smaller army north up the slope of Nu'uanu Valley. There they met a cliff, or pali, with a thousand-foot drop. Some say that Kalanikūpule's men were forced off the edge; others say they chose to jump rather than surrender. Either way, a few hundred guys fell to their deaths. Kamehameha and team had won the bloody Battle of Nu'uanu.

I'VE ALWAYS THOUGHT THAT FALLING TO YOUR DEATH WOULD BE A HALFWAY DECENT WAY TO GO. YOU'RE AFFORDED THAT FLEETING MOMENT OF BLISSFUL FREEFALL BEFORE SMACKING INTO THE GROUND AND EXPLODING LIKE A ZIPLOC FULL OF CHILI.

Shane, you're a madman.

One hundred years later, during the construction of the Pali Highway, workers uncovered eight hundred human skulls.

Whoa, I had no idea. I have family in Hawaii. We visited this highway a lot on account of it being preternaturally windy at all times. Really fun pictures to be had here. Had no idea about the skulls, though.

Today, you can take a five-minute drive from downtown Honolulu up to Nu'uanu Pali Lookout or hike up via a number of jungle trails. At the top, wind whips up the mountain at up to sixty miles per hour, making a whistling sound as it crests the top. Or is that the sound of the warriors' ghosts howling?

> I LOVE IT. THE WRETCHED BOOK IS BEING CHEEKY AGAIN. THE BOOK KNOWS IT'S THE WIND.

> Wrong again, stilts. You just don't know Pali wind. There's something going on on this cliff. Come to think of it, you don't really know much about elevation either. Gotta imagine the tallest "mountain" in Schaumburg belongs to the family that can Jenga the most haystacks.

> YOU KEEP SCHAUMBURG OUT OF YOUR MOUTH.

Locals wouldn't dream of going up to Nu'uanu Pali at night. The mere thought prompts chicken skin—Hawaiian slang for "the heebie jeebies"—and visitors are highly discouraged from staying near the site come sunset. That's because it is a known route of night marchers, or huka'i pō, the ghosts of warriors who marched to battles fought long ago. They carry torches, beat drums, and chant; some witnesses claim they float, while others have seen footprints in the dirt. Though the night marchers are merely protecting sacred ground, do not look directly at them, for those who do eventually die.

> Lol, my grandma used to tell me this story. Funny lady.

Even better, visitors are told to strip naked, lie down on the ground, and pee on themselves—though some suspect that recommendation might just be a locals' prank.

> INSTRUCTIONS SEEM A LITTLE VAGUE, BUT SAY NO MORE. I'VE PEED MYSELF.

> She left this part out, though. Assuming you're lying on your back. The instructions are basically to Bellagio yourself with piss?

The night marchers aren't alone in local lore. Another more prosaic yet gruesome legend is that of a brokenhearted teenage girl who hanged herself at Morgan's Corner on Nu'uanu Pali Drive and wasn't discovered for three days, by which point her head had separated from her body. Now she wanders the area, dragging her head by the spinal cord like a dog on a leash.

> JESUS FUCK!

> She's like one of the ghouls in Cabin in the Woods.

Then there's the ongoing clash between volcano goddess Pele and pig god Kamapua'a. Travel with pork products into Pele's territory at your own risk.

> I also recall hearing this a lot as a child. I wonder how I fell into ghost hunting?

The Creepy Dolls
of the Island of the Dolls

Lake Teshuilo, Xochimilco, Mexico City, Mexico

ONE DAY WE'LL PUBLISH AN ENTIRE NOVEL ABOUT OUR VISIT HERE. WHAT A JOURNEY.

It'll read like an exposé.

Sometime in the 1950s, Julian Santana left the barrios after getting busted for preaching without official anointment. Such was his devotion that he abandoned his wife and kids, eventually navigating a *trajinera* through the Xochimilco canals in search of a safe place to worship. He settled on a *chinampa*, a floating garden originally built by the Aztecs. But if he was hoping to escape his detractors—or his demons—Don Julian would be disappointed. Soon after his arrival, a drowned girl washed up—though no one else saw the body, and some, including his relatives, believe he imagined it.

DID HE JUST KACHOW HER BODY BACK INTO THE CANAL? SHE'S NOT A TROUT! CALL IT IN, DON!

Well, you've done it. A *Cars* reference in print. Say goodbye to whatever little integrity this book had.

PIXAR, CALL ME.

Not long afterward, a doll appeared in the same manner, which Julian took to be some kind of sign. To honor the girl and protect the island from malevolent spirits, he hung the doll on a tree as a talisman. The next day ushered in another weather-beaten doll, followed by the intermittent arrival of more plastic babies, some clothed and intact, others just heads with empty eyes and tangled yarn hair. Don Julian attached each doll or doll part to his hut or the surrounding trees with wire and string until the *chinampa* became La Isla de las Muñecas.

At no point did any of this sound like a good idea.

As the legend goes, during this time, Julian's perception of the dolls' supernatural role changed. Instead of them appeasing the drowned girl and protecting the island, he came to believe they were possessed by her, just as he seemed to be. His cousin Anastasio Velazquez, a frequent visitor to the *chinampa*, claimed, "They will move their heads and whisper to each other." Even so, visitors found the hermit and his spider-riddled isle to be friendly, even bringing dolls to trade for his homegrown produce.

WE CAN ATTEST TO THE SPIDERS AND THEIR RIDDLING. THEY SURE HAVE RIDDLED THAT ISLAND. A THOUSAND SPIDERS FOR EVERY DOLL.

The spider-to-doll ratio is really something there. Also, they're organized. Like the mob. Never going back.

For fifty years, Don Julian's collection grew to over 1,500 dolls, with the original occupying point-of-pride placement at the entrance to his shed. In 2001, Anastasio came to help his eighty-year-old uncle plant pumpkins. He found Don Julian strumming his guitar and singing to the mermaids, who, he said, were beckoning him. After a few hours in the garden, Anastasio returned to find him floating in the same spot in which he'd discovered the mysterious girl and the first doll.

Met this guy when we went back in 2016. Nice guy despite some clearly dark history.

ANASTASIO, HE MEANS. NOT THE FLOATING GUY.

Decades of punishment by the sun, wind, and rain haven't done the dolls any favors. Some claim to hear them laughing and whispering or to see them opening their eyes and turning their heads. Some believe it was the dolls that killed Don Julian.

IF YOU EVER VISIT, BE SURE TO SAY HELLO TO THE WET, MOLDY MICKEY MOUSE. HE SPEAKS IN BACKWARDS LATIN. IT'S A REAL KICK.

I still can't believe you touched it. So gross.

The Monster of Moon Lake

Uinta Basin, Utah

Scotland's Nessie isn't the only loch monster around. Moon Lake has its own monster, as well as a variety of ghosts, according to legends attributed to white settlers and to the local native Utes.

Shane's a big Nessie guy, actually. Fun fact.

I THINK CRYPTIDS ARE FUN TO THINK ABOUT, YEAH. SURE. SUE ME.

The area around the lake has been an on-again, off-again home to wandering tribes for a few millennia, but the Utes, who lived spread out around the region of Utah, were pushed into the Uinta region in the mid-1800s as Mormons settled near the Great Salt Lake. During that same period, tales of lake monsters were all the rage throughout Utah, according to *Deseret News*.

CAN'T JUST BE LUMPING IN CRYPTIDS AND GHOSTS LIKE THIS. PICK A LANE!

Sloppy lore is a bore.

Moonie the Moon Lake monster appears as a lone ripple near the north shore when the waters are still, in the quiet golden hour or blue hour. Is she a dinosaur? Perhaps, a possibility given credence by the proximity to Dinosaur National Monument, just one hundred miles away, where the bones of hundreds of ancient creatures lay undisturbed for nearly 150 million years. Is she some kind of evil spirit? Also maybe, if you believe an old legend about a giant hand pulling in some canoers who were returning from the burial ground after the funeral of their chief.

> Remember that boss fight in *Smash Bros.* vs. the giant hand? Terrifying.

Is she a force or a flesh-eating fish? Could be, according to the legend about a mother watching her two children go under, never to be seen again. Is she an ugly and bumpy critter of unknown origin who likes to follow and occasionally attempt to tip the boats and water weenies of day trippers and resort guests? According to said day trippers and resort guests, a resounding *yes*.

> I VIBE WITH MOONIE.
> Joshin' with tourists is just a funny thing to do.

Even if visitors stick to shore, they aren't guaranteed safety, at least not from getting spooked. There have been reports of a little girl, shivering and soaking wet, who approaches and asks for help only to vanish. Other hikers have heard the sound of a child's cries, frantic splashing, and silence-shattering screams with no corporeal source. This, too, has a corollary legend about an underwater village of "water babies" who cry in the night, only to pull into the depths anyone who attempts to rescue them.

> I VIBE WITH WATER BABIES.
> Seeing as how we have no physical details to go off of, I tend to believe that these are just some choppy, choppy waters.

Bigfoot: The Convincing Evidence

Pacific Northwest

> Was really hoping for a Madej family reunion in this ep. But couldn't find Mr. Foot.
> Sometimes people just fall out of touch. Sad.

Not all mysteries are made of ectoplasm—some are made of flesh and blood and lots of hair. In the fifteenth century, peoples of the Caucasus region called these mysterious creatures Alma and sometimes married them. Folks in the Himalayas call a white-haired version Yeti. For Australians they are Yowie, and Indonesian lore features the Ebu Gogo.

BECAUSE THERE'S ALWAYS SOME CONFUSION ABOUT THIS, I'LL CLEAR IT UP RIGHT HERE. I FIND CRYPTIDS WAY MORE COMPELLING THAN GHOSTS. AS THIS WRETCHED BOOK HAS POINTED OUT, WE'RE DEALING WITH HYPOTHETICAL BEINGS OF FLESH AND BONE. GHOSTS DEFY THE LAWS OF THE KNOWN NATURAL UNIVERSE, WITH EACH SPECTER PLAYING BY A WILDLY DIFFERENT CHERRY-PICKED SET OF RULES THAT CATERS TO WHATEVER HEARSAY EVIDENCE HAS BEEN GATHERED. I'VE SAID MY PEACE. LET'S HEAR ABOUT AMERICA'S MOST ELUSIVE BEEFCAKE.

This continues to baffle me. You'd think if there were a tribe of Bigfoot out there, we'd have seen him by now. Especially because he exists on land and not even the ocean, where 95 percent remains undiscovered. Really, all it boils down to is that one blurry-ass photo. Whereas with ghosts there's probably more photos and videos than you could watch in your lifetime. "Solid" or not. But they at least exist. Unless you're positing that the Bigfoot clan is akin to some insane John Wick society of spies. Maybe I'm judging a book by its cover, but the dude's measurables don't exactly scream "elusive."

BIGFOOT BIG. FOREST BIGGER. HE HIDE.

In the Pacific Northwest, he is often called Sasquatch, from the Salish word "Sésquac," meaning "wild men." These wild men went mainstream in 1958, when a tame man by the name of Ray L. Wallace discovered overly big footprints near his home in Bluff Creek, California, ushering in the term Big Foot, eventually shortened to Bigfoot in the *Humboldt Times*.

> Will never be unfunny to me that the reason this name was coined is because a dude saw a footprint in the dirt and thought, "Man, that's a big foot."

IF YOU DISCOVERED HIM, HE WOULD NO DOUBT BE KNOWN AS BIGASSFOOT.

The debate has raged ever since. Evidence includes a fifty-nine-second film shot in 1967, numerous big footprints, and unidentified DNA. Dr. Wolf Henner Fahrenbach, a retired zoologist who formerly worked at the Oregon Primate Research Center, has

analyzed over seven hundred footprints and concluded that, on average, Sasquatch's foot is 15.6 inches long and that he weighs up to two thousand pounds. "I've gotten close enough to smell him," he told the *New York Times* in 2003—apparently the creature smells like smegma.

YOU CAN'T JUST SAY STUFF LIKE THIS.

Still as gross as the first time I read it!

Dr. Jeffrey Meldrum, professor of anatomy and anthropology and author of *Sasquatch: Legend Meets Science*, believes that, based on smudges and skin whorls, these footprints could not be faked. Skamania County adds its authority, given the 1984 ordinance that states, "The Sasquatch, Yeti, Bigfoot, or Giant Hairy Ape are declared to be endangered species of Skamania County and there is hereby created a Sasquatch refuge."

Look, I'm not saying I absolutely think Bigfoot isn't real. I think it's plausible but not outright impossible like you suggest with ghosts. These footprints are interesting, but I do wonder if they could be from a completely different animal that's not Bigfoot?

Of course, the stinky creature cryptozoologists call Gigantopithecus could be a big hoax. Bigfoot hair has turned out to belong to sheep, dogs, raccoons, bears, and humans. In 2008, two Bigfoot hunters sold what they claimed to be a Bigfoot killed in the woods of northern Georgia. A couple of researchers in Atlanta paid a hefty price, thawed out the frozen Bigfoot, and discovered a rubber gorilla suit. Even more damning, or perhaps simply revealing of family dynamics, Ray L. Wallace's two sons came forward after his death in 2003 to say that it was all a prank. Before you weigh in, listen to one final word from beloved chimpanzee expert Dr. Jane Goodall: "Well, now you will be amazed when I tell you that I'm sure they exist."

JANE COMIN' IN CLUTCH! LOOK, I WOULDN'T PUT ANY MONEY ON IT, BUT I LOVE THE IDEA OF BIGFOOT EXISTING. SEEMS LIKE ONE OF THOSE THINGS THAT COULD BE PROVEN IN 2027 OR SOMETHING, AND FOR THE REST OF TIME ALL OUR GRANDCHILDREN WILL LAUGH AT WHAT DUMB SIMPLETONS WE WERE, NOT BELIEVING IN BIGFOOT FOR SO LONG. FINGERS CROSSED.

Wouldn't that be something?

The Swinging Specters of Lake Shawnee Amusement Park

Rock, West Virginia

In the summer of 1783, blood washed the land where the abandoned Lake Shawnee Amusement Park now sits. The Clay family had recently moved into the area and claimed eight hundred acres, encroaching on the territory of the Shawnee people already in residence. Cue violence. Three of the Clay children—Bartley, Tabitha, and Ezekiel—were killed in horrendous ways, and patriarch Mitchell Clay and friends retaliated. Blood and more blood fell upon the ground. In 1926, a man named Conley T. Snidow opened a park for amusement, featuring a circling swing set, a pond, a speakeasy, a water slide, and a Ferris wheel.

EVERY TIME YOU SEE FOOTAGE OF AN OLD-TIMEY AMUSEMENT PARK, IT'S LIKE A GIANT WOODEN DISC THE SIZE OF A ROLLER RINK VIOLENTLY WOBBLING AROUND A CENTRAL STEEL POLE AS HUNDREDS OF WOMEN DRESSED LIKE MARY POPPINS FLY OFF IT AND SEEMINGLY SHATTER ALL THEIR BONES. THE SNIDOW SPIN-'EM-UP!

Lmao. The dizzying hard cut from "horrendous stealing of land begets bloodshed" to "one ticket to the water slide, please!" really is something.

Coal-mining families went round and round and up and down for forty years, over the course of which six or so people lost their lives. Legend has it that a little boy drowned in the pond and a little girl was hit by a truck while on the circling swings, prompting the park's closure in 1966.

Look, it happens. People have died under the watchful eye of the mouse at Disneyland. Not surprising that the best carnies a corndog could buy struggled to erect a circling swing set to code.

BLAMING THE SWINGS FOR HITTING A TRUCK IN THEIR PATH FEELS A LITTLE BIT LIKE BLAMING JFK FOR BEING IN THE WAY OF THAT BULLET.

A man named Gaylord White bought the amusement park twenty years later, with dreams of getting in on that newfangled suburban sprawl. Then the construction crew allegedly unearthed a bunch of bones. Sadly enough, most of the bones were those of children.

Welp, that won't be on the brochure.

EASY REBRAND FOR A THEME PARK. BONE LAND! RIDE THE BONE COASTER! TAKE A PICTURE WITH BONEY THE BONE MAN! THIS IS ALL VERY SAD, THOUGH, OBVIOUSLY.

Now the park sits empty, swings and spokes creaking creepily while a partially deconstructed tractor, a school bus, an old van, and the ticket booth shed their paint onto the grass. Some have seen a little girl on the grounds, her cotton-candy-pink dress darkened by blood. On cold nights, heat spots on the swings mark the place where bottoms of yesteryear once sat.

In the rankings of "garments that are made horrifying by the presence of blood," cotton-candy-pink dress has gotta be near the top, no?

ONLY OTHER CONTENDER I CAN THINK OF IS A CHILD-SIZE CLOWN COSTUME.

The Jersey Devil of the Pine Barrens

Pine Barrens, New Jersey

Long before Rosemary had her baby, Mother Leeds spawned her own little bundle of hellfire. It was 1735, and the alleged sorceress was pregnant with her thirteenth baby.

> Weird how a witch conjures an image of the old witch from *Snow White*, but a sorceress seems much more svelte. Thirteen kids certainly proves that.

She was not happy. In a fit of pique, she shouted, "Let this one be a devil!"

> Lmao. Just a mom screaming at her thirteenth baby, "ENOUGH ALREADY!"
>
> SOUNDS LIKE SHE'S JUST CALLING HER SHOT HERE. I'M NOT ONE FOR SUPERSTITION, BUT I'M CERTAIN ANY DOCTOR WILL AGREE THAT IF YOU HAVE A THIRTEENTH CHILD, THE LAWS OF MEDICINE DICTATE THAT IT WILL BE THE UNHOLY HERALD OF THE APOCALYPSE. STICK WITH A DOZEN CHILDREN. EASIER TO BUY EGGS FOR.

Well, she learned a valuable lesson about being careful what you wish for. Baby Leeds had the head and hooves of a horse, the wings of a bat, glowing red eyes, sharp claws, and, apparently, an extra-long wingspan. It flew up the chimney and away to begin its centuries-long hobby of scaring the bejeezus out of people in the Pine Barrens and beyond.

> A real shame that they didn't have cameras in 1735. I'd kill for a jpeg of this little devil.

This is one of many stories. Another is that of the witchy Mother Leeds, who cursed a preacher who was trying to convert her, and he clapped back with his own curse.

> Wait, since when can preachers cast curses? How did I miss that in Bible study growing up? I woulda kept it going if that was the case! Just imagine Sunday Mass with this new info! A preacher turning a teen into a chubby little rabbit for being on their phone? Must-see TV.
>
> ISN'T THEIR WHOLE THING CURSING YOU TO DAMNATION UNLESS YOU FOLLOW THE RULES IN THAT OLD-ASS NOVEL?

There's also the girl who was cursed for sleeping with the British and then birthed a devil. Or the girl who was cursed for refusing to give a beggar food and then birthed a devil. The one tale that doesn't blame some poor overburdened woman is more of the academic variety and points to the tension between Quakers and other folks, specifically Daniel Leeds, who arrived in America in the late 1670s and set about antagonizing the locals with his heretical beliefs and bitchy exposés.

A late 1600s' Joe Rogan Experience. Sounds fun.

CURRENT-ERA JOE ROGAN IS ABOUT AS UP TO SPEED ON THE WORLD OF SCIENCE AS YOUR AVERAGE DIPSHIT FROM THE 1600S.

In fact, he pissed off his fellow Quakers so much that they started calling him Satan's Harbinger. This somehow, in this game of telephone we call history, became a bat-horse-devil thingy and the official state demon of New Jersey in 1936.

Wish every state had an official demon mascot.

I KNOW A GOOD CANDIDATE FOR ILLINOIS.

Though different folks believe different versions, everyone can agree that the Jersey Devil is real, and it—he? she? they?—wants to see you destroyed. It wants to destroy your crops, too, and your chickens and cows and goats and trees and the weather. It's been seen spreading panic and, some claim, the scent of dead fish within the 1,700 square miles of South Jersian forest and beyond. In 1909, Councilman E.P. Weeden went on record with the tale of being awakened by the sound of flapping wings outside his window and finding cloven footprints in the snow. After hundreds of people claimed to have seen the red-eyed devil, though, proof was not forthcoming. None of the hefty rewards offered for its capture have ever been claimed.

Sounds like the Jersey Devil needs some serious PR help. Could be a nice person, and we'd never know!

A FUN STORY, BUT WE CAN ALL AGREE: HOOEY THROUGH AND THROUGH.

SCARY CEMETERIES

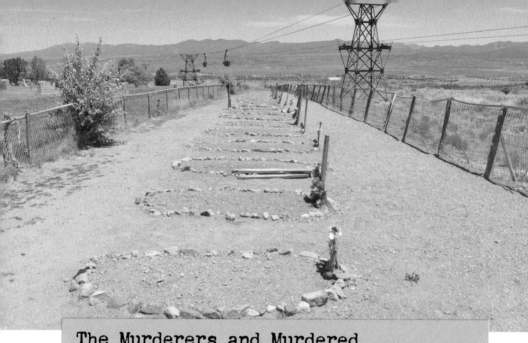

The Murderers and Murdered of Boot Hill Cemetery

Pioche, Nevada

"**D**ying with his boots on" is a cute way of saying "dude got murdered." In Boot Hill Cemetery rest a lot of guys who got murdered—and who murdered. In fact, there were seventy-two homicides before a single natural death in Pioche, and the cemetery includes a special section with one hundred graves called Murderer's Row.

> MURDERER'S ROW SOUNDS LIKE A REAL MURDERER'S ROW OF UH . . . MURDERERS. OKAY, I'LL GET OUTTA YOUR HAIR AND LET YOU FINISH READING THIS THING.

> Well, since you inexplicably brought us to a screeching halt for that, uh, joke, I'd love to take the opportunity to express how absolutely bananas it is that the first natural death was preceded by seventy-two MURDERS.

Pioche, Nevada, located 180 miles northeast of Las Vegas, was a quintessential boomtown. Silver ore was first discovered in 1864, and mines opened five years later. Pioche's population ballooned, and in 1871 and 1872, nearly 60 percent of Nevada's homicides happened there, making more famous Wild West locales like Tombstone and Dodge City look like your granny's knitting club. Such outrageous murderousness was the result of fierce competition for the best spots and confusion about the exact location of claims, and in a dusty desert town where guns were the go-to mediator, disagreements quickly erupted into violence. Many mine owners hired guards for the astronomical fee of $20 per day. The sheriff's office did its part in keeping the peace by accepting tens of thousands of dollars of bribes every year.

In a typical article in the *Sacramento Daily Union* from June 15, 1872, a drunken dispute over basically nothing between Morgan Courtney, who was known as "a very bad character," and Irish immigrant James Sullivan led to an argument. "You damned son of a bitch, I'll kill you yet," Sullivan said while reaching for his knife. "Take that back or I'll kill you," said Courtney, who then drew a pistol and shot the man through the left breast.

THIS SOUNDS LIKE THE SORT OF CONVERSATION RYAN AND I TYPICALLY HAVE WHEN WE'RE ON LOCATION OR AT THE AIRPORT OR OUT TO LUNCH AT CHIPOTLE OR REALLY DOING ANYTHING AT ALL.

I was about to say, why are my hands involuntarily clenching into fists as I read this?

The following summer, Courtney walked out of the Mint Saloon and was shot in the back by George McKinny. Courtney's marker is a favorite at Boot Hill Cemetery, with the inscription: "1844 – 1873 / Feared by some / respected by few / detested by many / Shot in the back 5 times from ambush."

ONE OF THE GODDAMN NASTIEST EPITAPHS I'VE EVER READ.

Also telling about this? The fact that he got shot FIVE times in the back. Normally, a shot in the back is one and done with a quick and cowardly retreat. You have to REALLY be hated to get shot five times in the back.

Throughout the cemetery, you can find metaphorically colorful but literally faded inscriptions on rudimentary wooden markers. John B. Lynch was killed by James Harrington, an event described as, "Shot during a dispute about a dog."

Loved the *John Wick* films.

John Bass's murder is summed up with "June 26 1875 / Shot by officers 5 times" while another comes with the odd editorial "Fanny Peterson AKA Panama Jack / Courtesan killed by lover Lymon P. Fuller / Damn shame / July 12, 1872." Then there's "Shot by a coward while he worked his claim / No one even knew his name."

ALRIGHT, I'M WON OVER BY THE FUNNY HEADSTONES. VERY HAUNTED MANSION. BOOKING AN EXTENDED STAY.

I could easily spend an afternoon strolling through this cemetery, reading every last inscription.

The departed are more likely to stick around if they've met bad ends, as did a majority of Pioche's boomtime residents. Some spirits haunt the Overland Hotel and the original jail cell at the Million Dollar Courthouse, and others walk the streets in the hazy light of morning. Some hang out with their trigger-happy pals on old Boot Hill.

Solid start to this cemetery section.

The Lost Infants of the Cemetery of the Lost Infants

Arlington, Texas

In the southwest corner of Doug Russell Park, next to the Varsity Circle of the University of Texas, Arlington, is a little cemetery. It is the only remnant of the Berachah Industrial Home for the Redemption and Protection of Erring Girls. The home was the third of its kind founded by Reverend James Tony and Maggie Mae Upchurch. By all accounts, this power couple was awesome, speaking out against the double standard held for the impregnated versus the impregnators.

AFTER ALL THE TALES OF COLD-HORNY MEN SHOOTING EACH OTHER IN THE STREET, IT'S VERY REFRESHING TO HEAR ABOUT PEOPLE COMMITTED TO A COMMENDABLE CAUSE.

Don't forget they shot each other in parlors, too. Anyway, eager to see how this will bum me out when it inevitably goes sideways.

Their first venture was the Berachah Rescue Society, opened in 1894 in Waco to help sex workers and fallen women. The community opposed this work, apparently preferring punishment and ostracism over aid, and chased the couple out of town. They set up another mission in Dallas then purchased land in Arlington that, over thirty-two years, grew to a self-sufficient village on sixty-seven acres. Pregnant young women, as well as those who were homeless or addicted to drugs, arrived from all over Texas and beyond to gestate and learn skills like gardening, printing, teaching, nursing, farming, cooking, and handkerchief making.

First off, this is a noble pursuit. I wanna make that VERY clear. But I do have just one small question. Is it not a little weird to lump in handkerchief making with things like nursing, teaching, and cooking? I've personally never thought of handkerchief craft as an essential skill in my tool box, but hey, maybe I'm alone here.

AS THE OWNER OF MANY FINE SILKEN HANDKERCHIEFS, I FEEL IT MY DUTY TO INFORM YOU THAT YOU ARE IGNORANT.

A print shop published the *Purity Journal,* which the goodly reverend used to report successful rehabilitations and to raise funds. A precept of the mission was to keep mothers and children together on Rescue Hill while the women learned to support themselves and care for their young. Then, in 1935, the home shut down probably because of a loss of donations due to the Great Depression as well as Reverend Upchurch's failing health. His daughter, Allie Mae, took over and converted it into an orphanage, which closed a few years later. The home was a safe haven, and women often arrived sick and starved—some didn't recover, or some died in childbirth or from the 1914 measles outbreak in the region. Babies died, too. Some of the women buried there include Eunice Williams, Pearl Carson, Jessie Weaver, Maude Trice, Dorothy Myrtle Carter, to name a few. Of the babies, some are remembered with first names like Darline, Juanita, Alfred, Frank, Cap, and Ruth. Other gravestones read "Infant" and a number or, simply, "Baby."

AT THE END OF THE DAY, SOUNDS LIKE MORE GOOD THAN BAD. THANKS FOR A LITTLE DASH OF HOPEFULNESS, BOOK!

Yeah, at last a facility where, sure, death happened, but at least it was from natural causes and not directly due to the facility's awfulness.

People have reported seeing shadowy figures among the graves, feeling watched, and hearing children's voices. Others claim to have their hair stroked, like that of a mother comforting a child. Toys randomly appear.

LIKE A NINTENDO SWITCH OR…?

Probably like a sack of marbles, but even the hauntings are pleasant here!

The Missing Miners of Dawson Cemetery

Cimarron, New Mexico

Today, all that's left of this booming mining town is the graveyard. From 1901 to 1950, this little city seventeen miles east of Cimarron was centered around a coal mine, purchased by Phelps Dodge Company in 1906. In its heyday, population ran to nine thousand, and the mines produced four million tons of coal per year. A community developed along with employment, including the homes of the workers and their families, a hospital, a hotel, and entertainment venues like a theater, swimming pool, golf course, baseball park, even a bowling alley. The high school had a celebrated (boys') sports program.

LET US CELEBRATE THE BOYS AND THEIR SPORTS FOR ONCE!

I'd still pay good money to see you dribble a basketball or swing a baseball bat.

IT LOOKS WEIRD.

Then on October 22, 1913, an unidentified miner set off an explosive while 284 miners were underground, killing 263 immediately and two rescuers later on, making it the nation's second-deadliest mining disaster on record. (The worst mining disaster killed 362 miners in Monongah, West Virginia, in 1907.)

NO QUIPS HERE! THAT'S A LOTTA DEAD FOLKS!

Mines really are the worst.

Ten years later, another explosion, this time when an electric mine car jumped its tracks and sparked the flammable coal dust, killed 120 miners. Many of these men were Italian and Greek immigrants who'd traveled to America to make a new life. In some cases, the two explosions killed two generations—the father and, a decade later, the son.

Not exactly a fun Snapple fact, book.

For a while, the wilderness encroached upon the cemetery in which these men were buried as well as the abandoned town itself. But renewed interest and a $65,000 grant allowed family members and other interested parties to reclaim and preserve the grounds. Today, row upon row of white iron crosses honor those who lost their lives on the job. Despite the recent caretaking, however, some believe that the ghosts of these miners are not happy about the way they went or, because of the suddenness, don't realize they're dead. The remote site is a popular tourist attraction, and visitors have reported hearing moans and voices carried on the lonesome wind and seeing ghostly figures in mining helmets and white lights among the crosses.

I'M STARTING TO THINK THE LEADING EXPORT OF THE COAL INDUSTRY IS GHOSTS, WITH COAL BEING A DISTANT SECOND.

Mine carts are essentially ghost machines.

The Witch of Yazoo

Yazoo City, Mississippi

KNOWING NOTHING, THE WITCH OF YAZOO IS MY FAVORITE PERSON.

10/10 name for sure. Nothing can bring me down now!

On May 25, 1904, the bustling town of Yazoo burned to the ground. In just a few hours, 324 buildings—churches, businesses, homes, the post office, and City Hall—were reduced to ash. While the villagers were assessing the damage the next day, a few people ventured to Glenwood Cemetery. They were the ones who hadn't forgotten the witch's legendary promise in 1894. "In twenty years," she had screamed as she sank into quicksand, the sheriff and his men watching in terror, "I will return and burn this town to the ground." Now the town was forced to remember. The heavy chains surrounding the grave were broken, her promise fulfilled.

You can't just casually mention quicksand and not provide any more info. How did she get into the quicksand? Did the town have a quicksand pit in lieu of a gallows? Or did she accidentally fall in the quicksand, and the town was like, "Well, works for us. We always thought she was a witch anyway."

QUICKSAND IS ONE OF MY OTHER GREAT FEARS. LUCKILY, IT'S NOT SOMETHING YOU ENCOUNTER ON THE REG, BUT I DON'T LIKE THE SOUND OF IT ONE BIT. I'VE READ ABOUT THE TECHNIQUES ONE MUST EMPLOY TO ESCAPE IT AND BELIEVE IN MY HEART THAT IF I WERE EVER ENSNARED, I'D HAVE AT LEAST A 60 PERCENT CHANCE OF SURVIVAL, BUT WHO KNOWS.

EXACTLY my point! It's not something you encounter regularly. So how is it seemingly chilling in the town square next to the sheriff's office?!

Who was the witch of Yazoo? According to local lore, she was an outcast who had the weird hobby of luring fishermen to her house to poison them with arsenic.

HOW VERY GIRLBOSS OF HER. (PLEASE ASK TUMBLR IF I'VE USED THAT SLANG APPROPRIATELY.)

One afternoon, a boy was floating down the Yazoo River on his raft and heard moaning. When he followed the sound to the witch's house, he discovered two dead guys and a bunch of cats, plus a woman who was "half ghost and half scarecrow, but all witch" as described by local author Willie Morris in his novel *Good Old Boy and the Witch of Yazoo*.

SOMETHING ABOUT "BUT ALL WITCH" SOUNDS A LIIIIITTLE TOO HORNY.

And also inaccurate? Clearly, they hadn't taught fractions yet 'cause after half ghost, half scarecrow, you're all out of lady to divvy up.

The boy fetched the law; the law found skeletons and other gruesome evidence of the witch's monstrous pastime; the law gave chase; the witch cursed the town. The sheriff then pulled her body from the quicksand and buried her in Glenwood Cemetery, where the townsfolk could keep an eye on her. As an extra cautionary measure, they laid chains around the grave to trap her spirit. The marker, now long gone, had the initials T.W. Perhaps it stood for The Witch?

Picturing a business card with small gold initials.

More than a century later, those chains, which are not made of string cheese but of strong metal, keep falling apart. Sometimes they get stolen, which makes current Yazoo residents nervous. One of the sexton's primary duties is to repair those chains because, as the legend goes, when the chains are gone, she will return for another taste of revenge.

If I ever come here, I'll discreetly break these chains myself. Worst-case scenario, I frighten the villagers. Best-case scenario, I meet the witch of Yazoo.

Satanic Panic at Bachelors Grove Cemetery

Midlothian, Illinois

It's likely the cemetery got its name from the town, which got its name from the Batchedler family. But over the years, the name has changed in no small part due to the claims of a Mr. Stephen Rexford, who arrived with three other single guys and decided to call it Bachelors Grove. Another spelling is an amalgamation of the two to form Batchelor.

ILLINOIS!

Home of the Shanester! You ever been to this cemetery?

I WAS CONCEIVED THERE!

The first burial at Bachelors Grove Cemetery took place in 1838 and the last in 1965, with the cremated remains of Robert E. Shields added to his family's plot in 1989. Only eighty-two people are buried there—or only eighty-two plots are on the map. If the stories of Team Al Capone using the remote area to dispose of finks and snitches are true, then there are more bodies as yet undiscovered. A few decades after Prohibition ended, the youth started listening to the rock-and-roll music and swiveling their hips. They began to use the isolated cemetery to consume booze and the devil's tobacco and make out, maybe play a little Dungeons & Dragons, rob graves, cut the heads off goats.

> HONESTLY? IF MY DEAD ASS IS ROTTING IN A CEMETERY, I CAN THINK OF NOTHING COOLER THAN PEOPLE USING THE SURROUNDING AREA FOR DRUGS AND SEX. I'LL BET THE GHOSTS THERE LOVE IT.
>
> Better than my loved ones sulking over my grave talking about my grandchildren getting an A in Algebra II or some elementary shit like that.

Vandalism did become a big problem during the 1970s, and the police routinely patrolled the grounds and spent a good amount of time dealing with graffiti and tracking down stolen gravestones. Some attribute the teenagers' wacky behavior to hallucinatory gas released by a nearby quarry pond. The limestone itself could be to blame; according to the stone tape theory, stone tends to "record" spiritual energy, so leftover occult issues get passed on. Or perhaps it's the other way around: All that ruckus pisses off the dead, a surefire way to get haunted.

> WE'RE SEARCHING FOR SUPERNATURAL EXPLANATIONS AS TO WHY TEENS WOULD GET UP TO SHENANIGANS? IT'S WHAT THEY DO! TEENS HAVE BEEN AND ALWAYS WILL BE DUMB AS HELL. IT IS THEIR RIGHT.
>
> Also, I think a lot of wacky behavior can be attributed to "hallucinatory gas," but lemme tell ya, ain't nothing supernatural about it. All natural, baby.

Whether it's due to gangster high jinks or kids' bad manners or gas-induced altered states of consciousness or paranormal stone storage, Bachelors Grove Cemetery is known as one of the most haunted cemeteries around. Many of these sightings have been caught on camera, the most famous one an apparition of a woman sitting on a gravestone, caught in August 1991 by Judy Huff. BGC curator Pete Crapia has a long and growing list of paranormal activity, including but not limited to a man dressed in yellow; a caretaker who went bonkers and killed his family; a disappearing house with a light in the window; phantom cars; a farmer and his horse, in the 1870s, who got spooked and ran into the pond, killing them both; a two-headed monster, who might also be said farmer and horse; a Woman in White holding a baby, known as the White Lady and the Madonna of Bachelors Grove; red streaking lights; dancing blue lights; a phantom dog; and a murderer with a hook for a hand.

> HAVING GROWN UP IN ILLINOIS, I CAN SPEAK ON THIS. EVERYONE THERE IS OFTEN BORED, AND THIS IS ALL MADE UP. ALSO, AGAIN WITH THE WHITE LADY?!
>
> Within that laundry list is an interesting thought: If you simultaneously enter the afterlife with an animal, do you re-emerge as a fused-together ghost? Kinda like Goldblum in The Fly? If that's the case, I know how I'm going out now.
>
> THE GOLDBLUM FLY MACHINE ALSO RESULTED IN THAT INSIDE-OUT BABOON. WOULD HATE TO SEE YOU THAT WAY. I MEAN, I DO WANT TO SEE YOU THAT WAY BUT IT WON'T BE PLEASANT.

The Vampire of Chestnut Hill Baptist Church Cemetery

Exeter, Rhode Island

When New Englanders weren't hanging witches, they were busy removing hearts from corpses. This, they believed, would stop the amalgamation of evil we now call vampires, who were blamed for all kinds of bad news, from the bubonic plague to goiters.

> WEIRD TO HAVE A GROWTH ON YOUR BODY AND JUMP TO "MUST BE A DRACULA THAT DONE IT."

> Dracula do be up to no good.

During the eighteenth and nineteenth centuries in the new colonies, vampires took the rap for consumption. A wasting disease that leaches its victim of life through a hacking, bloody cough and fever, it was so terrible and terrifying that, for those who didn't know about *Mycobacterium tuberculosis*, it could only be attributed to supernatural causes.

> Very thankful for modern medicine.

On a bitterly cold winter day in 1892, nineteen-year-old Mercy Lena Brown succumbed to consumption. Her mother and sister had died of the same disease six months apart almost a decade earlier, and her brother, Edwin, had struggled with it for five years. Although the cause of tuberculosis was discovered in 1882, at the end of the century, word of the discovery had not yet reached the small town of Exeter, which had greatly diminished under the blight of the white plague and the Civil War. So the townsfolk were looking for something on which to latch their frustration and grief.

Dracula do be a good scapegoat.

They exhumed the bodies of mother Mary, sister Mary Olive, and Mercy in March. All that was left of the two Marys was bone, but Mercy's corpse was preserved. Overlooking the fact that the former two had been dead for ten years and the latter's body had essentially been frozen since January, they decided that Mercy was a vampire who, if not stopped, would tug Edwin down the homestretch toward death. They removed her liver and heart—which still had clotted blood, another strike against her—burned the organs to ash, and then sprinkled it in her brother's tea, an elixir meant to ward her off. Then they reburied her body in the family plot next to her mother and sister. Despite the ritual, Edwin joined them a couple months later.

I'M GLAD THERE ARE MORE DISTRACTIONS THESE DAYS THAT PREVENT PEOPLE FROM GETTING CARRIED AWAY LIKE THIS. SEEMS LIKE MOST OF THESE WEIRD TRAGEDIES COULD BE AVOIDED IF YOU TRAVELED BACK IN TIME AND GAVE THESE KNUCKLEHEADS AN IPAD WITH CANDY CRUSH ON IT.

I got some anti-vax stats that beg to differ, sir!

AH FUCK.

Since then, many visitors to the Chestnut Hill Baptist Church Cemetery have seen an apparition of Mary wandering the grounds, sometimes wearing dirty or torn clothing. Some who stand at her well-attended grave are pushed violently away, while those who pray smell the fragrance of roses. Many pay homage to this teenage girl-slash-vampire, leaving plastic fangs and other occult doodads.

If tampering with final resting places is said to create paranormal activity, then I can only imagine what Jamba Juicing a person's remains does. I'd haunt the hell out of this place if I were Mary.

The Prisoners of Greenwood Cemetery

Canon City, Colorado

In June 1903, six convicts dynamited the gates of the Colorado State Penitentiary and, using the warden's wife as a human shield, attempted to escape. The men had stolen the clothing of a prison guard, the prison physician, and the prison pharmacists so as to disguise themselves, which bought them some time but not quite enough. One man was killed; the rest were wounded and recaptured. For James "Reddy" Armstrong, this was the third failed attempt. Fearing a life sentence, he tore electric wire out of the ceiling of his cell, secured it to a chair leg, and strangled himself, even going so far as to making a dummy and putting it in his bed to avoid detection by the guards long enough to die. The warden had Reddy's cell door buried over his coffin in Greenwood Cemetery, just six miles from the prison. Which begs the question: If Reddy couldn't escape in life, why did the warden take this extra measure to secure him in death? Whatever the answer, a metal detector has since been used to confirm this story.

> WARDENS SEEM PETTY, AND I WILL NEVER ROOT FOR THEM.
>
> Who in the hell would want to be a warden when they grow up?

There are approximately four thousand graves in this gold rush city's oldest cemetery, the final resting place of pioneer settlers, war veterans, and farmers since 1865. It wasn't until the 1930s that prisoners got their own special section called Woodpecker Hill, named for the wooden markers and the birds they attracted.

> Saw a woodpecker once. It was massively entertaining. Something inherently amusing about an animal that headbutts a tree for a living.
>
> YOU KNOW THEY'VE GOT LONG-ASS TONGUES? JUST A FUN WOODPECKER FACT.

Edward Ives was interred there after being hanged not once but twice—the rope broke on the first go-round—for killing a cop in 1930, as is William Cody Kelley, Colorado's first death by gas chamber in 1934. Convicted murderers John and Louis Pacheco asked to be executed together; the brothers are buried together. Joe Arridy, a man with a learning disability, is perhaps the most famous prisoner buried there. He was coerced into confessing to the murder of a fifteen-year-old girl, though the real killer, Frank Aguilar, swore Joe didn't do it. After nine stays of execution, an uncomprehending Arridy went smiling to the gas chamber in 1939. The governor posthumously pardoned him in 2011, and a marble gravestone has a picture of Arridy playing with his toy train and the words "Here Lies an Innocent Man." Aguilar is buried nearby.

It really took them over seventy years to pardon him? Not that that means anything, but yikes.

License plates made at the penitentiary's factory have replaced the wooden markers for these prisoners. These men, perhaps along with some of the thousands of others buried there, wander the grounds as shadowy spirits and mysterious orbs.

WHAT'S THE ORB TRANSFORMATION PROCESS LIKE? IS IT LIKE A SECOND PUBERTY BUT FOR GHOSTS? YOU DIE AND, WITH EACH PASSING DAY, NOTICE YOUR BODY BECOMING ROUNDER AND ROUNDER, YOUR LIMBS RECEDING, YOUR FACIAL FEATURES SMOOTHING. AND THEN ONE DAY YOU LOOK IN THE GHOST MIRROR AND REALIZE THERE'S NOTHING LEFT OF YOUR OLD SELF. YOU'RE A DISCO BALL.

I think it's more, like, that's what we on this plane of existence perceive them as. But I imagine on the ghost plane, they look in the mirror and appear perfectly normal? I'll acknowledge that I sound insane.

Buried Alive in Pikeville Cemetery

Pikeville, Kentucky

Jacob Hatcher was only a few hours old when he died in January 1891. His mother and father fell into mourning, but where James managed to carry on—as much as one can after the loss of a child—Octavia's state quickly worsened. The twenty-year-old took to her bed, where she declined further, eventually falling into a coma. In May, the doctor pronounced her dead.

James outlived his wife by almost fifty years, calling her the love of his life until the very end and never remarrying. Perhaps it was these two tragedies that allowed him to succeed in business and to feel free in his eccentricity—a no-fucks attitude brought about by having already experienced the worst possible thing. He owned the Hatcher Hotel in downtown Pikeville, where he established a museum of sorts, with a mishmash of antiques and modern miracles, like the newfangled iron lung and his own casket, which allegedly had some sort of special apparatus to prevent his being buried alive. Some claim it was a mechanism on the inside with which James could open his own casket, while others say that it was a bell he could ring if he were to wake up six feet under.

Seems random. Except, after Octavia's funeral, other Pikeville residents started going all catatonic, a condition some attribute to the tsetse fly, a parasite generally found in subtropical Africa that causes "sleeping sickness." But then they woke up, days or weeks later, and of course Hatcher freaked. He rushed to exhume his wife's casket, and when he flipped the lid, he came upon a horrifying scene: dead Octavia, her nails bloody and the lining of the coffin torn, her once-beautiful face a rictus of terror. Octavia, it seemed, had been buried alive.

> I HAVEN'T INTERRUPTED BECAUSE I WAS GLUED TO THIS STORY AND I GOTTA SAY: FUCK!
>
> SAME and I concur, FUCK. This is so insane.

James commissioned a life-size monument of his beloved over her grave, with a little stone infant lying on the ground next to his mother over the resting place of their baby.

> The mental fortitude of this man is wild. To suffer the death of his wife two times. Oof.

Today, the sound of a woman crying can be heard in the cemetery, and a mysterious haze sometimes surrounds Octavia's tombstone. On May 2, the anniversary of her death, the statue allegedly turns its back on the city that forsook her.

> AGAIN, NOT A THING. ANYBODY, I BEG OF YOU, GO HERE ON MAY 2 WITH A CELL PHONE IN HAND AND DOCUMENT THIS ALLEGED OCCURRENCE.

James died in 1939 at the age of eighty. He is buried next to his wife and son.

> Man . . . I hope this guy got reincarnated as a mouse in a cheese factory or something glorious like that.

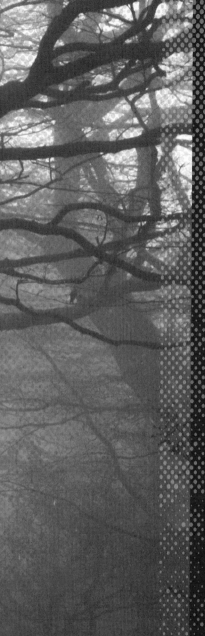

PARANORMAL PATHS

A Tombstone at Every Mile

Aroostook County, Maine

These days, with I-95 running almost two thousand miles between Miami, Florida, and the Canadian province of New Brunswick, the empty, winding road of Route 2A is easy enough to avoid. Which you definitely should. That's because, according to local lore, many a trucker has shuffled off his mortal coil on this section of road deep in the Haynesville Woods. So many, in fact, that the phenomenon was immortalized by the hit song "A Tombstone at Every Mile" by Dick Curless in 1965.

| Ah, the open road.

Originally, Route 2A was a military road built to connect Haynesville to Houlton twenty-five miles to the north, completed in the early 1830s. Once the need for military supplies dwindled, the remote road was used to transport lumber and potatoes. In that northern clime, temperatures drop below freezing for more than half the year, and when snow falls, it sticks. That, in combination with the road's windiness and remoteness—there are approximately 110 people within the town's forty-two square miles—means a high likelihood of accidents and a low likelihood of getting rescued. That's the practical explanation. The paranormal explanation hinges on the reported sightings of a strange black cloud that descends upon unfortunate trucks, seemingly swallowing them whole.

ICY ROADS ARE NOT SUPERNATURAL, BUT GO AHEAD. THE *UNSOLVED* CREW RAN INTO SIMILARLY TREACHEROUS CONDITIONS WHEN NAVIGATING THROUGH SNOWY MOUNTAIN PASSES AFTER OUR BIGFOOT HUNTING EPISODE. IT GOT A LITTLE HAIRY, BUT RYAN PUT ON THE SOUNDTRACK TO THE INDIANA JONES RIDE AT DISNEYLAND. THAT CHILLED EVERYBODY OUT.

And we lived. You're welcome.

The strange thing is that reported hauntings don't tend to feature the stereotypical teamster-turned-ghost—no apparitions with trucker hats and well-worn jeans and no flannel shirts and five o'clock shadows. Instead, most stories recall a Woman in White, though the particularities change.

WHY ALL THE WOMEN IN WHITE??

In one telling, a woman walks along the side of the road, but no matter how fast the vehicle goes, she stays the same distance ahead. Another tale involves a hitchhiker who vanishes as soon as the driver attempts to engage her in conversation. And then there's the distressed young woman who claims that she and her new husband have been in an accident and need help. Many believe that she is the spirit of a bride who froze to death by the side of the road after freeing herself from the wreckage in which her husband lay, already dead. As soon as the friendly motorist offers aid, she, too, disappears.

Always a fan of a hitchhiking ghost tale.

The Tragic Spirits of Trestle Bridge

Adrian, Michigan

The first rumble of a train could be heard in Adrian, Michigan, on October 1, 1836. Authorized by the territorial government of Michigan, the Erie & Kalamazoo Railroad planned to connect what is now Toledo, Ohio, to the Kalamazoo River. Construction stalled, however, and only the first thirty-three miles would be completed, making Adrian the last stop.

LOVING THIS PUBLIC INFRASTRUCTURE SECTION OF THE BOOK.

Hahaha.

The tracks would be the last stop, metaphorically speaking, for a family of three that lived nearby.

ABSOLUTELY TASTELESS.

Written like evil Rod Serling.

Sometime in the late 1800s—the dates as well as names have been lost to time—the family's barn caught fire. Even if somehow the Adrian Fire Department, established in 1841, got word of the blaze, response time was long and success was far from guaranteed. The firefighters themselves, then a team of horses in later years, had to pull the cumbersome steam pumper engine to the site. But dirt roads, including Bailey Highway that runs under the Trestle Bridge, are mud pits during the wet season and ridged as a dinosaur's spine come summer. Getting a steady, strong flow of water to the location was a whole 'nother feat.

Did these horse-powered fire trucks still have sirens?

I THINK THEY USUALLY JUST TICKLED THE HORSES SO THEY NEIGHED A LOT.

On that fateful night, Ma scooped up the baby and ran to get help while Pa tried to free the horses before they got barbequed. She made it to the Trestle Bridge, where she attempted to flag down the oncoming locomotive but, some say, accidently tripped onto the tracks and was squashed flat, along with the LO. Luckily, Pa didn't have to bear the pain of this loss because he died in the barn.

I HOPE MY EVENTUAL DEATH IS SO SENSATIONAL THAT PEOPLE REMEMBER EVERY DETAIL BUT MY NAME. "THE DATES AS WELL AS NAMES HAVE BEEN LOST TO TIME, BUT HE ACCIDENTALLY SAT ON A BIKE PUMP AND POPPED LIKE A BALLOON."

Third time you've mentioned that. Starting to think it's aspirational. Why do you want a bike pump shoved up your ass so badly? No shame here, just curiosity.

ACCIDENTALLY.

This isn't the only calamity caused by the iron horse. Some years later, in 1901, two trains collided five miles or so southwest of Haunted Trestle, killing almost one hundred Italian immigrants. They were buried in an unmarked grave in Oakwood Cemetery.

INCREDIBLY EASY TO PREVENT TRAINS FROM COLLIDING. IT'S LIKE THEIR WHOLE THING! ONE OF THOSE GUYS DID NOT READ THE MANUAL.

Yeah, it appears on a quick Google search that a train-to-train collision is quite rare. Train-to-car collisions, however . . . different story. I imagine trying and failing to jump the gap at a railroad crossing. Lot of people quite literally dying to be Vin Diesel.

Today, the old bridge stands, its walls covered in neon graffiti. Visitors report car and electronics-related trouble when parking in the vicinity. Others claim that, in the kind of darkness you can only find way down a country dirt road, the long-dead Pa wanders the area, looking for his wife and baby. Others say that, at the bridge, you can hear the sound of a woman screaming and an infant crying. Perhaps that's the sound of all those passengers screaming, too. According to one local source, "You might get so scared that you have to make out with whoever you're there with."

TO HORNY JAIL WITH YOU!

The Ghost Hound of Goshen

Goshen Hill, South Carolina

In the mid-1800s, a man and his best fur friend arrived in Goshen Hill via Old Buncombe Road, a remote path through Sumter National Forest. The large white mastiff had walked by the traveling salesman's side from town to town, two souls keeping each other company in a lonely, itinerant life.

LEGITIMATELY, IT TOOK ME A SECOND THERE TO REALIZE A "FUR FRIEND" WAS A DOG. THOUGHT MAYBE IT WAS A GUY HE SKINNED MUSKRATS WITH. OR HIS BUDDY WHO LOVED DRESSING UP LIKE A BIG, MUSCULAR CARTOON WOLF.

. . . What?

Bad luck would have it that the pair's arrival coincided with a murder, and the town's suspicions turned toward the stranger in their midst. Some accounts claim that the peddler languished in jail while his dog sat outside the jailhouse, silently waiting for his human's release. Instead of freedom, the townspeople gave the man a brief, perfunctory trial and death by hanging while the dog stood by. Another version skips the trial, with the townsfolks forming a lynch mob and, before their blood could stop boiling and reason could reassert itself, hanged the peddler from a tree. His body was left there.

Is there another version?

Night after night, the dog howled in anguish. Then the true perpetrator came forward. Or not. Either way, the bloodshed did not end. The townspeople couldn't handle the howling, which only reminded them of their haste, so they shot the dog.

I'M A CAT GUY.

Wow.

I JUST MEAN THAT I OWN A CAT. NOT THAT I DRESS UP AS, LIKE, A CARTOON CAT WITH RIPPED PECS.

The story goes on, of course. The ghost of the white mastiff—the Ghost Hound of Goshen—soon appeared on Old Buncombe Road to haunt the jerks who'd hurt his human. He chased the local doctor, who reported that the canine's eyes burned like coals and that his face bore a hideous grin, earning him another nickname: Happy Dog.

On foggy nights through the years, Happy Dog howls and gives chase, causing people to drive their Toyota Tacomas off the road, and foolish pedestrians to panic and run into barbed wire.

Good. Never much cared for Toyota Tacomas. Or foolish pedestrians, come to think of it.

The Sad Ghosts of Bellamy Bridge

Marianna, Florida

Eighteen-year-old Elizabeth Jane Bellamy died of malaria three years after her wedding night, as did her eighteen-month-old son, Alexander, a week later. Mother and son were buried under a grove of trees on her sister and brother-in-law's property along the Chipola River. Her grieving husband, Samuel, succumbed to alcoholism and slit his own throat with a straight razor fifteen years later in 1853. His final request was to be buried by his beloved's side, but since suicide was considered a sin, he was instead interred in an unmarked grave.

That certainly was an aggressively sad paragraph of text.

NEXT TIME I'M IN FLORIDA, I'LL BE SURE TO SQUEEZE THIS IN RIGHT AFTER DISNEY WORLD.

The Bellamy Bridge is located near Elizabeth and Alexander's final resting place, which was part of brand-new Jackson County, once occupied by the Creek Indians and the third county in all of Florida. Accounts of ghosts in the area have been around since 1890. Along with sightings of a sad, young lady ghost on dark foggy nights, the ghost of a young man believed to be Sylvester Hart has been seen. Sylvester was murdered there, reported the *Pensacola Journal* on May 15, 1914; he was shot in the back of the head by James Smith and his cousin Levi Hart over some moonshine.

That's the thing about moonshine; it gets you drunk.

Levi was sentenced to life on January 14, 1915. Other sightings include a mule-pulled wagon with a driver whose head vanishes on the return trip, accompanied by the sound of creaking wagon wheels, as well as a pair of inexplicable lights. These are believed to have something to do with a father who decapitated his daughter with an ax, then cut his own throat at Bellamy Bridge in order to get back at his wife. Of these legends, this is the only untraceable and most gruesome one.

FLORIDA REALLY DELIVERS ON THIS STUFF, HUH?

Let's hope untraceable means untrue.

The Seven Spirits of Seven Sisters Road

Nebraska City, Nebraska

Now known as the decidedly unterrifying designation Road L, this stretch of pavement leads to the Nebraska City power plant near the shore of the Missouri River. It's nondescript, with fields and some scattered trees on either side, and these days it's mostly used by trucks delivering chemicals and spare machine parts to or picking up waste from the facility. The ghost story starring this road is somewhat vague, yet reports of hauntings and other unexplained phenomena persist.

> EVERY TOWN'S GOT SOME NONDESCRIPT STRETCH OF ROAD THAT THE LOCALS LOVE TO PLAY UP AS HAUNTED. I THINK IT'S A VITAL MECHANISM OF LOCAL LORE. GIVES THE TEENS SOMEWHERE TO DRIVE TO AFTER THEY GET THEIR LICENSES.

> I think this is where believers and skeptics find common ground. Local lore is fun.

The story: A hundred-plus years ago, a young farmer down in Otoe County went bananas. Maybe it was a psychotic break or a demon taking possession. And so he hanged his seven sisters atop the seven hills that used to roll there. How exactly did he accomplish this? That's the question. Odds are against him, even if all seven of his sisters had to wear corsets or whatever it was that inhibited women's movement at the time—why wouldn't they just wrestle him to the ground and hogtie him or shoot him in the leg if need be? Did they all just go uncomplaining to their slaughter? Or did he trick them, put on his sane face, and entice them out one by one into the moonless night then murder them?

> NO WAY ONE OF THOSE WOMEN DIDN'T KICK HIM SQUARE IN THE BALLS. FICTION.

> Yeah, this reeks of bs. Not even because I'd prefer it to be fiction. Just seems like a lot of logistical hurdles.

Apparently, those seven hanging trees were chopped down before the road was built, and today only four hills remain. But ghost hunters who dare to drive down Road L report the sound of women's screaming as well as mechanical malfunctions like headlights blinking or dimming, speedometers freezing, windows rolling up and down, and engines stalling. Others have seen what appears to be white nightgowns flapping in the breeze.

> AGAIN, TEENS REQUIRE VENUES WHERE THEY CAN BE ROTTEN MISCREANTS. HAPPY FOR THE TEENS OF THIS TOWN.

> And again with the white nightgowns. God's really gotta buy the Sims expansion pack for these ghosts.

> IT'S ONLY GOTTA BE, WHAT, SIXTY-FIVE BUCKS? GET WRECKED, ELECTRONIC ARTS.

The Terrified Scream of Siren Bridge

Siren, Wisconsin

In Oak Grove Cemetery are three graves, their headstones engraved with the same date of death: March 7, 1985. Richard Arlen Kringle was a thirty-six-year-old Vietnam vet when he died. Rose Marie Kringle, identified only as "wife" on her headstone, was thirty. Jo Dee Kringle was eight. Other than that, information about these three has been lost to time. But legends abound.

> NOTHING FROM 1985 COULD *POSSIBLY* BE *LOST TO TIME*.
>
> I believe your calculations are correct. Let's get back to some serious shit.

On that winter day in early March, temperatures hovered around freezing, and more than a foot of snow shrouded the world in white. The Kringle family was driving east on County Road B when they came upon a bridge. Which bridge is unclear, and there are a lot of bodies of water over or near which Road B runs: Lost Lake, Clam Lake, and the stream that connects them; Windy Clam River and North Fork Clam River; Bashaw Lake; Little Bass Lake; Montgomery Creek, take your pick.

> SOUNDS LIKE THE FOLKS IN SIREN, WISCONSIN, GOT A CASE OF THE CLAM CRAZIES!

Or it could have been a dirt road alongside a marsh that, with all that snowfall, was deeper than usual. Anyway, as the story goes, the car hit black ice and slid off the road, through a guardrail, and into the water below. It landed upside down, trapping the passengers in the cold, shallow water, where they drowned.

> This is legit terrifying.

An entire family—two young parents and a little girl—wiped out in a single accident. What's liable to scare is the phenomenon that has reportedly occurred multiple times when folks drive across the bridge or along the dirt road. The radio begins to function as a spirit box, allowing those on the other side to communicate. Suddenly, the voice of a little girl—presumably eight-year-old Jo Dee Kringle—screams, "Help me, Mommy, I can't get out!"

> ALSO BONE-CHILLING REPORTS OF PEOPLE OVERHEARING RADIO CHATTER OF COUNTLESS PLEAS FOR HELP DIRECTED AT A WOMAN NAMED RHONDA.
>
> First organic spirit box appearance I've ever heard of in a ghost story. If that's possible, and I die before Shane, I'm totally going to turn every radio in his immediate radius into a spirit box, anywhere he goes. His home. His car. Lyfts he gets into. Bars he frequents. A sweet way for him to remember the ol' Bergmeister.

Hostess City with the Mostest Ghostess

Savannah, Georgia

Modern readers might be surprised to learn that the founding of Georgia was relatively peaceful. General James Oglethorpe landed on a bluff on the Savannah River in 1733, and, after metaphorically peeing on someone else's fire hydrant by naming the area after King George II, he pledged goodwill with local Yamacraw Indian chief Tomochichi. Slavery was forbidden, too.

Hard left incoming.

High hopes lasted only so long. White people brought bloodshed to the rich red-clay soil with the Revolutionary War and, along with it, slavery. The port in Savannah saw the sale of many human beings, who created a unique Gullah Geechee culture infused with ritual, cuisine, and language from West Africa.

History is not great.

Then came a couple ginormous fires and a yellow fever pandemic that killed one in ten, followed by the Civil War and ongoing racial strife as emancipated people fought for equal rights and freedom from oppression and violence. Suffice it to say that Savannah has seen its share of horror and heartbreak, making it home to all kinds of paranormal activity.

All this awfulness aside, I really enjoyed this town in modern times. Didn't get to have any peaches, though. Which, for the record, I was already after before the Bieber song.

BEAUTIFUL TOWN. MOSSY.

The Horrifying Sorrel Weed Haunted Mansion

RYAN'S PRETTY POSITIVE HE SAW A FULL-BODY APPARITION AT THIS LOCATION BUT, UNFORTUNATELY, DOES NOT HAVE THE FOOTAGE TO BACK UP HIS LUDICROUS CLAIM. CONVENIENT!

Also convenient is your omission that you're the reason I don't have the footage.

'TIS A SHODDY GHOST HUNTER WHO BLAMES HIS BIG, TALL FRIEND.

Like Savannah itself, the Sorrel Weed House hosted significant antebellum brutalities and Revolutionary War carnage. The home's first owner, Francis Sorrel, was born in Santo Domingo, Haiti, in 1793. His father, Colonel Antoine François Sorrel de Rivières, abandoned little Francis at age ten, and it's rumored that his mother, who died one month after his birth, was a free person of color.

This place is haunted as hell. Hated it here. It doesn't pick up too much in the episode, but we hear furniture and whatnot moving upstairs and what sounded like a dog. Shane, of course, thought there was some sort of vagrant or dog that had snuck into a museum guarded around the clock. A thing museums are known for.

YEAH, IT WAS A DOG.

Yeah, LACMA has a real stray dog problem.

Francis moved to Savannah in 1818 to operate his growing import-export business, and in 1822, he married his business partner's niece, Lucinda Ireland Moxley, who came from a wealthy slaveholding family in Virginia. In 1826, he included three enslaved people on his taxes—he would own, on average, six slaves per year. His wife died the next year of yellow fever, and Francis married her sister, Matilda, two years after that.

SEEMED VERY COMMON FOR PEOPLE TO CASUALLY MARRY THEIR DEAD SPOUSE'S SIBLINGS FOR A MINUTE IN HISTORY THERE. PRETTY FREAKY, TBH.

And even if somebody had somehow snuck into the building the night of our shoot, the floor above us was shut off and condemned because of safety reasons. As in, not walkable. Sooooo . . .

UPON RELEASE OF THIS EPISODE, NUMEROUS VIEWERS WHO HAD VISITED THE LOCATION AND MET THE STAFF COMMENTED THAT THE UPSTAIRS RESIDENCE WAS, AT THAT TIME, OCCUPIED BY A CARETAKER WHO LIVES THERE WITH THEIR DOG. IF A CARETAKER LIVES THERE WITH THEIR DOG, AND WE HEARD A PERSON AND A DOG WALKING AROUND, I'M GONNA ASSUME IT'S THE CARETAKER AND THEIR DOG. WHAT A CRAZY CONCLUSION I'VE JUMPED TO.

Ah, yes. The place where all go for their hard-hitting facts: the YouTube comment section.

Henry D. Weed bought the house in 1859, and Matilda died of a concussion in 1860, the result of exiting the balcony of the house next door and landing on her head in the shared courtyard. Whether she left of her own volition is unverifiable, as are the salacious tales surrounding her death. A popular story is that her husband was in a sexual relationship—the term "long-time affair" has been used, which ignores the power dynamics at play when one human owns another—with an enslaved person named Molly, and either Matilda suffered great mental depressions and died by suicide or was pushed. Then Molly was found hanged a week later in the carriage house.

> It was nuts. We heard the claws scratching the floor and everything. And clearly heard what sounded like a chair or an armoire being dragged.
>
> CAN CONFIRM. IT WAS SO CLEAR AND PRESENT, AS IF A PERSON WAS LIVING UPSTAIRS WITH THEIR DOG.
>
> I don't think you understand what *condemned* means.

That Matilda died of a head injury and that Francis did own a person named Molly are on record, but many believe that this purported love-murder triangle is a myth. Still, tour guides say that Francis hangs out in the dining room, Matilda haunts the courtyard, and Molly occupies the carriage house. A theory was circulating that Molly's remains were buried in a depression there, which a team of students at Georgia Southern University investigated in 2017. Turns out it was a trash pit.

Audio with screams and voices and images of strange orbs and human-shaped images have been captured, and one visitor took a photo that he believes shows the ghost of a soldier who died in the bloody Siege of Savannah in 1779. More than a thousand people lost their lives during that battle of the Revolutionary War, perhaps twelve of whom were killed by a cannonball while in a barracks on the site. Today, visitors report seeing shadowy soldier apparitions in the basement.

> This is where I saw a dude walk in front of me. Clear as day. Looked very much like a dude. Until he disappeared into a brick wall. Cool stuff. To be fair, I was barking about the redcoats getting dunked on in the Revolutionary War. So there's that.

The Ghostly Tears
of 17Hundred90 Inn & Restaurant

According to the hotel, Anna in Room 204 is a friendly ghost. There are multiple versions of her story: Sometime in the early 1800s, Anna's folks put her on a ship bound for America to marry an old rich guy. He locked her in Room 204 to prep for their wedding, but the young Irish girl decided death was preferable, and so she flung herself out the window. Or maybe what actually happened was that she was betrothed and yet fell in love with a sailor, who was either single or married. Then, unable to deal with the heartbreak of his ship leaving harbor or the impending doom of marrying some parent-approved doofus, she killed herself. Then again, it could be that her arranged fiancé got wind of her cavorting and killed her himself. Either way, she has apparently chosen to spend her afterlife moving guests' clothing and jewelry around and ruffling bed covers. Some reports describe her as less friendly and more melancholy, even angry. Guests have reported answering the ringing phone to hear a woman sobbing and being awakened at night by droplets of water thought to be Anna's tears.

If I awoke to this sight, I'd die instantly.

WELL, NOW I WISH WE'D GONE HERE AND SPENT THE NIGHT.

Sometimes she turns on the TV or makes glasses explode, particularly when a beautiful woman is present.

Genuinely curious if Anna has a favorite TV show now that she's channel surfing in the modern age. Probably something surprising, like *Sons of Anarchy* or *Bones*.

IT'D BE FUN TO SIT HER DOWN AND FREAK HER ASS OUT WITH *TENET*.

Anna is not the only ghost in the establishment that was named to honor the year of the first free election and the formation of the city government. It is the oldest inn in Savannah, though the structure itself was destroyed in the city's big fires of 1796 and 1820, leaving only the brick foundation. Today it occupies three buildings built in 1823 and 1888, plus a three-story guest house built in 1875. The restaurant and tavern serve Southern specialties like fried green tomatoes and pecan pie. Thaddeus, another friendly ghost, exudes a warm presence and leaves shiny pennies around; presumably this would be a decent tip in the nineteenth century. A less friendly spirit who remains nameless throws spice jars in the inn's kitchen. Staff have reported the sound of clinking, which has been linked to the metal bracelets worn by a cook in the 1850s. She, too, seems to get mad when other women are around.

I'll say it, fried green tomatoes are gross.

MORE FOR ME. GOOD GOD, I LOVE 'EM.

The Spirits of Moon River Brewing

Perhaps one of the most inactive places at the time of our investigation in this show's history.

THE PLACE WE ALWAYS POINT TO WHEN PROVING THAT WE DON'T FABRICATE EVIDENCE, EVEN AT THE COST OF AN EXTREMELY BORING EPISODE. (BUT A GREAT ESTABLISHMENT TO VISIT.)

One year after the Great Savannah Fire of 1820 destroyed 463 buildings, the City Hotel opened its doors on West Bay Street. Branded as a luxury establishment, politicians and businessmen met to discuss politics and business and, inevitably, got drunk and quarreled. One such fight occurred in 1832 and resulted in one of the locale's first deaths. James Stark, a known anti-Semite, got into it with a local Jewish doctor, Philip Minis. Stark then allegedly reached into his pocket, at which point Minis drew his gun and shot him dead. Minis was charged with "justifiable homicide" and went on to a successful career, while Stark stayed dead.

A much less noble death than another Mr. Stark I know.

A couple decades later, Peter Wiltberger bought the hotel and put a live lion and lioness on display to attract guests.

NONE OF THE HOLIDAY INN EXPRESSES WE'VE STAYED AT IN OUR YEARS OF GHOST HUNTING HAVE FEATURED ANY LIONS WHATSOEVER. CANCEL CULTURE RUN AMOK.

Northerner guests and Southerner locals began to play out the mounting national tension, and as the Civil War erupted, the hotel was converted into a hospital to treat patients from both sides of the aisle. Presumably, many soldiers expired within its walls; the building officially closed in 1864 as General Sherman marched toward the sea.

Tough time to be a business owner during the Civil War. Seems like every building became a sniper's nest or a hospital. Kinda strange that most of the western US didn't see a single battle, too.

Over the next hundred years or so, the building went through a few boring iterations—coal storage, general storage, office supply store—until Hurricane David ripped its roof off in 1979. For nearly twenty years, the building sat empty except for all the ghosts. Moon River Brewing returned the establishment to libatious tradition in 1999, without the new owners knowing that the place was haunted until after the papers were signed and the check was cashed.

Well, they certainly put a lid on the paranormal activity the night we were there. I danced on a staircase for Christsakes.

CONTENT, BABY.

One presence is a lady in 1800s attire who has been spotted around the bar, often mistaken for an actor or reenactor until she vanishes into thin air. As a whole, however, the ghosts seem to prefer pushing, and tour guides warn visitors not to taunt them. Obnoxious James Stark pushes a lot. A ghost called Toby, who is thought to be a negative spirit and/or the ghost of a small boy, hangs out in the billiards room and also pushes people. An apparition believed to be a former hotel employee pushed the foreman's wife down the third-floor stairs.

Undoubtedly, a punk-ass move.

NOT SURE IF WE SHOULD BE HONORED OR OFFENDED THAT THESE NASTY LITTLE FREAKS WANTED NOTHING TO DO WITH US.

City of Cities of the Dead

New Orleans, Louisiana

Three hundred years ago, European settlers began to tame the river delta that is now New Orleans. As engineers developed complicated drainage systems, the city sprawled into former swamps and marshlands. Technology had conquered the environment!

Except obviously not. Hurricane Katrina was not the first storm to expose modern man's hubris to show that water goes where water wants to go, despite levees and floodwalls. Early settlers faced this fact while digging graves, which started filling much less than six feet under. Even when weighted down with stones, caskets would float in their graves, and further flooding would push them up and out and away. Boring holes in the coffins to let the water in was tried but abandoned due to the ick factor. Eventually, locals decided to build aboveground vaults to house their departed. In time, these mausoleums and crypts filled cemeteries, lining up like houses on a street, inspiring Mark Twain to call them "cities of the dead."

New Orleans is my favorite US city. Place rules.

THE ONLY TIME I'VE EVER SEEN RYAN BERGARA FULL AFTER A MEAL IS NEW ORLEANS. THAT'S A HUGE ACCOMPLISHMENT. HE ALMOST PASSED OUT.

The Occult of Bloody Mary's Haunted Museum and Voodoo Pharmacy Spirit Shop

What a wonderful lady. Super hospitable and friendly, and she taught us how to dance in a haunted voodoo temple. Good times.

Priestess Miriam Chamani and Priest Oswan Chamani opened the Voodoo Spiritual Temple at 826 North Rampart Street in 1990. Located one block from Congo Square, on the first floor of a two-story Creole cottage built in 1829, the couple set about bringing the community "West African spiritual herbal healing practices" known as voodoo. Believed to have traveled with enslaved peoples from the west coast of Africa or Haiti, this ancient ideology and its rituals were maligned primarily by stans of white supremacy, who cast it as devil worship and made it illegal.

Sounds about right.

The Voodoo Spiritual Temple had zero connection to tenants Addie Hall and Zack Bowen, who lived upstairs in the early aughts. In 2006, Zack murdered Addie, dismembered her body, and then, eleven days later, jumped off the New Orleans Hotel. He left a detailed murder-suicide note and the spray-painted words "I'm a total failure" and "Please help me stop the pain" on the walls of the apartment the couple shared.

I really, really did not enjoy being in this place.

IT'S ONE OF THE FEW PLACES WE'VE BEEN TO THAT HAD A VERY *RECENT* CRIME, AND THAT CERTAINLY MADE IT, FOR LACK OF A BETTER WORD, A BUMMER.

To reiterate, one had nothing to do with the other—one was a space for spiritual practice and education, one a gruesome scene wrought by domestic violence, substance abuse, and mental illness. In fact, the temple didn't move until after an electrical fire in 2016. But some still believe—as does museum proprietor and eleventh-generation Creole mystic Bloody Mary—that the combo of this horrific crime, years of voodoo ritual, and two hundred years of French Quarter history has made the building a paranormal hot spot. Add to that a doll nursery, a Victorian séance room, and a psychic spa. Bloody Mary claims that thirteen resident ghosts haunt the location, including those of Addie and Zack.

Horrible house. Horrible tragedy. Bloody Mary rules. Next.

The Haunted Quarters
of the Dauphine Orleans Hotel

Another old haunt of ours. The place where I heard the infamous footsteps. When I told Shane about them, we were walking back to our off-site hotel where the crew was staying, and he told me that it must have been the people above me. I said it was highly unlikely that the folks above stomped and walked around nonstop all night like a bunch of maniacs. He thought otherwise. So that's why I walked back to the Dauphine to ask the people upstairs if they had, in fact, walked around all night, and of course they told me they had not and that they had heard the footsteps, too. And that's how that clip made it into the show. Now that I think of it, I wonder if that couple ever watched the ep.

IF I HAD A DOLLAR FOR EVERY GHOST THAT WAS CONVENIENTLY CONFINED TO AN INACCESSIBLE ROOM, I COULD BUY THE DAUPHINE ORLEANS HOTEL AND TURN IT INTO MY PING-PONG ROOM.

In an attempt to curtail gambling and prostitution in the Crescent City, Alderman Sidney Story proposed a designated debauchery zone within a sixteen-block radius in 1897. Not all that into YOLO himself, the council member would come to accept the honor of inspiring the red-light district's nickname of Storyville.

You can't designate a debauchery zone and then sit on a tower of self-righteousness. Speaking of debauchery, boy, did we get up to some shenanigans on Bourbon Street the night before the shoot.

WE GOT BOURBON-FACED ON SHIT STREET, AS THE LOCALS SAY.

May Bailey's bordello on the precinct's fringe had long been in operation by the time it was made official. Just a couple blocks east of Bourbon Street party central and a few blocks up from the Mississippi River, it was a favorite hangout of Confederate soldiers, who stopped by for one of May's famous cocktails and some nookie before marching out. Ladies of the night led their johns up the stairs to what is now known as the bordello suite above the bar to give them what they'd paid for. On the way home, injured soldiers returned to the adjoining hotel, perhaps feeling less amorous, to recover.

That bordello suite had a weird-ass vibe.

SMELLED LIKE A GAMESTOP, YEAH.

Today you can see the establishment's city license, signed in 1857 by the madame herself and the mayor and spotlighted with a little red light. Patrons report being touched on the leg—just the leg—under the bar and getting locked in the bathroom.

Hey, I wasn't even going there, pal. Don't you push your perviness on me.

I WAS GOING THERE. THIS WRETCHED BOOK READ MY PERV MIND.

The presence of a particular working girl can be sensed, and a man believed to be an angry soldier can be heard pacing and stomping at all hours of the night.

ahem

Guests have seen a bridal-themed apparition known as the Lost Bride of the Dauphine Orleans Hotel, who, according to legend, is May Bailey's sister Millie. As the story goes, Millie's fiancé was shot during a gambling dispute on the morning of their wedding, and, consumed by grief, she refused to relinquish her wedding dress and so wears it for all of eternity.

Nice place, honestly. Full of ghosts.

YEAH, HORRIFYING. SLEPT GREAT. TUB DIDN'T WORK.

Interring Well Is the Best Revenge

From the sky, the Metairie Cemetery looks just like the race track it once was. Metairie Race Course was built on rare high ground in 1838, but the investors made one big mistake: They refused membership to Louisiana State Lottery Company founder, suspected shyster, and devout grunge-holder Charles T. Howard. Unused to not getting his way, he vowed to turn the exclusive jockey club into a graveyard.

| You gotta almost respect the pettiness.

Which he did, eventually. During the Civil War, the track was closed for use as a Confederate campsite, and in the hard economic times of Reconstruction, Howard saw his chance. He planned to keep it classy, sectioning off a portion of the former infield for the affluent's final resting place, or Millionaire's Row. Regular folk would be buried within the 150 acres, too, along with military men, famous restaurateurs, politicians, and musicians. PBS Pinchback, Louisiana's only Black governor, occupies one of the seven thousand tombs, as does Popeyes Fried Chicken magnate Al Copeland.

Can only hope his casket is sprinkled with that incredible Cajun Sparkle. Can't get enough of it. God, I love Popeyes.

THIS IS AS GOOD A TIME AS ANY TO GET THIS PSA OUT THERE. THE FINE FOLKS AT POPEYES AREN'T GONNA BEND OVER BACKWARD AND JUST HAND OUT THE CAJUN SPARKLE. YOU HAVE TO ASK FOR THOSE LITTLE PINK PACKETS BY NAME. DUST OF THE HEAVENS, THAT STUFF.

Rumor has it that Charles T. Howard himself makes awkward noises from within his tomb. Police Chief David Hennessey, sporting his uniform, roams the grounds, serving justice from beyond the grave. He'd made the mistake of conflating all Italians with mafia, stirring up international ire and getting himself shot. Unable to wait for a fair trial, fifty or so equally confused people stormed the jail in which the Italian and Italian-American suspects were being held for a retaliatory mass lynching. Those eleven are not buried in Metairie Cemetery.

Uh, what just happened?

HISTORY OR SOMETHING. I'M NOT SURE. ALL I CAN REALLY ASCERTAIN IS THAT EVERYBODY INVOLVED IS DEAD, AND CHARLES T. HOWARD FARTS FROM HIS GRAVE.

Then there's Josie Arlington (née Mary Anne Duebler), a renowned madame who died on Valentine's Day 1914. There are multiple versions of the story of Josie's rise to fame; in her youth, her name was regularly featured in the newspapers. Through chutzpah and elbow grease, she went from bruiser madame of a blue-collar bordello to wealthy madame of a gorgeous four-story mansion named the Arlington.

Good on ya, Josie.

Perhaps she took her cue from Charles T. Howard when she decided to purchase a plot among those who had used her services but socially shunned her. She commissioned a red marble mausoleum, with two flaming pillars and a bronze statue of a woman holding a bouquet of roses, her other hand outstretched toward the tomb's entry. Josie's remains attracted vandals and eventually were relocated, but her mausoleum still stands. Many claim that the stone flames atop the pillars appear to be burning at night, and the statue itself has been known to move among the graves of those who considered themselves her betters.

I believe in ghosts, but I draw the line at cemetery statues going full *Night at the Museum*.

ALWAYS LOVE TO HEAR WHERE THE GHOST PEOPLE DRAW THEIR LINES.

Literally a Witch Hunt Village

Salem, Massachusetts

The Puritans left England and its loosey-goosey church in 1630, hoping to found a colony of people who took things seriously in America. They established a legal code in 1641, with hierarchy of crimes, from most worst to least worst: idolatry, witchcraft, blasphemy, murder, poisoning, and bestiality.

> GLAD BLASPHEMY IS BACK ON THE MENU THESE DAYS. EXTREMELY FUN TO BLASPHEME. CHECK THIS OUT: GOD IS A BUTTHOLE.

> "Murder" sneaking onto this list at #4 is a real underdog story.

So, theoretically, you would get in less trouble for killing a person and/or making love to a donkey than you would for saying mean things about the Man Upstairs or engaging in the ill-defined practice of witchcraft.

> JC doesn't mess around. (Initials used to avoid blasphemy.)

Four hundred years of witch-hunting in Europe had seen the execution of tens of thousands of people, mostly women, but the craze there was no longer at fever pitch by the time it reached New England. In Salem, from the winter of 1692 to the spring of 1693, there were over two hundred accusations of witchcraft, twenty executions, and possibly thirteen more deaths in jail.

> Yoooo, I'm straight up not having a good time right now.

Why? Well, there are a few theories:

Theory #1: Economic/environmental issues: A "little ice age" caused economic hardship in the region, for which someone needed to be blamed.

Theory #2: Medical issues: The accusers were exposed to the ergot fungus, found in grains like rye, which can cause hallucinations, seizure-like muscle contractions, vertigo, and crawling and tingling sensations.

Theory #3: Mass hysteria.

Theory #4: Sociopolitical issues: Men in power stirred up paranoia in order to maintain power.

Theory #5: Witches are real.

> Theory #6: Humans are stupid.

Whether one or more of these theories are true (though probably not Theory #5), we will never know for certain. Today, the city honors the victims of the Salem Witch Trials by keeping their stories alive.

The Ministerial Ghost
at Samuel Parris Archeology Site

In perverse Puritan logic, it was actually a feather in Reverend Samuel Parris's cap that the witches targeted his household—that meant he was super holy. He certainly needed the boost, as well as the distraction. He'd taken over the ministry post in Salem only a few years earlier, in 1688, and from the start he'd rubbed folks the wrong way. He wanted to make getting full membership to the church more difficult, and he wanted to own the ministry house outright rather than just occupying it when he was serving. So perhaps it was a relief when his nine-year-old daughter, Elizabeth, and eleven-year-old niece, Abigail Williams, started acting strangely in a freezing January 1692. They screamed and contorted themselves and threw things, claiming that an invisible being was biting and pinching them. Even worse, they skipped prayers and interrupted sermons.

All of this because two children started wiggin' out. Pretty wild. Humans aren't complicated folks.

PROBABLY JUST DIDN'T WANNA GO TO CHURCH BECAUSE IT'S BORING.

The village's sole and partially illiterate doctor diagnosed witchcraft, and other girls soon followed suit, including twelve-year-old Ann Putnam and Elizabeth Hubbard, the sixteen-year-old niece of the esteemed doctor, landing on poor and pregnant Sarah Good, old and grumpy Sarah Osborne, and enslaved person Tituba as the source of their malarky. Of the accused, Tituba was the only one to offer a confession, which she did with enough gusto to satisfy the court that she was at least trying to fight off the devil. She survived her year in prison, while the two Sarahs died, of hanging and while in jail, respectively.

If he couldn't read, then how did he learn to be a doctor? Textbooks are obviously out, so what's he going off of? I imagine this dude just stared at that rudimentary chalk-line diagram of the human body for three years and continuously muttered, "Interesting, interesting . . ." and then one day someone called him a doctor.

I THINK DOCTORS IN THOSE DAYS MOSTLY JUST HAD TO BE ABLE TO DECIPHER WHETHER OR NOT A PERSON WAS DEAD.

Some believe that Samuel Parris could have nipped the hysteria in the bud but instead chose to feed it, delivering sermons with titles like "Christ Knows How Many Devils There Are" and "These Shall Make War with the Lamb" and saying outright that there were witches in Salem. After the trials, Samuel refused to pay Tituba's bail, and it is believed that she was eventually sold. Some of the family members of the killed blamed him and tried to get him fired, instigating a series of lawsuits. Although he never apologized, he did express regret over the weight given to spectral evidence. He died at the ripe old age of sixty-seven in the house of his daughter and former witch trials accuser, thirty-five miles away from Salem. But does his spirit still reside in the home he was so desperate to own?

I hope so, so I can pay him a visit and give him a paranormal punch in the balls.

HERE, HERE!

The Magisterial Ghost
of the Jonathan Corwin House

Though it's called the Witch House, no known witches resided there. Instead, Judge Corwin, heir to one of the largest fortunes in New England, and his family moved into the stately home in 1675 and occupied it until his death in 1718. Built in 1642, it is the only remaining structure from that era.

A crazy lookin' house, by all accounts.

GENUINELY LOVE THE VIBES OF THIS HOUSE. IF WE SELL ENOUGH OF THESE BOOKS, I WILL BUY THAT HOUSE.

Magistrates Corwin and John Hathorne were the ones to push the afflicted girls to name names. After Sarah G., Sarah O., and Tituba came Martha Corey and Sarah G.'s four-year-old daughter, Dorcas, who acted especially suspicious by being shy when a bunch of grown men yelled at her.

"Hey, that little girl has skin flaps that intermittently cover her eyeballs. Gotta be a witch."

BABIES AIN'T WITCHIN'.

Over the next few months, the hysteria grew and family members accused one another. The accused had no legal counsel, and at each trial, Hathorne and Corwin would ask, "Are you a witch?" "Have you seen Satan?" "If you are innocent, then why are people acting all wonky?"

WHAT A MASTERFUL TRAP THEY LAID WITH "ARE YOU A WITCH?"

People trying to clean house before the holidays.

Officially, 152 people were accused of witchcraft, blamed for everything from pinching to spoiled produce to night terrors. One accused witch, Rebecca Nurse, even had the gall to lecture a man for allowing his pig to root in her garden. Then that man died. Eighty-year-old Giles Corey was the only one of the accused who died by torture rather than hanging. He was accused while standing up for his wife after she was accused, but instead of protesting his innocence or confessing his guilt, he simply refused to stand trial. His penalty was getting smooshed to death by heavy stones. Corwin ordered him to be buried in an unmarked grave on Gallows Hill.

Undeniably tough way to go.

IT'S BEEN ON MY TO-DO LIST FOREVER, BUT ONE OF THESE HALLOWEENS I INTEND TO DON SOME PURITAN GARB AND FASHION GIANT MARSHMALLOWS AND GRAHAM CRACKERS TO HANG ON EITHER SIDE OF ME. GILES S'MOREY! IT WORKS ON MULTIPLE LEVELS BECAUSE HE WAS SMOOSHED! (NOT INTENDED AS A SLEIGHT. I THINK THE GUY WAS A BALLER.)

Absolutely tasteless. You. Not s'mores.

Presumably, after a long day of examining the accusers and the accused at the Salem Village Meetinghouse, Judge Corwin would come home, take off his steeple-crowned hat, loosen his jerkin, and do whatever it was that Puritans did to relax.

Pray, probably. Lest they want to be accused of witchcraft themselves. If I lived in this era, I'm making a necklace with a full-ass Bible as the pendant. Just to leave no doubt.

I WOULDN'T EVEN BOTHER. I'M AS GOOD AS SMOOSHED.

Soon after the trials, Judge Sam Sewall apologized for his part. The jury apologized. Ann Putnam, who had accused sixty-two people, apologized. (Even the state of Massachusetts apologized in 1957.) Corwin never apologized, not even the "I'm sorry you felt bad about all those executions" variety. He is buried in a marked grave at Broad Street Cemetery.

Pretty ballsy to baselessly crush someone's bones with stones and then be like, "Hey, my b, that one's on me."

The Innocents of Gallows Hill

"I am as innocent as the child unborn," said gossipy tavern owner Bridget Bishop, which is obviously something a guilty person would say. She was the first to be hanged on Gallows Hill, on June 10, 1692. Next for the rope, on July 19, were Rebecca Nurse, Sarah Good, Susannah Martin, Elizabeth Howe, and Sarah Wildes. All but Sarah Good were over the age of fifty-five, and most had been accused of witchcraft before. Grandmother Rebecca Nurse just so happened to have a longstanding dispute with accuser Ann Putnam's family about borders between their land holdings, and her poor opinion of Samuel Parris was well known. Sixty-five-year-old Sarah Wildes had once been accused of wearing a silk scarf.

> Kinda nuts that in the book of American history, one that includes two World Wars, the most batshit and indefensible chapters we did to ourselves.
>
> I WISH THIS WERE LIKE THE THIRD ACT OF *A MUPPETS' CHRISTMAS CAROL* WHERE GONZO AND RIZZO ARE LIKE, "THIS SUCKS. WE'RE GONNA LEAVE FOR A WHILE."

Hanged one month later were Martha Carrier and the male contingent: Reverend John Proctor, George Burroughs, John Willard, and George Jacobs Sr. Most of them were critics of the trials, and thirty-three-year-old Carrier was involved in a land dispute; her children were coerced into testifying against her. Mary Easty, Ann Pudeator, Alice Parker, Mary Parker, Wilmott Redd, Margaret Scott, Samuel Wardell, and Martha Corey were the last to die on Gallows Hill, on September 22. None of the executed ever admitted to witchcraft. The bodies of these nineteen people were buried in unmarked graves and, to this day, have not been discovered. No wonder Gallows Hill has a reputation for being haunted. Visitors claim to hear disembodied screams and the crack of ropes suddenly stretched. Others have seen a Lady in White.

> Oh yeah, this is a book about ghosts. Almost forgot as we took a walk down memory lane of one of humanity's greatest embarrassments.
>
> LADIES IN WHITE JUST GETTING CHUCKED INTO EVERY ONE OF THESE GHOST STORIES LIKE BONUS FRIES IN A FIVE GUYS BAG.

Today, a memorial to these victims is located on Liberty Street, a mile and a half from Gallows Hill, half a mile from the house of the man who ordered the graves to be unmarked, and six miles from the home site of the man who might have put a stop to it. Four-foot-high granite walls surround granite benches with the names, means of execution, and date of death etched into the stone.

> Still can't believe this happened. Get me out of this town.

The Town Too Tough to Die

Tombstone, Arizona

Thank god, a town with some order.

Nine years before Geronimo surrendered to General George Crook, aka the Tan Wolf, prospector Ed Schieffelin joined a scouting mission against the Chiricahua Apaches in 1877. When off duty, he stayed at Camp Huachuca, choosing to spend his free time rock hunting in the surrounding desert. This hobby puzzled his fellow scouts, who insisted that instead of rocks, he'd "find his tombstone."

"They're minerals, Marie."

HEY, FROM THAT SHOW, YEAH!

Ed found silver. As a big eff you to the haters, he called the first mine the Tombstone.

Petty points to Ed. Love to see it.

IT'S SIMULTANEOUSLY A GREAT RAZZ AND A METAL NAME FOR A TOWN.

With brother Albert Schieffelin and friend Richard Gird, he developed a bunch of claims in southeastern Arizona, which they dubbed the Graveyard, the Ground Hog, the Owl Nest, the Lucky Cuss, the Tough Nut, and the Contention.

You sure the Tough Nut wasn't a brothel in town? Sorry, let's keep going here.

A town officially formed in 1879 and was named for its proximity to that first mine. Ed sold his share of the claims for $500,000 in 1880, presumably laughing all the way to the bank. In a single year, Tombstone grew to six thousand residents, capping at twenty-seven thousand just a few years later. Of course, the promise of silver attracted prospectors, adventure-seekers, outlaws, and people who generally didn't get along in civilized society or had a reason to run from it. With such speedy development came the usual class tensions and political power struggles. Throw in lots of booze and testosterone—at Tombstone's height, it had at least one hundred saloons and a thriving red-light district—and you have yourself a recipe for a Wild West showdown.

I don't know why I love the West so much. By all accounts, it was violent and awful, but I can't help but daydream about roaming the open plains on my horse and stoppin' in town for a nice stiff glass of bourbon.

I'VE BASICALLY LIVED IT ON ACCOUNT OF MY PLAYTHROUGH OF *RED DEAD REDEMPTION 2*. HAD A HORSE NAMED JINGLEJOHN.

The Shootout That Haunts the O.K. Coral

Early in Tombstone's founding, two factions emerged: that of the ranching Clanton and McLaury families, who aligned themselves with Sheriff John Behan; and that of the business elite, including the mayor, a mining magnate, and a minister backed by the Earp family and their friend Doc Holliday. Each of the "lawmen" Earp brothers—Morgan, Wyatt, and the town's marshal, Virgil—had a stupendous mustache, while "cowboys" Ike Clanton and Frank McLaury sported goatees that would make the devil proud. Billy Clanton and Tom McLaury were the cleanest cut of the bunch.

When they cast Sam Elliot to play you, they're basically handing you a certification that you have an excellent, excellent mustache.

On the morning of October 26, 1881, everyone was grumpy after a long night of drinking and gambling. Rude words were exchanged, and the McLaury brothers and the Clanton brothers went to the vacant lot behind the O.K. Corral, with one gun per family. An unarmed friend named Billy Claibourne joined them. The Earps and Doc Holliday arrived, one gun per man, plus a bonus shotgun.

"Throw up your hands! I've come to disarm you!" yelled Marshal Virgil.

"Don't shoot, I don't want to fight," said Billy Clanton.

"You sons of bitches have been looking for a fight," said Wyatt Earp, "and now you have it."

It is unclear who fired the first of the nearly thirty gunshots that killed Billy Clanton and Tom and Frank McLaury. Morgan got a bullet in the leg, Virgil in the shoulder, Doc in the hip. Ike Clanton and Billy Claibourne had turned tail and run and so were unscathed.

Tough to get murked five days before Halloween.

IT'S LIKE BECOMING SANTA FIVE DAYS BEFORE CHRISTMAS.

Uh, yeah.

Wyatt Earp, also unharmed, Virgil Earp, and Doc Holliday were charged with murder but acquitted. Eight weeks after the fight, on December 28, Virgil was ambushed but survived; in March 1882, Morgan died after being shot in the back by Ike Clanton and four other cowboys during a game of billiards at the Campbell & Hatch Saloon, what is now the Red Buffalo Trading Company. Wyatt, a very pissed deputy marshal, went on a month-long vengeance tour that left two dead before he and Doc rode off into the sunset. Some believe, however, that though they died elsewhere, the lawmen's spirits can be found still fighting the cowboys at the O.K. Corral, the feed and livery stables that started it all.

What a treat that we got to see this crazy little town.

GREAT TAFFY!

The Wild West Ghosts of Big Nose Kate's Saloon

Did Big Nose Kate have a big nose? Perhaps. But some believe Kate Elder was given that nickname because of her nosy ways, including sticking her nose in the business of her SO Doc Holliday. As in, acting as his accomplice and getting him out of trouble, despite the severe beatings he regularly gave her.

> Weird, they didn't show that in the movies.
>
> I'M STARTING TO SUSPECT THAT MAYBE WESTERNS ARE NOT THE MOST ACCURATE OF HISTORICAL DOCUMENTS. *RANGO* WAS THE TIPPING POINT FOR ME.

Whatever the reason for the nickname, the building named in her honor was originally the site of the Grand Hotel, which was indeed grand until a fire destroyed it only two years after its construction in 1880. In that time, however, the McLaury brothers stayed as guests, their signatures on the registry the night before their big gunfight. Also during that time, Big Nose either owned a saloon and brothel or just worked in one. A career sex worker, she met Doc in 1870 and worked in brothels wherever they found a decent town for drinking and gambling.

> We actually investigated this place ourselves. The site rep is caught in the background of one of the shots and probably scared half the audience to death. Scared me, too, when I saw it. Alas, no ghost. Just a person.
>
> RYAN GENUINELY NEVER INTENDS TO LET STUFF LIKE THAT SLIP PAST, BUT IT HAPPENED ONCE OR TWICE. ALWAYS SO FUN TO EXPLAIN IT AWAY.

The locale at 417 East Allen Street has had a drinkery in some form since 1882. One bartender reported seeing a "breathtaking" woman in a dark 1880s-style dress, holding a parasol, and watching the crowd before disappearing. The ghost believed to be that of Doc Holliday has been spotted. Cowboy spirits have been seen standing at the bar and in doorways. One manager claims to be frequently physically assaulted by ghosts, and many have felt the touch, pinch, shove, and even choke of unseen hands.

> Just once, I'd like to see a ghost put someone in a sleeper hold. Not to me, of course—to Shane. If anybody could reach him, that is.

Drinks levitate to hit servers in the chest or face. The sound of voices and dancing boots can be heard from the dance floor. A local photojournalist captured an image of what appears to be a horse apparition at the bar.

> Ghost horse is a wild thing to claim, I won't lie. Also, this suggests that back in the day horses walked into establishments and parked it by the bar on the reg? Don't know about that one.

> IT'S LIKE THAT OLD JOKE. HORSE WALKS INTO A BAR AND THE BARTENDER IS LIKE, "A HORSE? AT THE BAR? WHAT'S HE DOING HERE? HOW'D HE GET IN HERE? DOES THIS HORSE BELONG TO ANYBODY? HE'S EATING ALL THE PEANUTS!"

In the basement lives the specter of the Swamper, a former janitor whose bedroom occupied one dark corner. It is said that he dug tunnels from the basement to the mine shafts that ran underneath the town and that he would go to the mines at night to steal silver. His spirit remains to guard his treasure trove, rumored to be buried under the saloon, and his moans of distress can be heard by anyone who dares to enter his tunnel.

> Swamper sounds like a nasty dude. I like him.

The Wickedest Spirits of Bird Cage Theatre

"**H**er beauty was sold for an old man's gold," wrote Arthur Lamb for his and Harry Von Tilzer's 1899 song "A Bird in a Gilded Cage," thought to be inspired by the Bird Cage Theatre. This gambling hall, saloon, and brothel operated around the clock and year-round from 1881 to 1889. Sex workers welcomed their clients into the cage-like compartments on the second-story balcony, then drew the drapes so that they could get down to business.

The cacophony of debauchery here was probably mindnumbing.

ALMOST LIKE A PROTO-RAINFOREST CAFÉ BUT SWEATIER.

The main stage and orchestra pit offered other entertainment, occasionally with performances by some of the era's hottest acts. In the basement was a poker room that once hosted the longest poker game in history, which had a $1,000 buy-in and supposedly lasted eight years, five months, and three days, ending only because of the building flooding with the same groundwater that was seeping into the mines.

They were banging it out to a soundtrack in this joint!? Wonder if the music was sultry and moody, like an old-timey equivalent to the Weeknd. Hard to imagine the typical goofy-ass Western piano not ruining the mood. Then again, you're in a bird cage. I guess all bets are off.

WOULD BE COOL IF THEY ONLY PLAYED "SANDSTORM."

During that time, there was an exchange of over $10 million. No wonder the *New York Times* allegedly called the Bird Cage Theatre "the wildest, wickedest night spot between Basin Street and the Barbary Coast."

This entire place was probably as sticky as your hands after roasting marshmallows.

The venue shut down when the town went bust, and the soiled doves were forced to pack up their purses and move along. Forty-five years later, in 1934, the new owners found everything exactly as it had been left, including the poker table. There are reportedly 140 bullet holes in the building's walls and ceilings, and it is rumored that a total of twenty-six people were killed there. One murder involved a courtesan named Gold Dollar, who stabbed colleague Margarita with a stiletto knife for flirting with her client. Margarita haunts the building to this day, along with thirty other ghosts, some of whom are topless for all of eternity.

We didn't get to investigate here when we were in town, which was an enormous bummer. I love a good theme.

WE TOOK A TOUR, THOUGH! OBVIOUSLY, IT WOULD HAVE BEEN COOL TO HUNT THERE, BUT SOMETIMES IT'S JUST NICE TO TAKE IN A PLACE WITHOUT CARRYING AROUND A STUPID SCREAMING RADIO.

The Old Smoke

London, United Kingdom

For the last few thousand years, it wasn't all tea parties on the southwest side of what is now England. Seems that the various peoples who lived there weren't always all that nice to one another, and when folks weren't dying of disease and childbirth and horse accidents, they were cutting off one another's heads and hanging each other by the neck and ripping one another limb from limb.

'ALLO 'ALLO!

The ol' foggy town across the pond. Boy, did we have fun here. Too much fun . . . I digress. Let's talk proper ghosts.

The Headless Specters of London Bridge

The first London Bridge was made of wood and built around 80 CE by the Romans, who abandoned it in 410 CE when they left Britain. Records covering the next few hundred years are scarce, but there is a 984 CE record about an accusation of witchcraft, which resulted in the drowning of a widow at London Bridge.

> Ah shit, here we go again.
>
> I MEAN, FOR ALL OF AMERICA'S WITCHCRAFT SINS, EUROPE'S GOT US HANDILY BEAT. BONA FIDE SICKOS OVER THERE.
>
> Great castles, though.

Storms and general weathering required repair and replacement of the wooden structures every few decades, as did the aftermath of a battle between the Danes and the Saxons and Vikings in 1014, an event that inspired Fergie's "London Bridge."

> Can confirm, it still slaps. What's she up to nowadays?

London Bridge has seen untold number of drownings, suicides, and death by warfare, as well as pre-executions and post-executions. The first stone bridge was completed in 1209, and it came to be used not only for traversing the River Thames but for the display of decapitated heads and dismembered limbs. This was especially popular from 1304 to 1678, when horses were used to draw and quarter traitors and a Keeper of the Heads was kept on staff to tar the heads and stick them on spikes.

"It's a modest living, but I've learned to add my own artistic flair to it."

HOW DOES A PERSON EVEN LAND THAT GIG? THOUGH, I GUESS I'M A SKEPTIC GHOST HUNTER. SO. NEVER MIND.

Body parts were sent elsewhere—not sure what the title for that job was.

DeadEx.

HEY-O!

Famous decorative heads included those of Braveheart William Wallace, Catholic conspirator Guy Fawkes, Peasants' Revolt leader Wat Tyler, and Lord Protector Oliver Cromwell, whose body was exhumed two years after his death so it could be posthumously beheaded.

Pretty much a skull by that point, no? I imagine that takes some of the umph away, if that's what you're into.

KIND OF ON PAR WITH REPLAYING AN ARGUMENT IN YOUR HEAD AFTER THE FACT AND THINKING OF A ZINGER IN THE SHOWER.

These decaying visages might have overlooked the bridge crossing of those who'd been sentenced to die by hanging, a trek from the prison in Southwark to the scaffold at Wapping. Over four hundred pirates, smugglers, and mutineers made this final march, traditionally stopping at a pub on the way for a last drink. Some of the heads, once they were as thoroughly rotted as jack-o'-lanterns in June, were taken none too far for disposal—to the London Tombs below.

Is it weird that I wouldn't mind being one of these heads? Preferably after I died of natural causes, of course. But I think it would be neat to be one of these heads. Just posthumously catching some rare London rays.

YOUR HEAD WOULD LOOK GOOD ON A PIKE, HONESTLY.

The Subterranean Terrors
of the London Tombs

What a nightmare it was to walk through this place alone.

Throughout London's long history, there have been several epidemics. From 1347 to 1351, the Black Death killed an estimated 1.5 million Britons, a third of the population; the bubonic plague wiped out one hundred thousand Londoners in 1665. The departed were buried without coffins, ceremony, or much by way of long-term planning in order to prevent further spread of infection.

There's a clip floating around of Shane from this episode where it seems like he predicts the Covid-19 pandemic. I'm not saying that he's Nostradamus or anything, but it definitely is eerie.

NO COMMENT.

To manage all the dead bodies, mass graves known as "plague pits" were dug, seemingly at random, their locations rarely recorded. John Stow's 1598 Survey of London suggests that up to 150,000 bodies had been buried in plague pits throughout London—and that was sixty-seven years *before* the Great Plague. According to urban legend, this is why the London Underground, the world's first underground railway, opened in 1863, takes such a meandering route. This may be based on a kernel of truth; according to the author of *Necropolis: London and Its Dead*, "Excavations for the Piccadilly Line between Knightsbridge and South Kensington Underground stations unearthed a pit so dense with human remains that it could not be tunneled through. This is said to account for the curving nature of the track between the two stations."

Absolutely bonkers. But shoutout to the Tube. Might be number 1 for me in my public transit rankings. Sorry NYC, I know you get all hot and bothered anytime you hear the word subway, but I think the Tube is better.

ALSO, JUST EXQUISITE TILE AESTHETIC ON THE UNDERGROUND. I KNOW YOU DIDN'T PICK UP THIS BOOK TO HEAR US GET ALL HOT AND BOTHERED ABOUT TILE, BUT IT'S REALLY GREAT TILE. I HOPE IT'S NOT TAKEN FOR GRANTED THERE.

One particular catacomb had been sealed for decades before becoming the tourist attraction London Tombs. The developers claim that while they were excavating the location in 2007, they uncovered hundreds of bodies plus a second "haul of bones" found under concrete. Police pathologists reportedly dated the bones to the mid-seventeenth century, the time of the Great Plague. But some of the skulls sported holes, suggesting death by spike impalement rather than plague. This scared construction workers, who reported strange noises, disappearing tools, electricity surges, and the hair-on-the-back-of-your-neck feeling of being watched. Still, the London Bridge Experience, featuring the London Tomb, is now open to tourists. There have been reports of hideous visions, poltergeist attacks, bodiless faces suspended in air, and dark figures roaming the hallways.

We got some pretty good stuff here. One incident of note happened off camera while we changed batteries, when we heard what sounded like walking or talking, if I recall. Unfortunately, couldn't scramble fast enough to get the cameras on.

SUCKS!

Haunted Viaduct Tavern

A lovely bar. Shoutout to my dude Liam. Made one of the best gin drinks I've ever had.

ABSOLUTE MANIAC, LIAM. BASICALLY HANDED US FISHBOWLS FULL OF GIN. ONE OF LONDON'S GREATEST MEN.

For two hundred years, six hundred sheep and fifty bulls were slaughtered daily at the major meat market on Newgate Street. It moved in 1869, the year that Queen Victoria officially opened the Holborn Viaduct, and the gin palace Viaduct Tavern opened its doors soon thereafter. The diverse clientele included everyone from lawyers and government officials to the working class to criminals and those going to and from the nearby centuries-old Newgate Gaol.

Will never forget Shane pronouncing this as "Gayowl." It's pronounced *jail*, but it was nice to be on the other end of a mispronunciation for once.

SOMEBODY'S GOTTA INTRODUCE OLD-TIMEY LONDONERS TO MY FRIEND CLIPPY. IT LOOKS LIKE YOU'RE TRYING TO SPELL JAIL.

These patrons swilled gin, which was cheap—cheaper than beer—due to some patriotic legislation meant to irritate the French and diminish French brandy sales and encourage more at-home spirit production.

Here we are patting ourselves on the backs for normalizing working from home, and the French had us beat by over 250 years.

I WONDER HOW MUCH ENGLISH LEGISLATION WAS DRAFTED UP WITH THE EXPRESS PURPOSE OF IRRITATING THE FRENCH?

People henceforth got faced. Entertainment occasionally took the form of executions at the gallows across the street at 8 a.m., as the bells of Holy Sepulchre Church tolled. (Unlike nearby Magpie & Stump, the Viaduct Tavern did not offer "hanging breakfasts.") Serial baby killer Amelia Dyer was hanged there in 1896 and haunted the gaol thereafter.

"Serial baby killer" is as unpleasant as a three-word combination can get.

ALSO, LOW-HANGIN' FRUIT FOR A SERIAL KILLER.

Occasionally, customers shot off their guns, as did an off-duty World War I soldier, whose ricocheting bullet tore a hole in a grand painting and the ornate ceiling. That soldier is now a ghost, of course, who keeps company with another thirsty ghost who steals drinks at the bar when patrons aren't paying attention. The ghost of the landlady occupies the cashier's booth—she didn't trust her staff, so customers had to exchange their pence for gin tokens before heading to the bar. Upstairs, in the loft, the ghost believed to be that of a murdered sex worker runs on the stairs, slams doors, pokes electricians, and elevates rolled-up carpeting.

Lmao at "pokes electricians." This ghost has a type!

THIS GHOST REPEATEDLY TYPES "5318008" INTO CALCULATORS. WHAT CAN IT MEAN?

Less cute ghosts occupy the cellar, which houses cell rooms that some think are the last remaining cells of either the abysmal next-door gaol or abysmal next-door Giltspur Street Compter, a debtor's prison demolished in 1854. Haunting is heightened by the underground stream—paranormal experts believe that water carries energy that catalyzes paranormal activity.

Paranormal expert here. I don't believe this.

THIS IS WHY I RESPECT YOU.

In the 1980s, the lights went out and the door slammed closed, trapping the landlord. A voice then said, "There's just us two down here now."

Genuinely chilling note to end this book on, as there really is just us two here now. Writer's gone, just you and me, big guy, with a lot of blank pages left. They can't stop us now.

YOU'RE RIGHT! LET'S STOP NOW.

FURTHER READING AND LISTENING

Ghostland: An American History of Haunted Places, Colin Dickley
Haunted America series, Arcadia Publishing
Most Haunted series, Matthew Clark
The New England Grimpendium: A Guide to Macabre and Ghastly Sites,
    J.W. Ocker
*The New York Grimpendium: A Guide to Macabre and Ghastly Sites in New
    York State,* J.W. Ocker
*Weird California: Your Travel Guide to California's Local Legends and Best
    Kept Secrets,* Greg Bishop, Joe Oesterle, Mike Marinacci
*Weird Oregon: Your Travel Guide to Washington's Local Legends and Best
    Kept Secrets,* Jefferson Davis and Al Eufrasio
*Weird Washington: Your Travel Guide to Washington's Local Legends and
    Best Kept Secrets,* Jefferson Davis and Al Eufrasio
History Goes Bump podcast
Legends of America podcast
New England Legends podcast
Southern Gothic podcast

ACKNOWLEDGMENTS

We are grateful to the many, many ghost hunters, ghost storytellers, ghost legend curators, historians, historical record keepers, and ghost researchers—there are too many to name. Many thanks to BuzzFeed researchers Mariana Uribe, Kari Koeppel, Leena Gundapaneni, Leo Chiquillo, Adriana Gomez, Alaina Rook, Rachel Schnalzer, Micki Taylor, Lauren Woelfel, Tatiana August-Schmidt, Ben Purdy, Tasbeeh Herwees, Zoë Sherman, and Nina De Salvo.

Amy Levenson of Blue Heron Literary Agency.

Running Press editor, Jordana Hawkins.

Designer Rachel Peckman, illustrator Matt Hollings, copyeditor Hope Clarke, and proofreader Adaobi Obi Tulton.

Big thank you to Lisa Petion and Jody Kuehner. And Troy Lucero.

FOR SARA, MOM, DAD, SCOTT, AND OBI. FOR THE RESEARCHERS, EDITORS, POST TEAM, AND OUR RAGTAG TRAVELING CREW WHO MADE THE SHOW POSSIBLE. FOR EVERY WEIRD, WONDERFUL STRANGER WHO LET US STOMP AROUND THEIR HAUNTED ABODES. FOR THE FANS WHO WERE THERE FROM THE FIRST EPISODE, AND THOSE WHO JOINED ALONG THE RIDE. FOR STEVE, WHOSE BRIDGE I NOW OWN, AND FOR THAT CANDY-ASS ZERO, ANNABELLE. AND, LASTLY, FOR GENE, MAY HE REST IN PEACE.
—SHANE

Just beyond grateful for the opportunities that this show has continued to give me. Thank you to everyone at BuzzFeed who made the show possible, including the editors, the researchers, the writers, the producers, the boots on the ground squad, and the people up top who allowed the show to happen. Thank you to Anna for writing a lovely case file of a book, and to everyone she already listed in terms of making this book possible! Thank you to my parents, my family, my friends, and, of course, my fiancé—who, by the time you're reading this, will be my wife—for always supporting me! And lastly, thanks to YOU, reader. I imagine this book wasn't your first foray into *Unsolved*, and frankly, because of that, it's the reason this book exists. So thank you!

—Ryan

(continued on next page)

Special thanks to the *BuzzFeed Unsolved* researchers:

Season 1

Three Horrifying Cases of Ghosts and Demons: Leena Gundapaneni

The Spirits of the Whaley House: Kari Koeppel

The Haunted Decks of the *Queen Mary*: Adriana Gomez

Season 2

The Ghosts and Demons of Bobby Mackey's: Kari Koeppel

Bigfoot: The Convincing Evidence: Kari Koeppel

The Haunted Halls of Waverly Hills Hospital: Micki Taylor

The Murders That Haunt the Lizzie Borden House: Kari Koeppel

The Spirits of the Salem Witch Trials: Rachel Schnalzer

The Haunted Quarters of the Dauphine Orleans Hotel: Micki Taylor

The Bizarre Voodoo World of New Orleans: Adriana Gomez

Season 3

The Ghost Town at Vulture Mine: Alaina Rook

The Captive Spirits of Eastern State Penitentiary: Micki Taylor

The Horrors of Pennhurst Asylum: Lauren Woelfel

The Mysterious Disappearance of Roanoke Colony: Kari Koeppel

London's Haunted Viaduct Tavern: Lauren Woelfel

The Subterranean Terrors of the London Tombs: Alaina Rook

Season 4

The Search for the Mysterious Mothman: Adriana Gomez, Rachel Schnalzer, and Lauren Woelfel

The Shadowy Spirits of Rolling Hills Asylum: Adriana Gomez

The Demonic Bellaire House: Alaina Rook

The Phantom Prisoners of Ohio State Penitentiary: Lauren Woelfel

The Spirits of Moon River Brewing: Alaina Rook

The Horrifying Sorrel-Weed Haunted Mansion: Rachel Schnalzer

The Mystical Villa Montezuma Mansion: Lauren Woelfel

Season 5

Return to the Horrifying Winchester Mansion: Micki Taylor

The Demon Priest of Mission Solano: Alaina Rook

The Terrors of Yuma Territorial Prison: Rachel Schnalzer

The Haunted Town of Tombstone: Alaina Rook

Season 6

The Haunting Shadows of the St. Augustine Lighthouse: Lauren Woelfel

The Lost Souls of the USS *Yorktown*: Alaina Rook

The Hollywood Ghosts of the Legendary Viper Room: Lauren Woelfel

The Unbelievable Horrors of the Old City Jail: Micki Taylor